TITLES IN  SERIES

STORIES AND POEMS

Little Red Riding Hood
Goldilocks and the Three Bears
Nursery Rhymes from Mother Goose
Hansel and Gretel
The Three Little Pigs
Songs in Signed English (with record)
The Night Before Christmas
Three Little Kittens
Mouse's Christmas Eve
The Ugly Duckling
Little Poems for Little People
The Tale of Peter Rabbit
Jack and the Beanstalk
The Gingerbread Man
The Three Billy Goats Gruff

POSTERS

Rock-A-Baby (17″ x 43″)
Jack and Jill (17″ x 43″)
Manual Alphabet (23″ x 36″)

GROWING UP BOOKS

Tommy's Day
Mealtime at the Zoo
I Want to be a Farmer
Happy Birthday Carol
Spring is Green
Questions and More Questions
We're Going to the Doctor
Cars and Trucks and Things
Night-Day. Sleep-Play
The Holiday Book
Sand, Sea, Shells and Sky
Stores
Julie Goes to School
Bobby Visits the Dentist
Matthew's Accident
How To (in Signed English)
Little Lost Sally
The Clock Book
Oliver in the City
Be Careful
Good Manners
At Night

BEGINNING ONE BOOKS

A Book About Me
Count and Color
My Toy Book
Baby's Animal Book

BEGINNING TWO BOOKS

I Am A Kitten
With My Legs
All By Myself
Things I Like To Do
The Pet Shop
Circus Time
Policeman Jones
Fireman Brown

REFERENCES

Signed English for the Classroom
The Signed English Dictionary

For a free copy of A Guide to the Selection and Use of the Teaching Aids of the Signed English System *write to:*

Gallaudet College Bookstore
Gallaudet College
Washington, D.C. 20002

NUMBERS

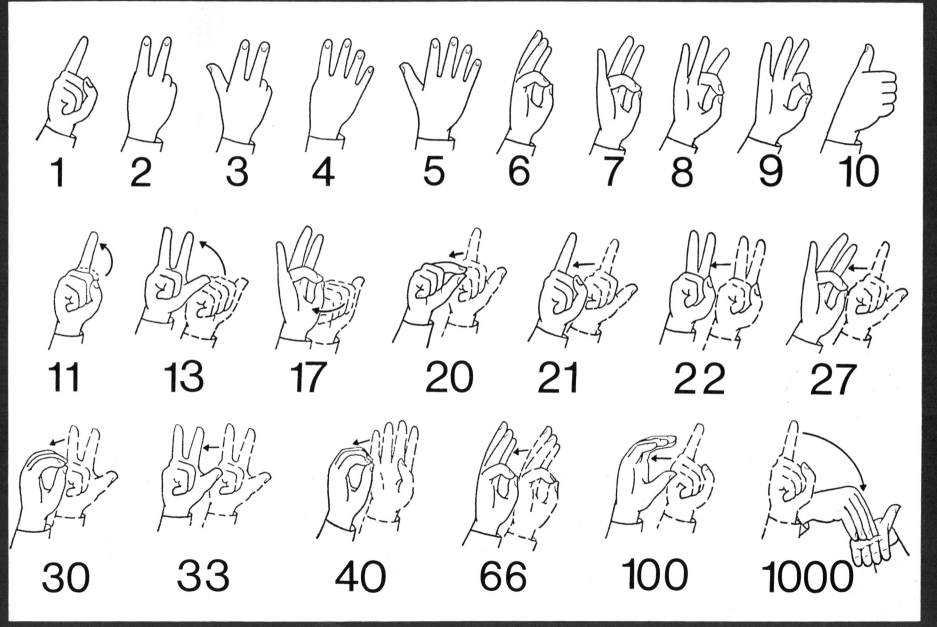

SIGN MARKERS

 past regular verbs: walk*ed*, talk*ed*, want*ed*, kiss*ed*, learn*ed*

 past irregular verbs: *saw*, hea*rd*, blew, forg*ot*. *came*

 participle: spok*en*, eat*en*, brok*en*, fall*en*, g*one*

 ing verb form: speak*ing*, sing*ing*, play*ing*, rain*ing*, danc*ing*, talk*ing*

 adverbs: ly quick*ly*, neat*ly*, angri*ly*, strong*ly*, deep*ly*

 adjectives: y sleep*y*, sunn*y*, cloud*y*, rain*y*, dream*y*

 regular plural nouns:

bear*s*, chair*s*, house*s*, table*s*, book*s*

plural irregular nouns: [repeat the sign word twice]

child*ren*, *feet*, s*heep*, *mice*, *geese*

 third person singular: walk*s*, talk*s*, lead*s*, eat*s*, sing*s*

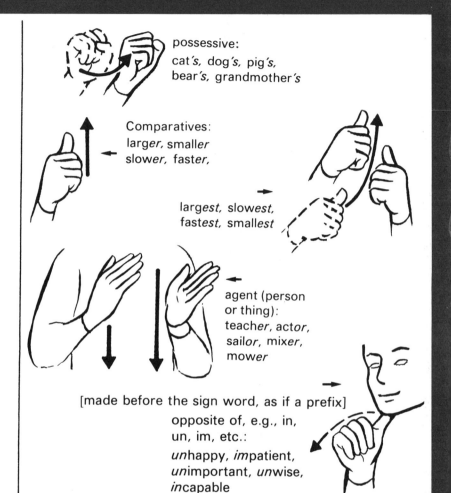

possessive: cat*'s*, dog*'s*, pig*'s*, bear*'s*, grandmother*'s*

Comparatives: larg*er*, small*er* slow*er*, fast*er*,

larg*est*, slow*est*, fast*est*, small*est*

agent (person or thing): teach*er*, act*or*, sail*or*, mix*er*, m*ower*

[made before the sign word, as if a prefix]

opposite of, e.g., in, un, im, etc.: *un*happy, *im*patient, *un*important, *un*wise, *in*capable

---

Signed English uses two kinds of gestures or signs: sign words and sign markers. Each sign word stands for one English word from a basic vocabulary of 2500 words used by and with young children. These are words such as mother, house, play, eat, think, etc. These sign words are used in the same order as words in an English sentence.

The sign markers are used when you wish to show that you are talking about more than one thing, show that something has happened in the past, or show the possessive. At this writing, we recommend that you use the 14 sign markers pictured above.

All but one of these markers are signed after the sign word. The marker which stands for "opposite of" is the only marker signed before the sign word.

In *Signed English* you use either a sign word alone or a sign word and *one* sign marker to represent a given English word. When this does not adequately represent the word you have in mind, use the manual alphabet and spell the word.

If you use these markers properly, you will be able to offer a better and more complete English model for the child.

The
Signed English
Dictionary

FOR PRESCHOOL AND ELEMENTARY LEVELS

signed
ENGLISH

2nd Printing, November, 1976
3rd Printing, June, 1977
4th Printing, May, 1978

● A small proportion of the sign words in this book are original with this work. These signs, as well as the others included, have been in general usage for some time and should be regarded as nonproprietary. Reproduction of the pictures of signs in this book without written permission, however, is prohibited.

ISBN 0-013-580-46-5

Library of Congress Catalog Card Number 75-24685

Gallaudet College is an Equal Opportunity Employer
Programs and services offered by Gallaudet College receive substantial financial support from the Department of Health, Education, and Welfare.

edited by

Harry Bornstein

Lillian B. Hamilton

Karen Luczak Saulnier

Howard L. Roy

signs drawn by

Linda C. Tom

Nancy L. Lundborg

cover and layout by Ralph R. Miller, Sr.

Gallaudet College Press
Washington, D.C.
1975

PREFACE

This dictionary is a revised and expanded replacement for the *Basic Preschool Signed English Dictionary*. Since it contains approximately 2200 sign words, we believe that it will meet some of the language needs of elementary levels of education as well as the needs of our primary target, the preschool years. Still other, smaller, and more specialized reference works, such as *Signed English in the Classroom,* are being prepared and will provide additional vocabulary for users of the *Signed English* system.

In preparing this educational tool, we have tried to work with the American Sign Language (ASL) and to build upon the work of those scholars who have dealt with similar educational problems. The most prominent of these are mentioned in the Appendix.

It is very difficult to attribute with complete accuracy the origins of the signs in this book. The American Sign Language is a natural language with considerable regional variation. Much of it is still unrecorded. And, so far as we can tell, deaf people are not disposed to think of any person or book as authoritative.

It is clear that those who have devised systems to represent English or have merely attempted to enlarge ASL, have borrowed freely from one another. In part, this is due to the fact that dittoed materials have been in informal circulation for many years.

Given the above cautions, we believe that 1353 signs in this book are taken unchanged from the American Sign Language. In addition, there are 134 ASL signs which have been slightly modified. We have invented or adopted from those used in the Gallaudet community, 317 more signs. We have selected 255 signs from the several "SEE" systems: *Seeing Essential English, Signing Exact English,* and *Linguistics of Visual English*. And, there are an additional 97 compound signs listed in the index.

Although this is largely a new work, it, of course, includes most of the previous dictionary. In this regard, we wish to thank Barbara M. Kannapell for compiling the ASL signs and for coordinating sign invention by members of the Gallaudet community.

While all members of the Preschool Signed English Project contribute to every phase of the work, it is possible to describe the principal contributions of each to this volume as follows:

Karen Luczak Saulnier compiled the English vocabulary.

Lillian B. Hamilton wrote the descriptions of the signs and organized the sign presentation and index.

Howard L. Roy acted as consultant and made suggestions on system design and presentation.

Harry Bornstein wrote the introduction, the appendix, and the endpapers, and is the principal system designer.

Linda C. Tom and Nancy L. Lundborg prepared the final sign drawings. They used many of the earlier drawings by Ann Silver and Jack Fennell.

Ralph R. Miller, Sr., designed the book layout, endpapers, and cover.

Rosemary Weller, Shirley Stein, and James M. Pickett developed the "Model for the Visual Representation of Speech."

These Gallaudet students assisted in sign invention and tracing:

Reba Poole, Mary Ann Schoenberg, Carolyn Ball, Bill Collins, George Pehlgrim, Shirley Manning, Jane Matuszak, Barbara Burg, Deborah Lentz, and Wendy Nelson.

Gallaudet faculty members who assisted:

Willard Madsen and Gilbert Eastman. Mr. Madsen also helped us resolve a series of difficult decisions about choice of signs.

As director of the project, however, I am responsible for any of its deficiencies.

HARRY BORNSTEIN

CONTENTS

ABOUT SIGNED ENGLISH

Introduction

We will describe to you the purpose, nature, and use of *Signed English*. *Signed English* is an educational tool meant to be used while you speak and thereby help you communicate with deaf children. It is a way of presenting meaning by gesture or sign along with speech. Learn and use *Signed English* with your child *as early as possible in his life*. By doing so, you will help him develop better English and we think that improved English should result in better speech.

Let us first give you the basic reason for developing a manual parallel to speech. Deaf children must depend on what they see to understand what others say to them. They must somehow get more information than do hearing children from what can be *seen* in other people's behavior. What does each of us see when we speak with one another? We see lips move, changes in facial expression, different body postures, and natural gestures.

Can most deaf children get enough information from these "signals" to learn English well? The answer to this question is very clear and very well documented. It is NO. Most deaf children do not learn English well. Recent surveys of the educational achievement of older deaf children show them on the average equalling the reading performance of hearing fifth graders. (Not all deaf students do this well.) This has caused many to consider using a manual parallel to speech. *Signed English* is just one of several manual systems, most of which are modifications of the American Sign Language. A brief history of this work is given in the appendix of this book. More technical discussions can be found in journals which deal with the education of the deaf and the sign language. As far as you are concerned, however, none of this other material is needed for you to use *Signed English* well. All you need is included in this section of the book.

Signed English uses two kinds of gestures or signs: sign words and sign markers. Each sign word stands for the meaning of one English word (an entry in a standard English dictionary) from a basic vocabulary of 2500 words used by and with young children. These are words such as mother, house, play, eat, think, etc. They have been assembled from published lists of children's spoken vocabulary and from parent and teacher logs of deaf preschool children word needs. The sign words are used in the same order as words in an English sentence. This book shows about 2200 sign words. It should meet your essential needs. Additional vocabulary will be presented in smaller, more specialized reference works. There is only one available at this printing. We have also prepared a large number of teaching aids. These stories and nursery rhymes contain some words which are not included in the references. You do not need to worry about this because every teaching aid contains all the information you need to use it effectively.

Sign markers are used when you want to show that you are talking about more than one thing, show that something has happened in the past, or show the possessive. We now recommend that you use 14 sign markers. All but one of these markers are signed after the sign word.

In *Signed English* you use either a sign word alone or a sign word and one sign marker to represent a given English word. When this does not represent the word you have in mind, use the manual alphabet and spell the word. (More about the manual alphabet later.)

Although we have tried to keep *Signed English* simple, we know that learning an artificial language is not easy. If you find there are parts of our system you are not able to use, then learn to do without that part or element. Basically, we want to say to you that *Signed English* is a tool for your use. Some of you will learn to use it very well, some reasonably well, and some only in a very limited way. Do not worry about it. Do the best you can to make it work for you and your child.

Nature of *Signed English*

Before we describe *Signed English* in more detail let us introduce the manual alphabet which is shown on Endpaper I. As you can see, there is a manual representation of every letter in the English alphabet. There are two reasons why you should learn the alphabet. First, you can use the manual alphabet to spell any English word for which we do not have a sign. If you continue using *Signed English* with an older child, however, you will surely have a greater need to use the manual alphabet. Second, a great many sign words have a manual letter as a basic part of the sign. Many of the sign markers are simply manual letters. If you know the manual alphabet, it will be easier for you to form and to read the signs. Manual letters are also used in our word descriptions of the signs pictured in this book.

Since you can reproduce any English word by spelling it, you may wonder why signs are necessary. These are the reasons: Spelling is slow. It is relatively difficult for a very young child to form and to read letters. It is a strain on both children and adults to attend for too long a time to such a fine signal. Finally, and perhaps most important, asking a child to read the manual alphabet is skipping a step in the usual order of things. Hearing children know English *before* they learn to read. If you fingerspell to an 18 month old deaf child, you force him to read and learn language at the same time. We do not know how many children can do this.

The basic unit of *Signed English* is the sign word. Most of the sign words in this system are taken from the American Sign Language. But these signs are now used in the same order as English words and with the same meaning. We use American Sign Language signs where possible because it should make it somewhat easier for the child to communicate with people who use that language. The American Sign Language is different from English, so do not be surprised if you have difficulty in communicating with deaf adults who depend exclusively on ASL.

Our sign words are words which are used frequently with children, not adults. We have signs for words often found in fairy tales and nursery rhymes, for animals on the farm and at the zoo, and for aspects of the major holidays. Of course the most commonly used words by adults are also used by children and are included here. Another example of our focus on a child's needs is the way we treat contractions such as "I've", "you'll", and so on. Each contraction is treated as if it were a single and separate word because that is how a pre-school child meets such words. It is only much later when he begins to read, that he learns that "I've" is really a combination of "I and have". Aside from these points, there is nothing unusual about the vocabulary of *Signed English*. Sign words are presented in this book in singular, non-past form.

At this point we want to describe the second kind of sign used in *Signed English,* the sign marker. It is used to represent certain very basic and common English word form changes, usually inflections and endings, which change the meaning of the word.

When we say that you use a sign word and a sign marker to change a word such as *look* to *looked,* exactly what do we mean by this? First, of course, you must form the sign word for *look* as shown in the body of the text. Second, as smoothly and as quickly as possible, you form the regular past sign marker described below and pictured on Endpaper III. It takes additional time and effort to form this second gesture. How can you minimize these? Consider

the diagram illustrated below. It shows the approximate position assumed by the hands of a signer when he pauses. It is reasonable to suppose, therefore, that on the average, a signer can execute his next sign with least effort from this position. Consequently, all of the frequently used sign markers are formed by the right hand in the area bounded by the rectangle. These sign markers are all newly developed. Those sign markers which are formed outside this area are used much less frequently in speech and, interestingly enough, are those which have been adopted from the American Sign Language. These are the comparative, the superlative, the agent, and the opposite prefix. Now to discuss each of the 14 sign markers more specifically.

The most important words in an English sentence are usually the nouns and the verbs. A noun can stand for one (singular) or more (plural) things. Most often a noun is made plural by adding an *s,* e.g., bear becomes bears, house becomes houses, etc. As can be seen in the sign marker chart on Endpaper III, *Signed English* uses a manual alphabet *s* for this purpose. We call this the regular plural marker. When you want to show this kind of plural, you first form the sign word and then form the sign marker *s.* Now there are many other ways that nouns can be changed into plurals, e.g., child becomes children, foot becomes feet, mouse becomes mice, etc. The sign marker for all of these ways of showing plural is simply repetition of the sign itself. We call this the irregular plural marker.

We turn our attention now to verbs, those words which express an action or the existence of something or the occurrence of an event. We find it necessary to distinguish between things that happen in the past and those which do not happen in the past. The manual alphabet *d,* stands for the most frequent past ending, *ed.*

It is also formed after the sign word is made. There are many other ways that a verb is changed into a past form, e.g., see becomes saw, hear becomes heard, blow becomes blew, etc. There is a special verb marker which represents all of these irregular past forms. It is a manual alphabet *b,* palm left, tips out, swept from the center of the body to the right side.

There is a third class of actions which take place in the past prior to some specified or implied time. In English, the past participle conveys this meaning. Examples include *gone, broken, eaten,* etc. The participle sign marker is represented by the manual letter *n.*

Aside from the past and not past distinction, verbs have two other very common endings, i.e., *ing* and *s.* Thus work becomes working or works, play can become playing or plays, etc. A native speaker of English knows when these forms are used without needing to think about it. When using *Signed English,* he adds a manual alphabet *i,* which he swings to the right, for *ing,* and the manual alphabet *s* for *s.* All he need learn is to associate the hand signal with his normal use of these endings.

There are three other important ways that English words change that are represented by sign markers. A noun has a possessive form *'s* which can be seen in boy's house, girl's doll, etc. This ending is represented by the possessive marker which is a twisted manual alphabet *s.* Some nouns and verbs acquire a *y* ending when used as adjectives, e.g., cloud becomes cloudy, sleep becomes sleepy, etc. The manual alphabet *y* is the sign marker for this ending. Finally, words can become adverbs by the addition of *ly,* e.g., quickly, happily, etc. The sign marker for this ending is a simultaneous combination of the manual alphabet letters *l* and *y* twisted down.

So far we have described ten markers. They are the basic aspects of English structure which are represented in *Signed English.* If you are a hearing person, you already know this structure and use it without thinking about it. Just add the markers to your normal speech.

There are four other markers on the sign marker chart which parallel frequent word form changes in English. These are the comparative (er), the superlative (est), as in taller and tallest, and the agent (person or thing) as in worker, sailor, librarian, mixer, and mower. The fourth marker, the "opposite of" marker, is a prefix and is the only marker formed before or ahead of the sign word. It represents the prefixes *in, un, im* as used in words such as *incapable, unhappy, impatient,* etc. The "opposite of" marker is formed by placing a right A shape hand, knuckles left, thumb extended, under the chin, then moving it out. These last markers are taken directly from ASL and are very useful in speech.

It should be obvious to you that these 14 sign markers will not permit you to parallel all of the changes in English word form. Why stop with a "small" number? There are two important reasons: First, small children do not often use most of the other changes in word form. Second, since each sign marker must be used in combination with a sign word, a large number of markers becomes a heavy learning burden on you and could make the *Signed English* very cumbersome to use. For the last reason, users of *Signed English* are urged, with one exception, not to add more than one marker to a sign word at any one time.

There are a few more things that we wish to say about these markers which may make it easier for you to learn. It is usually easier to recognize something than it is to recall it from memory. So we will continue to show all 14 markers in our teaching aids. You may be able to recognize them even if you can't remember them when you try to communicate. For those who have difficulty learning to use all 14 markers, we suggest a reduced set of seven. These are the irregular past, the irregular plural, the "ing" verb form, the third person singular, the adverbial, the adjectival, and the possessive.

In those situations where seven markers still appear to be too many, we would suggest that three markers be used: the irregular past, the irregular plural, and the "ing" verb form. The best that can be said for the suggested reduced systems is that they are at least consistent with one another.

Exceptions

While exceptions almost always complicate a system, there are a few signs which are so well established or so colorful, that we thought it appropriate to make these exceptions to our basic rules.

One sign for each English word: There are two phrases, two proper names and 19 compounds, of two or more words, in this dictionary which are represented by a single sign word.
These are:

> after a while, of course, Santa Claus, United States, Band-Aid, bubble pipe, chewing gum, French fries, guinea pig, hot dog, ice cream, ice-skate, jack-in-the-box, jack-o-lantern, merry-go-round, Ping-Pong, polar bear, rolling pin, teddy bear, tightrope walker, walkie-talkie, X-ray, and yo-yo.

One sign word for a separate English dictionary entry: There are two signs for each of the following English dictionary entries: blind, brush, fall, and right.

One sign word plus only one sign marker: Since use of the agent marker does not preclude a noun from further assuming a plural or possessive form, we permit the use of two sign markers in this one instance, e.g., work + agent + plural, or speak + agent + possessive, etc.

One meaning for a sign marker: The agent marker is used to change the name of a country to the name for its people, e.g., England, France, Germany and Russia become English, French, German, and Russian, respectively. In English this letter word form change also stands for the language used in these countries. The distinction between the two meanings comes from context only. And this is how the distinction is made in this system.

In the short time that *Signed English* has been used, it has become quite clear that using the sign markers all of the time is a difficult habit to acquire. We are speaking now of those adults who have no difficulty learning to use the markers. Some teachers and parents appear to use them when they think a language lesson is "in order" or when they think it is especially important to communicate to the child the information inherent in the marker. Logically, such practices merely reduce the frequency with which the child is exposed to these word form changes and increase his uncertainty as to when he should use them. In spite of the fact that it may take years before you see these sign markers incorporated accurately into the child's productive language, it still appears that the best strategy is to use all of the markers all of the time.

Changes

During the last four years, we have felt obliged to change some signs and to make some exceptions to our rules. This section will detail the changes and the reasons for those changes.

Sign Words: There are about a dozen very important English words for which we were only able to devise rather clumsy signs in the past. They are: *could, would, should,* their contractions, and the contraction forms of the *do* verb. After repeated efforts we have succeeded in developing what we believe are simple and easy-to-make signs for these words. For the above contractions, we simply add the appropriate markers to one or another contracted forms. Endpaper V outlines and illustrates the entire contraction subsystem. *Could, would,* and *should* are now shown, respectively, in the text as repeated movements of *can, will,* and *must.*

There are 23 other sign words that have been changed either because they were esthetically objectionable to some deaf adults, were too easily confused with other existing signs, and/or were not as clear as an alternative sign. All changed sign words are marked with asterisks in the index. These changes will be incorporated into the teaching aids as each is reprinted. We recognize that changing signs is a nuisance and an inconvenience to users, but we felt that continuing to use clumsy and unattractive signs would prove harmful in the long run. While we anticipate fewer changes in the future, we would like to note that a language-like tool such as *Signed English,* will change through usage in ways that we may not be able to predict. It is both pointless and useless to resist such change.

While on the topic of changing signs, there are certain other features of signing that are worth noting. Experienced signers do *not* always form a sign in the same way. For example, the first five numbers (Endpaper II) and many of the signs for the days of the week are formed either with palm in or palm out. Often the movement is dependent upon the sign made just prior to that for the number or day. Normally, a signer will make the smallest possible number of wrist twists because it is easier and less awkward.

While all signs drawn in the dictionary and teaching aids are formed as if by right-handed persons, there are many signs which can be executed with either hand without a change in meaning. Also, the direction of the movement of a sign varies in importance. For example, when you use the sign for *pull* or *turn* or *push* the direction in which you pull or turn or push may or may not be important. As you become more adept in using *Signed English* you will attend more and more to those features of a sign which add to meaning or to fluid movement. To simplify your task of learning these signs, however, we have tried to show each sign being formed in exactly the same way each time it appears in our teaching aids. Occasionally, our artists, all of whom are deaf, unconsciously draw a sign in a manner which reflects the esthetics of the Sign language rather than our patterns. We sometimes fail to catch these "deviations".

As noted in the preface, the Sign language is largely unrecorded. There is considerable age, regional, and socio-economic variation in signs used throughout the United States. Consequently, you and your children will sometimes encounter different signs for some of the words in this dictionary. We suggest that you use them just as you might use two English words that have the same meaning, e.g., *small* and *little.* Debates about which sign is the "right" sign usually stem from differences in taste and past experience but, as in any language, correctness rests upon usage.

Sign markers: We began our work using 14 sign markers, reduced the number to 12, and return to 14 in this book. Thirteen of the original 14 remain the same. The new 14th marker, the participle, is an important, although relatively infrequent, verb form change. The "ful" marker was dropped because of low frequency of use. As noted earlier, for those who have difficulty learning to use all

14 markers, we suggest a reduced set of seven; the irregular past, the irregular plural, the "ing" verb form, the third person singular, the adverbial, the adjectival, and the possessive. At one time we recommended that the regular past and the regular plural be used in reduced marker systems. However, it seems more appropriate to use the irregular past and plural since these cover many different forms. The regular markers would be subsumed as another form with the same meaning.

How to Learn *Signed English*

We recommend that you learn *Signed English* by using the teaching aids, especially the story books and posters, which have been developed for the system. Each of these teaching aids is completely self contained. Everything you need is in the teaching aid itself. The sign markers are used as they should be without any reference to grammar or to the explanations given in this introduction. You do not need to learn grammar to use *Signed English*. With practice you will begin to use the markers in the right way without thinking about grammar. Also use the teaching aids to learn the vocabulary of *Signed English*. Virtually all of the vocabulary in this book will be in those teaching aids. Learn by reading the stories to your child. Not only can this be a delightful experience for both of you, but it is really a more pleasant way to learn this artificial language than to try and memorize lists of loosely connected words.

On page i you will find the titles of the teaching aids so far produced in the *Signed English* series. The subject matter of each of these aids has been developed to serve needs beyond those related to language development.

The *Stories* deal with some aspects of our heritage which should be familiar to all children. While these stories were designed to be read to children, they are also useful as scripts for skits and plays.

The *Poetry* and *Song* books offer both parent and child an opportunity to practice signing parallel to spoken English rhythm. This language rhythm is important to English and often precedes specific vocabulary acquisition.

The *Beginning* books are small and sturdy enough to be given to the smallest child. With the *Beginning One* books, the child can look at, point to, and describe important parts of his environment. The *Beginning Two* books contain slightly more advanced language and describe behavior and things more important to toddlers.

The *Growing Up* books are efficient tools for acquainting the child with the complex world around him. Apart from *Tommy's Day,* which should be the very first book used by parents because it provides the family, especially the mother, with the language needed for a typical day, most *Growing Up* books depict experiences important to the child. It is usually helpful to the child if he can be exposed to these experiences through the medium of these books before the actual experience takes place. He need not fully understand the contents of a book to profit from that exposure. Not only does a book such as *Bobby Visits the Dentist* show him the proper way to brush his teeth, but it also permits him to become familiar with the people, and the things that happen, in a dentist's office. This should make him feel more comfortable and secure when he makes his first visit. Similarly, exposure to *Julie Goes to School* should begin before a child enters school so that he can anticipate the school routines and be comfortable with them from the very first day he attends. In short, the carefully developed descriptions in the *Growing Up* books are designed to increase a child's understanding of, and his ability to cope with his environment. These, in turn, should aid in his personal adjustment and enhance his language behavior.

The *Posters* are designed to be used as decorations for home and classroom. The Manual Alphabet poster is particularly flexible in this regard. The letters are often cut out and rearranged in a variety of decorative patterns pleasing to the child and parent.

In addition to this dictionary there is one other *Reference, Signed English for the Classroom,* which provides a vocabulary for the teacher's use in the classroom on a typical day. Other references covering additional specialized vocabulary are in preparation.

One teaching aid, *Tommy's Day,* has been filmed. The film is cartridge-loaded and used with a hand-held viewer. This viewer enables the user to vary the rate of presentation, reverse the film, or stop as he chooses. This film is probably most useful for introducing the sign words to the beginning signer. If it proves effective, more films like it will be prepared.

We would like to comment on the drawings of the sign words and markers in the dictionary and teaching aids. There are two principal problems in drawing signs: First, there is the problem of sequence. We use arrows to show the movement of the hands and/or the fingers. When a sign requires two different hand positions, the starting position is shown by means of dashed lines. The final position is drawn with solid lines. This means that the marker is shown on the signer's right (your left) because that is where a right-handed signer would usually make it. It is drawn this way because the sign and the sign marker represent a single English word. English print, on the other hand, goes from left to right. This "mirror image" or reversal may confuse you at first, but with a little practice it should cause you little trouble. For some words, you may find it helpful to turn the book upside-down and align your hands with those of the signer.

The second problem, showing movement through three dimensions, is difficult to solve by means of drawing alone. We have found that a verbal description is often helpful in the interpretation of some signs. This leads to what is perhaps the primary purpose of this book. It is a reference book. We suggest that you refer to the pictures and word descriptions in this book when the drawings in the teaching aids are not clear or if you just wish to browse while looking up a word. Otherwise depend on the teaching aids to learn the signs.

If you will remember, we stated that if you know the manual alphabet, it will help you to recognize and form the sign words. It will also help you to understand the word descriptions of a sign. In addition, the numbers one - ten and several other handshapes are also part of many signs. It will help you to read the word descriptions if you are familiar with all of these handshapes. They are shown in the Key to the Word Descriptions and on the endpapers of this book.

Final Words

We hope that we have given you enough information to learn and use *Signed English*. It is not an easy way to communicate for a person who has used speech all his life. But we think it will be an effective way for your deaf child to develop his English and transition into reading for further language growth and pleasure. We also think that his speech and his ability to read speech will be enhanced by a better knowledge of the English language. If for any reason a manual signal system such as *Signed English* proves ineffective or irksome, you can always stop using it. But remember, the critical years of a child's life spent with little or no language, can never be recovered.

Good Luck!

Key to Word Descriptions

In order to use this dictionary easily and effectively, you should be familiar with the names of your fingers, the manual alphabet, the numbers one through ten, and certain handshapes that are frequently used when making the sign words.

Positions of the handshapes are described by saying that the palms, (finger)tips, and or knuckles, whichever the case may be are facing: in, out, up, down, right, or left. Directions for movements are given as clearly as possible.

Study the handshapes on this page and the letters and numbers on the endpapers. The positions and movements are described with the picture of each sign.

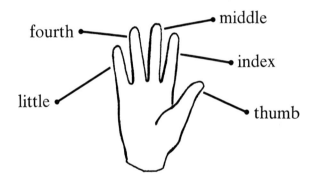

Sample letter shape "a". See complete alphabet on endpaper

Sample number shape 1. See numbers 1-10 on endpaper

Open B

Bent B

Bent V

Claw shape (or hand)

Flat O

A

signed ENGLISH

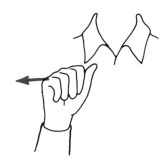

a

A shape RH. Move to right.

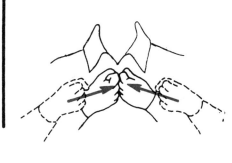

about

Point left index finger right, palm in. Circle with right index.

above

Open B both hands palms down, left tips right, right tips slanted left. Place RH on back of LH, arc out and up.

accept

Five shape both hands palms down, tips out. Draw back into flat O's toward chest.

accident

S shape both hands knuckles facing. Strike knuckles together.

1

ache
A shape both hands thumbs extended, knuckles out. Move thumbs back and forth toward one another.

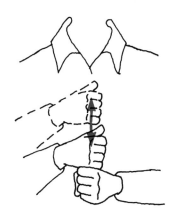

acorn
S shape LH knuckles right. A shape RH knuckles left. Tap left S with right A. Repeat.

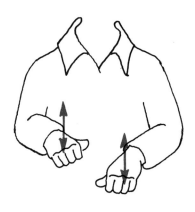

acrobat
A shape both hands knuckles down. Move up and down alternately as if balancing.

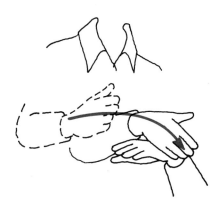

across
Open B LH palm down, tips slanted right. Slide little finger edge of right A across back of LH.

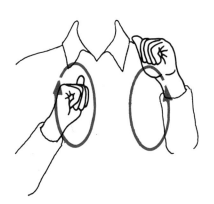

act
A shape both hands. Move alternately in circles toward body.

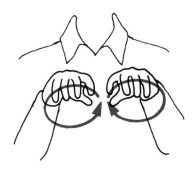

active
Claw shape both hands palms down. Circle RH down and to the left and LH down and to the right simultaneously.

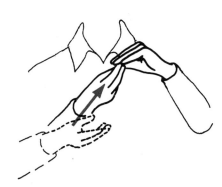

add
Hold left flat O, tips down, over right open palm. Close RH into flat O and bring up to left tips.

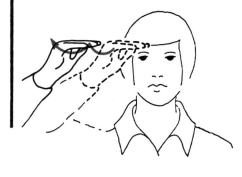

adult
Flat O RH tips left. Hold at forehead then step up several times.

afford
F shape RH palm down. Mime placing in pocket and drawing out again.

afraid
Open 5 both hands palms in, tips facing. Move back and forth several times as if shaking in fright.

Africa
Hold right A at right side of face. Circle face to left ending with thumb on mouth.

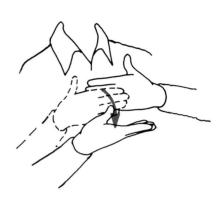

after
Open B both hands palms in, left tips right, right tips left. Place right B on back of left. Turn out ending with palm up.

after a while
Open B LH palm right, tips up. Place thumb of right L in left palm and circle forward (about ¼ turn).

afternoon
Hold left arm before you palm down, tips right. Now place elbow of right open B on back of LH and lower slightly.

again
Open B LH palm up, tips out. Bent B RH palm up. Arc to left and place tips in left palm.

against
Open B LH, palm right, tips up. Strike palm with tips of right bent B, palm down.

3

ago
Open B RH palm left, tips up.
Flip over right shoulder.

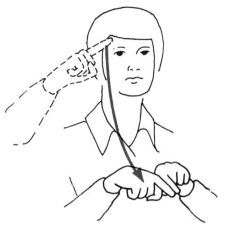

agree
Place tip of right index finger
on forehead. Bring down and
place against left index which
is held tip out, palm down.

ahead
A shape both hands thumbs up,
knuckles facing. Place right
knuckles on left wrist and move
ahead of left A.

aid
A shape both hands knuckles
facing, right thumb extended.
Place right A under left and
push up.

aim
One shape both hands, right
hand palm down. Place tip of
right index on forehead then
move directly to tip of left index.

air
A shape RH. Move in wavy motion from left to right.

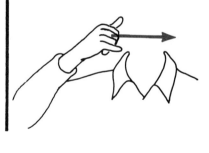

airplane
Y shape RH. Zoom to left.

4

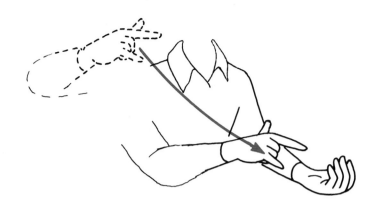

airport
Cupped shape LH palm up. Y shape RH index finger extended. Hold at right shoulder and "zoom" down into left palm.

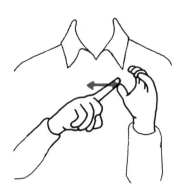

alarm
C shape LH palm right. Tap left thumb with right index several times.

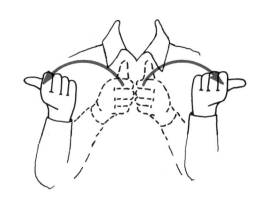

album
A shape both hands thumbs extended, knuckles touching. Separate as if opening a book.

alike
Y shape both hands thumbs almost touching. Move apart and back again.

alive
A shape both hands, thumbs up. Place knuckles on chest and move up.

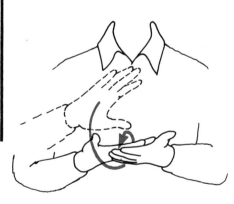

all
Open B both hands, left palm up, right palm down. Circle left with right ending with back of RH resting in left palm.

alligator
Five shape both hands, left palm up, right palm down, tips out. Place right palm on left interlocking fingers, then lift RH up (indicating huge jaws).

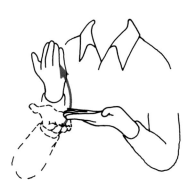

almost
Open B LH palm up, tips slightly right. Stroke back of left fingers with right fingers, bringing RH up above LH.

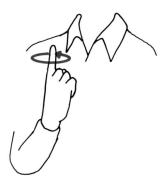

alone
One shape RH, palm in, tip up. Circle counter-clockwise.

along
A shape RH, knuckles down. Place on back of left wrist and slide up forearm.

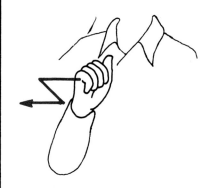

alphabet
A shape RH. Move down in "Z" motion.

already
Five shape RH palm in and slightly to the right. Twist out so that palm faces out.

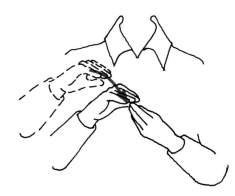

also
Flat O shape both hands tips up, right O a little higher than left. Arc right tips over to left tips.

always
One shape RH, palm left, tip out. Circle continuously.

am
Place right A on mouth and move out.

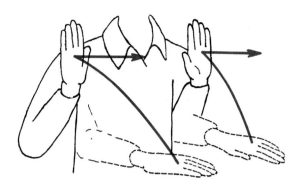

amaze
Open B both hands palms down, tips out. Draw back to body palms out, tips up and push forward.

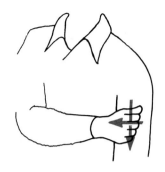

ambulance
Make cross on upper left arm with right A.

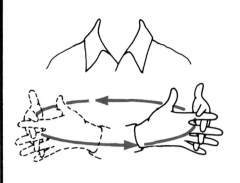

America
Interlock fingers, palms in, and circle from right to left.

among
Five shape LH palm slightly left. Weave right index finger in and out of left fingers beginning at little finger.

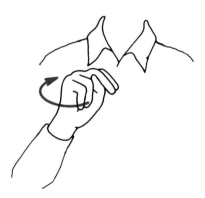

an
N shape RH palm in. Twist outward.

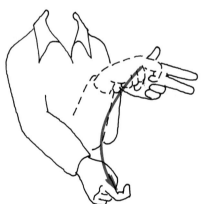

anchor
Three shape LH palm right, tips out. Place index finger of right X against left palm, swing down, then turn up as if hooking anchor.

and
Five shape RH palm in, tips left. Move from left to right closing into flat O.

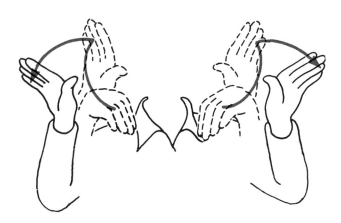

angel
Place tips of curved open B's on shoulder. Turn palms out then down, i.e., wings.

angry
Claw shape both hands palms in, tips facing. Place on chest and draw up to shoulders in forceful manner.

animal
Place tips of claw hands on shoulders and move back and forth toward one another.

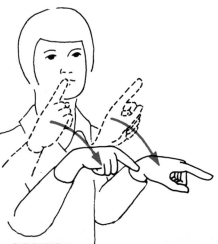

ankle
A shape right hand knuckles left. Place against side of left wrist which is held before you palm down.

annoy
Open B both hands left palm right, tips out; right palm up, tips left. Slide RH back and forth between thumb and index of LH.

another
A shape RH knuckles down, thumb pointed left. Turn over so that knuckles face up.

answer
One shape both hands right index on mouth, left index a little in front of face. Move both forward ending with palms down.

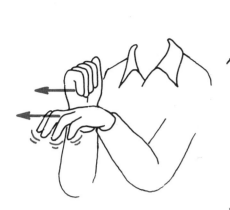

ant
Place base of right A on back of left claw hand which is held palm down. Move left claw forward in crawling motion.

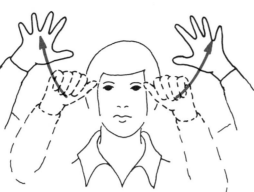

antler
A shape both hands. Place thumbs on temple and move up opening into five shapes.

any
A shape RH thumb up. Turn to left.

anyway
Open B both hands palms in. Slap left tips back and forth with right tips.

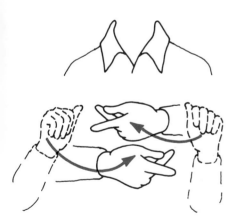

apartment
A shape both hands. Change into P's bringing left P behind right P.

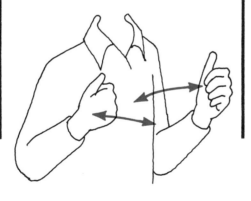

ape
A shape both hands knuckles in. Beat alternately against chest.

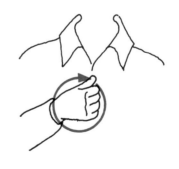

apologize
Circle right A on chest.

appear
Open B LH palm down, tips out. Push right index up between left middle and index fingers.

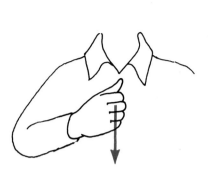

appetite
Place knuckles of right A on chest and move down.

apple
Press knuckle of right index finger into right cheek and twist forward.

apricot
Place thumb of right A on right cheek. Twist forward and down into P shape.

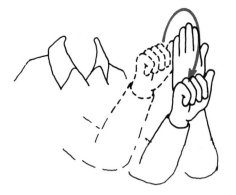

April
Open B LH palm in. Place knuckles of right A against left palm, slide over fingers and down back of hand.

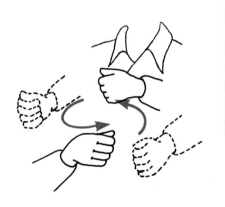

aquarium
A shape both hands palms facing. Move right in front of left palm in, and left behind right palm in.

are
Place right R on lips, then move forward.

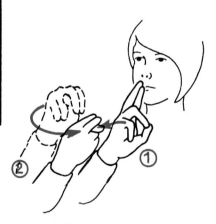

aren't
Place right R on lips, then move forward forming N shape. Twist in.

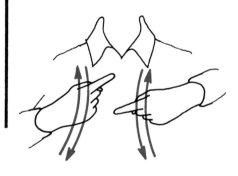

argue
One shape both hands palms in, tips facing. Shake up and down at one another.

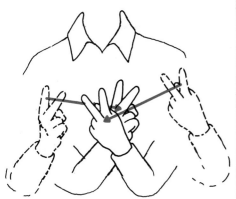

arithmetic
V shape both hands palms in, tips up. Cross one another twice.

arm
Clasp left wrist with right C and run C up to left elbow.

around
One shape LH palm in. Circle with right index which is held tip down.

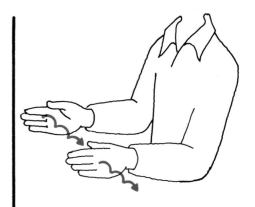

arrange
B shape both hands palms facing, tips out. Move in short jumps to the left.

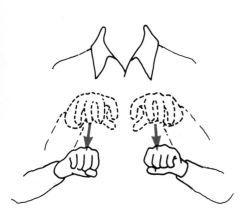

arrest
Claw shape both hands palms down. Drop forcefully into A shapes.

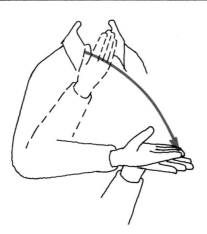

arrive
Open B both hands palms up, tips out. Place back of right B in left palm.

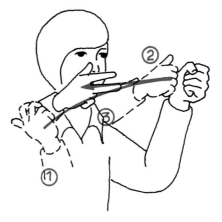

arrow
Mime pulling arrow from holder over shoulder, placing in bow string and shooting.

art
Open B LH palm in, tips up. Draw right little finger straight down left palm. Repeat.

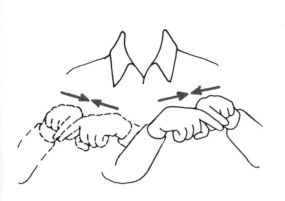

as
One shape both hands knuckles down, tips out. Place index fingers together and move to left.

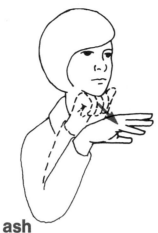

ash
Place back of right A under chin and open into five shape.

ashtray
Mime smoking cigar or cigarette then tapping ashes in cupped left hand.

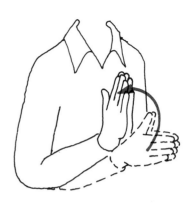

ask
Palms together tips out. Arc back to body ending with tips up.

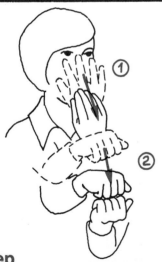

asleep
Draw fingers of RH down over face, form A shape knuckles down, and place on upturned left A.

asparagus
H shape RH palm in, tips left. Place tips on left A.

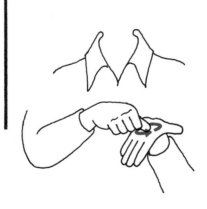

aspirin
A shape RH palm down, thumb extended. Place thumb in upturned left palm and circle.

astronaut
A shape both hands knuckles out, thumbs touching. Thrust right A forward and up forcefully.

12

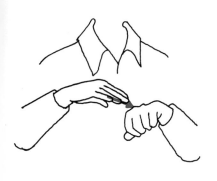

at
Touch back of left A with right finger tips.

athlete
A shape both hands. Push up above shoulders as if pushing up weights.

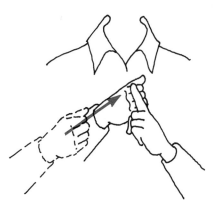

attack
Strike left index finger with right A.

attention
B shape both hands palms placed on temples. Move forward parallel to one another.

audiology
Circle right A at right ear clockwise.

August
Open B LH palm in. Place knuckles of right A against left palm, slide over fingers and down back of hand changing into G shape.

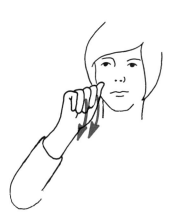

aunt
A shape RH. Place thumb on right cheek and stroke twice.

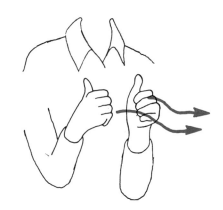

avenue
A shape both hands palms facing, thumbs extended. Move forward in wavy motion as if following path.

13

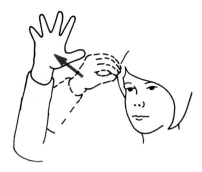

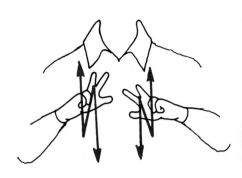

awake
Place tips of forefingers and thumbs at sides of eyes.

away
Open B RH palm in, tips left. Flip away and out.

awful
Flat O shape RH. Place on temple and snap open into 5 shape palm out.

awkward
Three shape both hands palms down. Move up and down alternately once or twice.

axe
Open B both hands left palm right, tips out; right palm and tips slanted left. Chop left index finger with little finger side of RH backward then forward.

B

baby
Place right arm in left arm at waist and move as if rocking a baby.

back
Open B LH palm in, tips right. Touch back of LH with tips of right curved B.

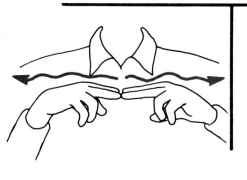

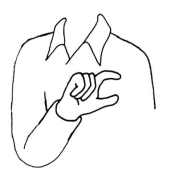

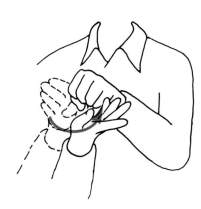

bacon
H shape both hands palms down, tips touching. Draw away in wavy motion.

bad
Open B RH palm in, tips up. Place tips on chin, twist out and down.

badge
Place index and thumb side of right C on upper left chest (other fingers closed).

bag
S shape LH, knuckles down. Place index finger of right B on left S and circle under.

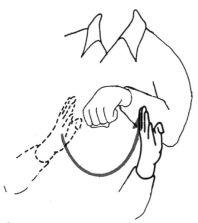

baggage

S shape LH knuckles down, arm extended. B shape RH palm down, tips out. Place index side of right B on left thumb and circle under to left.

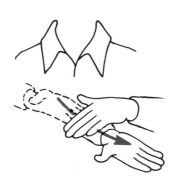

bake

Open B's both hands left palm down, tips slanted right. Right palm up, tips slanted left. Slide RH under LH.

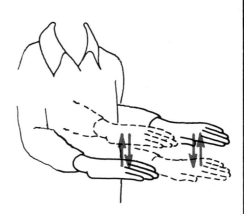

balance

B shape both hands palms down, tips out. Move up and down alternately.

bald

Circle crown of head with right middle finger.

ball

Curved B shape both hands palms facing. Outline shape of ball ending with palms up.

balloon

Mime blowing up a balloon until it is filled.

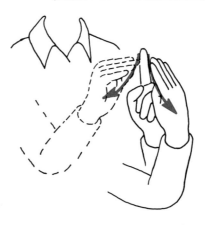

banana

Hold left index finger up. Go through motions of peeling a banana with tips of right flat O.

band

B shape both hands, index fingers touching. Move out in semi-circle until little fingers touch.

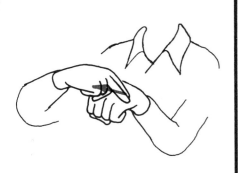

Band-Aid
S shape LH knuckles down. Draw right H over back of left S.

bang (verb)
B shape LH palm right, tips up. Hammer with right A.

bang (noun)
Claw shape RH palm down. Place fingers on forehead imitating bang(s).

banjo
B shape LH palm and tips slanted right. Mime plucking banjo strings with right fingers.

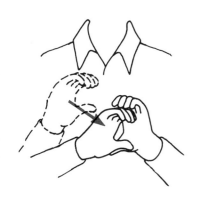

bank
C shape both hands, left palm out, right palm left. Place right C into left C.

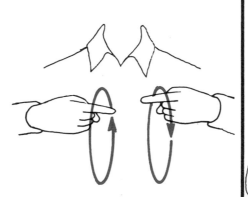

barbeque
One shape both hands palm in, tips facing. Move in circular motion (i.e. spit turning).

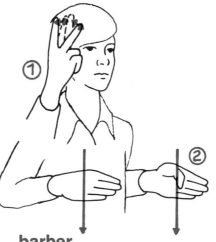

barber
Mime cutting hair with fingers of right V. Follow with agent marker.

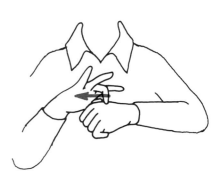

bare
S shape LH knuckles down, arm extended. Slide right middle finger forward over back of left hand to knuckles.

17

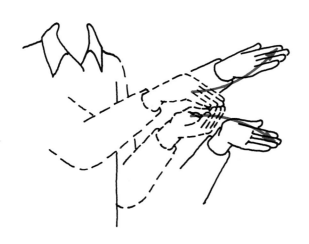

bark

Bent B shape both hands right palm down, left palm up. Move forward opening fingers so that tips point out. Repeat.

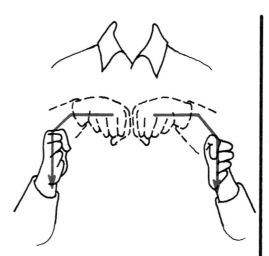

barn

B shape both hands palms down tips out, index fingers touching. Draw apart and down (palms facing) outlining shape of barn.

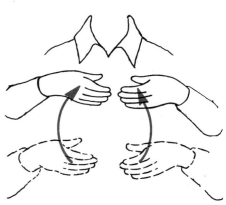

barrel

Curved open B both hands palms and tips facing. Move up indicating shape of barrel.

base

Open B both hands palms down, tips opposite. Circle right B under left B counterclockwise.

baseball

S shape both hands, right knuckles left, left knuckles right. Place right S on left and move forward (i.e. swinging a bat).

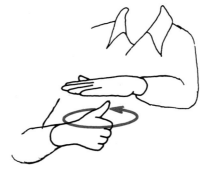

basement

Open B LH palm down, tips right. Circle right A, thumb extended, under right B counterclockwise.

bashful

Place backs of A's on cheeks and twist forward opening fingers.

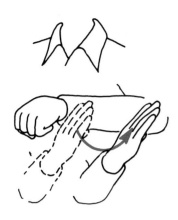

basket
Place index finger of right B under left wrist and arc to elbow.

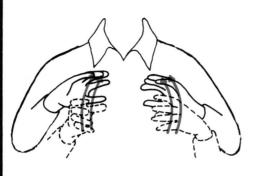

basketball
Mime holding and twisting ball.

bat(animal)
Cross arms on chest holding hands with thumbs and index fingers touching. Flick index fingers up.

bath
A shape both hands, knuckles in, thumbs up. Make scrubbing motion on chest.

batter
C shape LH palm and tips right. Stir tips of right B in left C clockwise.

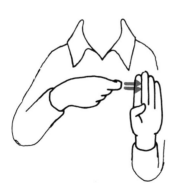

battery
B shape LH. Strike left index finger with knuckle of right index finger.

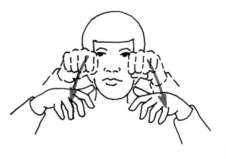

bawl
S shape both hands. Hold just under eyes and drop into five shapes palms down.

be
B shape RH palm left, tips up. Place index finger on mouth and move out.

beach

Open B both hands palms down, left tips slanted right, right tips slanted left. Circle right B over left hand up to elbow and back.

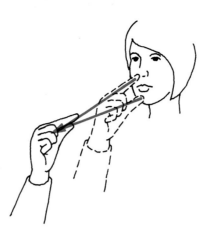

beak

Place tips of right G on nose and chin. Draw away closing fingers.

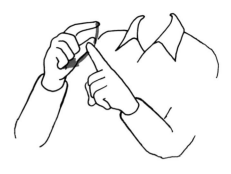

bean

One shape LH palm right, tip out. Strike once with tips of right G.

bear

Cross wrists of claw hands and scratch shoulders twice.

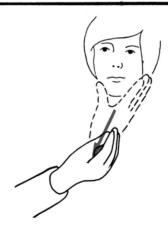

beard

Grasp chin with open B and draw down into flat O.

beat

Hold left index finger up and slap with right open B several times.

beautiful

Five shape RH palm in, tips up. Circle face from right to left ending in flat O. Then spread fingers palm in, tips up.

beauty

Five shape RH palm in, tips up. Circle face from right to left closing fingers into flat O shape. Follow with Y shape.

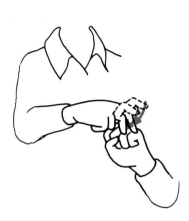

beaver

S shape LH knuckles down. Place tips of right bent V on back of left S and scratch back and fourth.

because

Open B RH palm in, tips left. Place tips on forehead and draw back to right ending in A shape, thumb up.

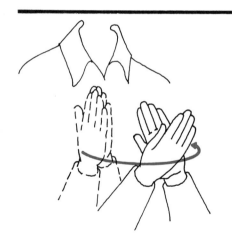

become

Open B both hands left palm in, right palm out. Place together and reverse positions.

bed

Place right palm on right cheek and tilt head slightly.

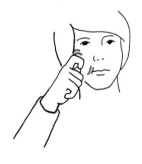

bee

Nibble right cheek with index finger and thumb of right X.

beef

Open B LH. Grasp between thumb and index with right thumb and index and shake.

21

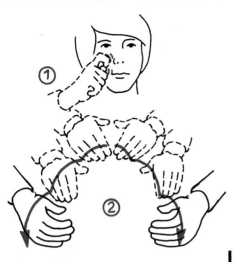

beehive
Nibble right cheek with index finger and thumb of right X. Then, open B both hands palms down. Move down outlining shape of hive.

been
Place index finger of letter B on lips. Move out and form letter N.

beer
Place right B against right cheek and circle forward.

beet
B shape both hands left palm right, tips up; right palm left, tips out. Slice palm of right B down palm of left.

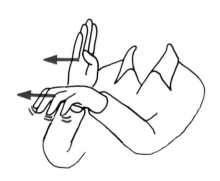

beetle
Rest base of right B on back of left claw hand which is held palm down. Move left claw forward in crawling motion.

before
Open B both hands palms in, thumbs up. Place RH inside LH and move back toward body.

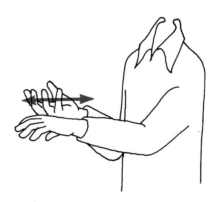

beg
Claw shape both hands left palm down, right palm up. Place back of right claw on back of left and draw back toward body in pleading manner.

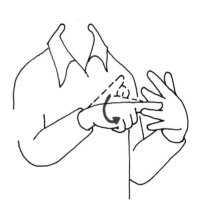

begin
Five shape LH palm right, tips out. Place right index between left middle and fourth fingers and make half turn.

22

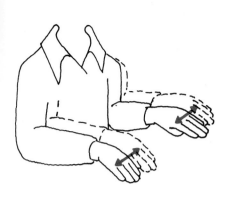

behave
B shape both hands palms down, tips out. Swing from left to right.

behind
A shape both hands knuckles facing, thumbs up. Place knuckles together and draw RH back of LH.

believe
Place right index on forehead then clasp both hands together.

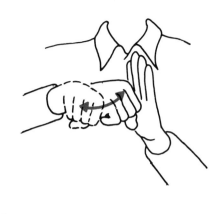

bell
Open B LH palm right, tips up. Strike right S against left palm and pull away.

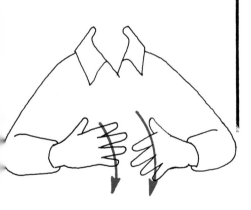

belly
Place hands on stomach then arc out and down outlining "big" stomach.

belong
F shape both hands fingers spread, palms facing. Hook right right index and thumb into left index and thumb.

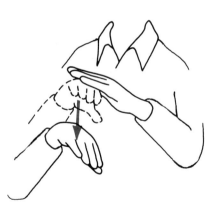

below
Open B both hands palms down, left tips slanted right, right tips slanted left. Place RH under LH and move down.

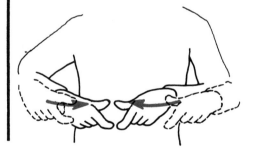

belt
Run index fingers and thumbs from each side of waist to middle of stomach (i.e. fasten buckle).

23

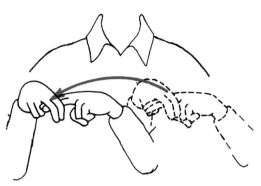

bench

H shape both hands palms down, left tips out right tips left. Hook right tips over left, lift up slightly, move both hands to right, and hook fingers again (i.e. long chair).

bend

Open B LH palm right. Grasp tips with RH and bend down.

beneath

Open B LH palm down, tips right. Place right A beneath left palm and describe a small circle.

berry

F shape RH palm in. Twist out into nine shape.

beside

B shape both hands tips out, left palm right, right palm left. Place right B on left then move off to right ending with palms opposite.

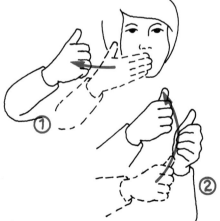

best

A shape LH knuckles right, thumb extended. Place fingers of right open B on lips, bring down in A shape below LH, then brush upward and past LH.

bet

B shape both hands palms up, tips out. Flip over toward one another ending with palms down. (Sometimes made with open B's).

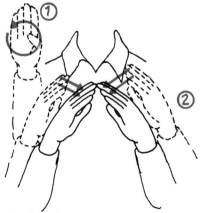

Bethlehem

Circle right B at shoulder. Then tap tips of both B's (palms facing) together.

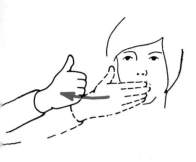

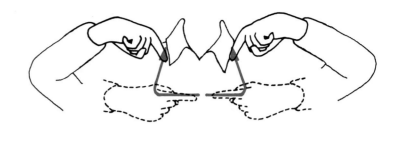

better
Open B RH, palm in, tips left. Place tips on chin then move upward into A shape with thumb extended.

between
Hold cupped LH in front of body. Place little finger edge of right open B in palm and move from fingers to thumb.

bib
One shape both hands palms in, tips facing. Move up to collar outlining bib.

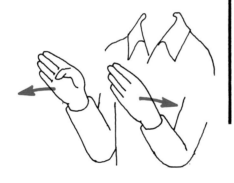

bicycle
S shape both hands knuckles down, LH below RH. Circle up and down as if pedaling.

big
B shape both hands, palms facing, tips out. Move away from one another.

bill
B shape RH palm up, tips out. Move forward.

bill (bird)
Place back of right G on mouth.

binoculars

C shape both hands palms facing. Place on eyes and twist as if adjusting binoculars.

bird

G shape right hand, tips left. Place on chin and snap index and thumb together twice.

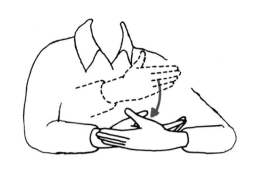

birthday

Open B both hands left palm up, tips right; right palm in, tips left. Flip right B over and place in left palm.

biscuit

Open B LH palm up, tips slanted right. A shape RH knuckles down, thumb extended. Twist right A in left palm.

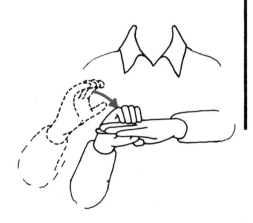

bite

B shape LH palm down, tips right. "Bite" with fingers of right C.

black

Draw index finger across forehead from one brow to the other.

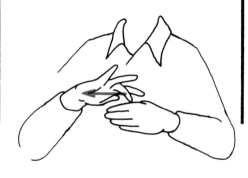

blade

B shape LH palm and tips slanted right. Slide right middle finger forward off left index.

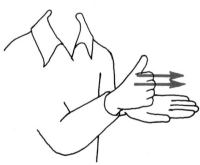

blame

B shape LH palm down, tips out. Slide right A, thumb extended, over back of LH twice.

blanket
B shape both hands palms down, tips facing. Move toward chest as if pulling blanket up to neck.

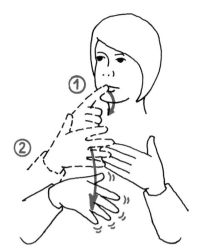

bleed
Open B LH palm in, tips right. Place right index finger on lips then flutter right fingers across back of left fingers.

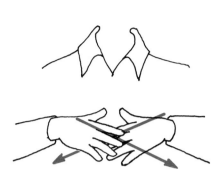

blend
Five shape both hands palms in, tips facing. Place right fingers on back of left fingers.

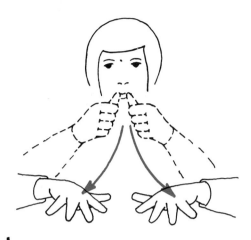

bless
A shape both hands knuckles facing, thumbs extended. Place on mouth then move out into five shapes palms down.

blind
Touch eyes with bent V.

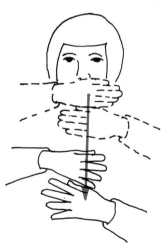

blind (window)
B shape both hands palms in, left tips right, right tips left. Hold in front of face then drop and spread fingers.

blindfold
C shape both hands palms facing. Place on eyes and move back to temples as if putting on blindfold.

blink
Snap right flat O in front of right eye.

blister
B shape LH palm down, tips out. Place tips of right claw on back of LH and draw up into O shape.

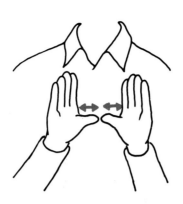

block
Open B both hands palms out. Tap thumbs together twice.

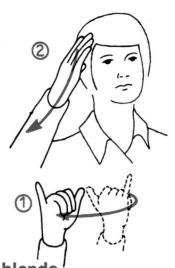

blonde
Y shape RH knuckles left. Twist so that knuckles face out. Change into B shape, place fingers on hair and move down.

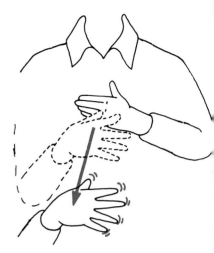

blood
Open B LH palm in, tips right. Trickle right fingers down back of left (i.e. blood dripping).

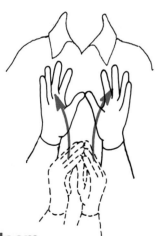

bloom
Place tips of flat O's together and open into five shapes, thumbs touching.

blossom
Place tips of flat O's together and open into five shapes, thumbs touching. Repeat.

blouse
Bent B both hands palms down held at upper chest. Turn out and over.

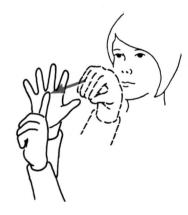

blow
Place right O on right edge of lips. Bring out into open 5 toward left index finger which is pointed up.

blue
B shape RH palm left, tips up. Shake slightly.

bluejay
B shape RH palm left. Shake slightly. Then place right G on head and move up closing index and thumb.

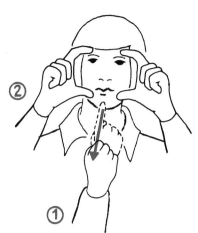

blush
Brush mouth with right index finger, then place index fingers and thumbs on cheeks.

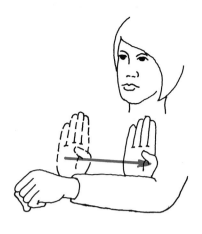

board
Run base of right B up left arm from wrist to elbow.

boat
Place little finger sides of open hands together, tips out, to form shape of boat. Move forward twice.

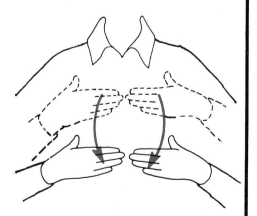

body
Open B shape both hands palms in, tips facing. Pat chest, then stomach.

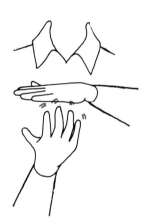

boil
Open B LH palm down, tips right. Flutter fingers of RH beneath LH.

boloney
B shape both hands right palm left, tips out. Slice down left index with palm of right open B.

bone
Three shape both hands palms in. Cross wrists in front of chest.

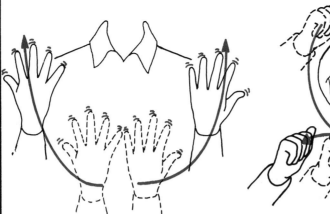

bonfire
Five shape both hands palms in. Flutter fingers while moving up in semicircular motion.

bonnet
A shape both hands. Mime putting on bonnet and tying strings under chin.

book
Palms together thumbs up. Open as if opening book.

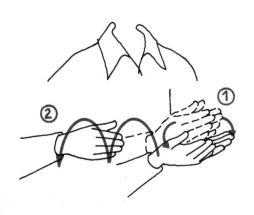

bookcase
Place palms together, thumbs up, and open as if opening book. Then form right open B palm left, tips out and move to right while dipping up and down.

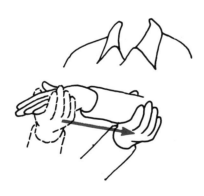

boot
B shape LH palm down, tips out. Place in right C which is held palm up, then slide right C up to left elbow.

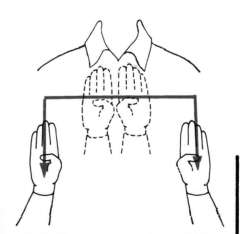

booth
B shape both hands held together. Move apart and down.

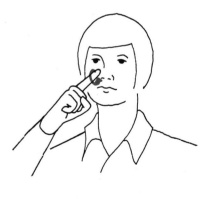

bore
Place right index on right side of nose and twist to left.

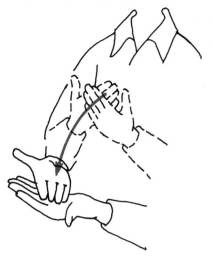

born

Open B both hands palms in. Cross in front of chest and move away turning palms up.

borrow

V shape both hands left palm right, tips out; right palm in, tips left. Place right V on left and draw back to body.

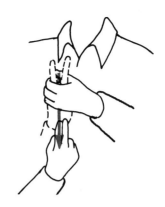

both

V shape RH palm in. Place in left C which is held palm in, then draw down and out.

bother

Open B both hands, left palm right, tips out; right palm in, tips left. Strike right little finger several times on left hand between thumb and forefinger.

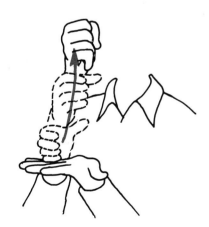

bottle

Place right C in left palm. Lift up closing into S shape.

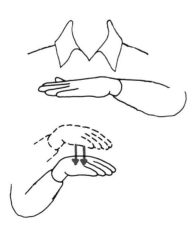

bottom

B shape both hands palms down, left tips right, right tips left. Place B under left and lower. Repeat.

bounce

Five shape RH palm down, tips out. Bounce up and down as if bouncing a ball.

bow

Place knuckles of bent V's together palms in. Draw apart into straight V's.

31

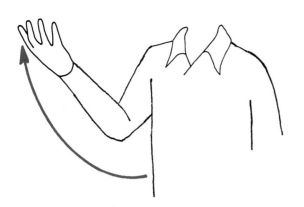

bowl (verb)
Mime throwing bowling ball.

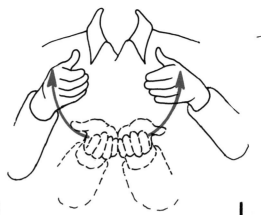

bowl (noun)
Hold cupped hands together palms up. Move apart and up outlining shape of bowl.

box (v)
Move fists in circular motion as if getting ready to box.

box
Open B both hands palms facing, thumbs up. Turn LH right and RH left to form shape of box.

boy
Snap flat O at forehead twice (indicating brim of cap.)

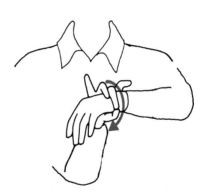

bracelet
Circle left wrist with right middle finger and thumb and twist slightly.

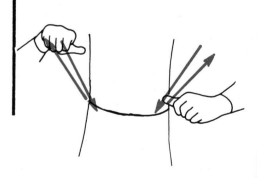

brag
A shape both hands knuckles down, thumbs extended. Punch sides of body with thumbs alternately.

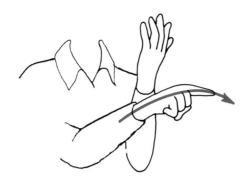

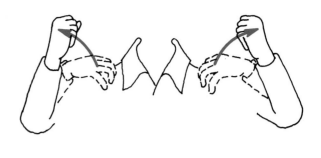

brake

A shape RH. Move forward quickly as if pushing brake.

branch

Open B left hand palm in. Slide right index across back of left wrist.

brave

Place claw hands on shoulders. Move out in strong movement ending in fists.

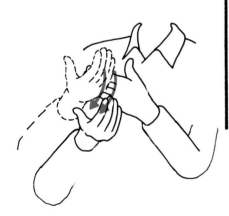

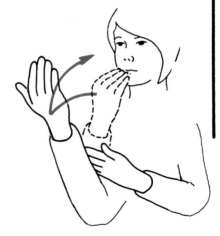

bread

Open B LH palm in, tips right. Draw little finger side of right hand down back of left fingers several times.

break

S shape both hands knuckles down, thumbs and index fingers touching. Break apart.

breakfast

Place tips of right flat O on lips then move out into open B. Now place little finger side of left open B, palm in, tips right, in crook of right elbow and bring right arm up.

breathe

Place tips of claw hands on chest and move in and out.

breeze
Open B both hands palms in, tips up and slanted toward one another. Fan toward shoulders.

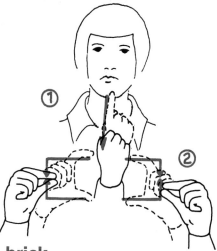

brick
Brush right index tip down chin. Then outline shape of brick with index fingers and thumbs.

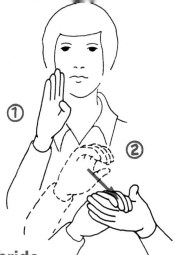

bride
Place index side of right B on right cheek then clasp hands together.

bridegroom
Place right G on forehead, tips left, then clasp hands together.

bridge
Hold left open B in front of body palm down, tips right. Place tips of right V under left wrist then arc to elbow.

bright
B shape both hands palms facing, tips up. Spread fingers and turn palms out.

brilliant
C shape RH palm left. Place thumb on forehead and move out.

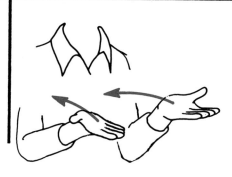

bring
Open B both hands palms up, one slightly behind the other. Move toward body as if carrying something.

34

broccoli

B shape LH. H shape RH palm in, tips left. Touch index finger of left B with tips of right H.

broil

Open B LH palm down, tips right. Flutter fingers of RH over back of LH.

brook

Open B both hands tips out, left palm up, right palm left. Slide little finger side of right B across left palm in wavy motion.

broom

S shape both hands. Mime holding broom and sweeping.

brother

L shape both hands, thumbs up; left palm right, right palm left. Touch forehead with right thumb then place right L on top of left L.

brown

B shape RH palm out, tips up. Place on right cheek and bring down a little.

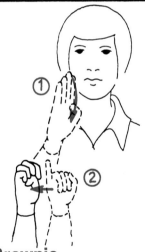

Brownie

Place the right B against the right cheek. Slide down and quickly form the letters I and E.

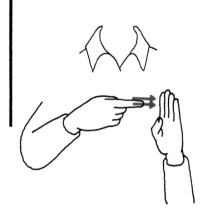

bruise

B shape LH. Touch left index with tip of right index.

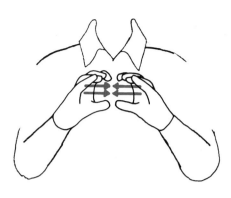

brush
Open B LH palm down, tips out. Brush tips of RH forward over back of left B.

brush (teeth)
Rub right index finger back and forth on teeth.

bubble
C shape both hands palms and tips facing. Tap tips together quickly.

bubble pipe
Place thumb of left Y on lips. Shake right fingers over left little finger and move up.

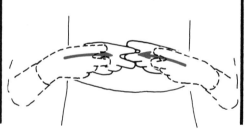
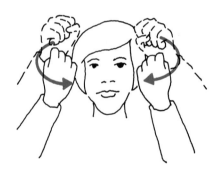

bucket
Hold left fist up as if holding handle of bucket. Place right index on thumb side then circle under to little finger side.

buckle
Bent V's both hands palms in, knuckles facing. Interlock at waist.

buffalo
S shape both hands. Place index sides on temples and reverse so that little finger sides touch temples.

bug
Place thumb of right 3 on nose and crook index and middle fingers down.

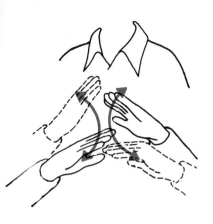

build
Open B both hands palms down, tips facing. Alternatively place one hand on top of other moving upward.

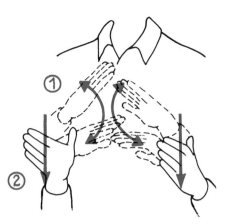

building
Open B both hands palms down, tips facing. Alternatively place one on top of other moving upward. Then form sides of building, palms facing.

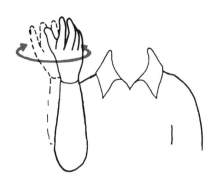

bulb
Mime screwing in light bulb.

bull
Place knuckles of right Y on forehead.

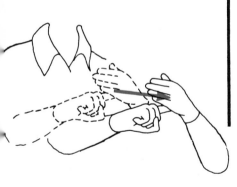

bulldozer
Open B LH palm in, tips right. Place right index in left palm and push forward.

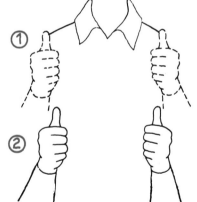

bulletin
A shape both hands palms facing, thumbs extended. Hold before chest, punch forward, drop and punch again.

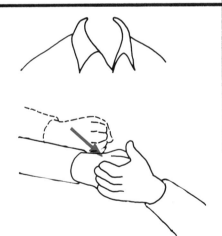

bump
Curved open B LH palm right, tips slanted out. Hit left palm with knuckles of right S.

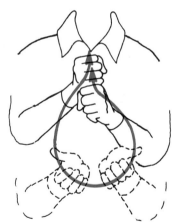

bundle
Hold cupped hands in front of body. Circle up, right above left closing into S shapes. Rest right S on left.

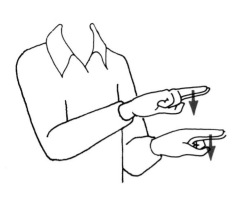

bunk

H shape both hands palm down, tips out. Hold left above right.

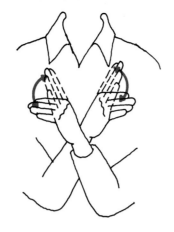

bunny

B shape both hands palms in, tips up. Cross wrists and flick fingers back toward body.

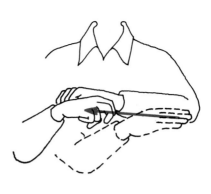

burglar

Place right B palm down, tips left, against left elbow then snatch back to wrist ending in bent V.

burn

One shape LH palm down tip right. Flutter fingers of RH beneath left index.

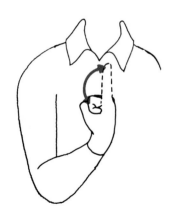

burp

Hold right S on chest and pop index finger up several times.

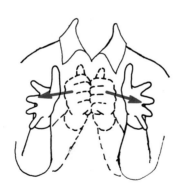

burst

A shape both hands knuckles touching. Draw apart and push forward into five shapes.

bury

B shape both hands palms facing, tips slanted down. Move down until tips face all the way down.

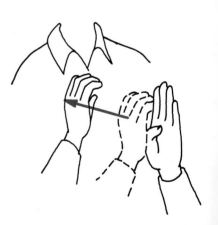

bus

B shape LH palm slanted out, tips up. Place little finger side of right C against left index and draw back to right.

bush
Five shape RH palm left, tips up. Place tips of left B on right wrist and wiggle right fingers.

business
B shape both hands left palm in, tips right; right palm left, tips up. Slide base of right B back and forth on left index.

busy
B shape both hands left palm in, tips right; right palm left, tips up. Place base of right B on inside of left index and flick back and forth.

but
Cross index fingers and draw apart.

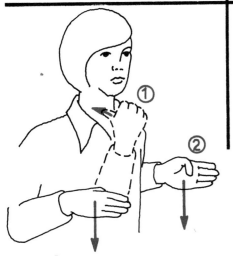

butcher
A shape RH knuckles down, thumb extended. Jab throat with thumb. Follow with agent marker.

butter
Open B LH palm up, tips out. brush twice with tips of right H.

buttercup
Place index side of right B on right cheek. Move over to left cheek ending in C shape palm left.

butterfly
Hook thumbs palms in, and flap fingers.

butterscotch

B shape LH palm down, tips slanted right. B shape RH palm left. Place base of right B on back of left B and make small circular motion.

button

Curve index finger inside thumb. Tap three times on chest beginning at top.

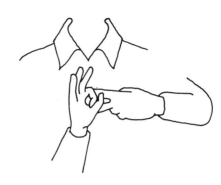

buttonhole

V shape LH palm in, tips right. Place on chest. Curve right index finger inside thumb, palm down, and place on left V.

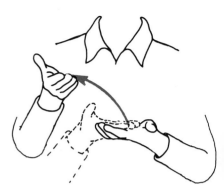

buy

Place back of right hand in left palm. Lift up and out.

buzz

Place right index finger on ear then zig-zag away to the right.

by

Form the letters B and Y in quick succession as if one movement.

C

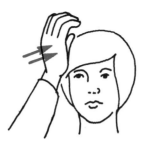

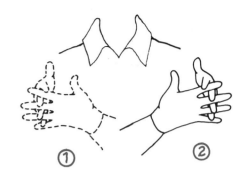

cabbage
Tap base of right C against right temple twice.

cabin
Interlock fingers and move from right to left.

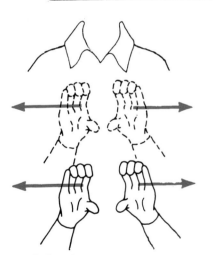

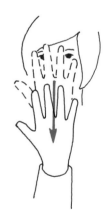

cabinet
C shape both hands palms out held close together. Move apart, lower and repeat motion (i.e. shelves).

caboose
H shape LH palm down, tips out. C shape RH palm and tips left. Rub base of right C back and forth on left H.

cafeteria
Place tips of flat O on mouth. Then form A shapes both hands palms facing, and move from right to left.

cage
Hold right 5 in front of forehead palm in. Drop to chin.

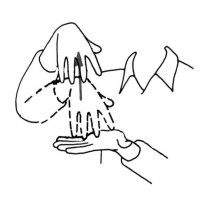

cake
Open B LH palm up, tips out. Hold right claw, tips down, over left palm then lift up spreading fingers.

calendar
Open B LH palm in. C shape RH palm and tips left. Place in left palm, slide over tips and down back of hand.

calf
Pace thumb of right Y on right temple and twist forward. Then hold right bent B over left bent B palms facing, and bend fingers slightly.

call
Place right C at right side of mouth and move out.

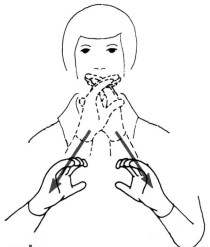

calm
C shape both hands left palm right, right palm left. Cross at mouth, draw down and apart.

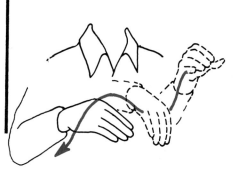

camel
C shape RH palm left. Beginning at left slide down toward right, come up and down again outlining hump.

camera
Mime holding camera in front of face and clicking shutter.

camp
V shape both hands palms facing, tips touching. Draw apart ending with palms down. Repeat.

42

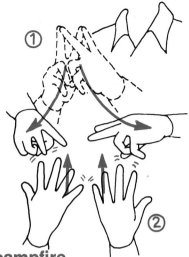

campfire
V shape both hands palms facing, tips touching. Draw apart ending with palms down. Change into five shapes palms up, and flutter fingers.

can (verb)
S shape both hands knuckles down. Move down in forceful motion.

can (noun)
Open B LH palm up, tips right. Place little finger side of right C in left palm and lift up.

Canada
Tap right upper chest with right A several times.

canary
Open B LH palm up, tips out. C shape RH palm left. Place thumb of right C on chin then swing over left palm.

candle
Place left index finger against back of right L. Flick right L into G shape.

candy
Place right index finger just below right side of mouth and twist.

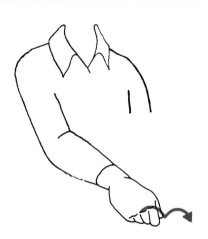

cane
Mime holding and using a walking cane.

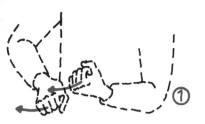
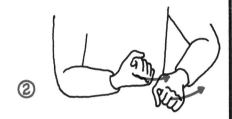

canoe
Mime paddling a canoe.

can't
One shape both hands palms down, tips slanted toward one another. Strike tip of left index with tip of right passing on down.

cantaloupe
C shape LH palm down. Thump back of left wrist with right middle finger.

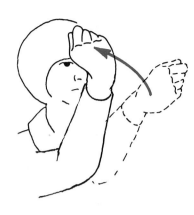

cap
A shape RH. Mime putting cap on head.

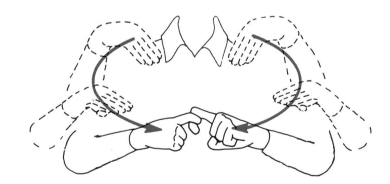

cape
Place curved hands on shoulders. Move forward in semicircles and hook index fingers.

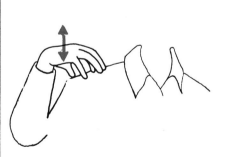

captain
Tap right shoulder with tips of right claw hand.

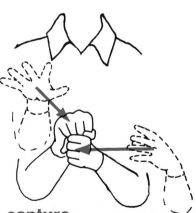

capture
Five shape both hands left palm and tips slightly right, right palm down, tips out. Bring together quickly closing into S shapes, right on top of left.

car
C shape both hands. Place little finger side of right C on index side of left C and draw away.

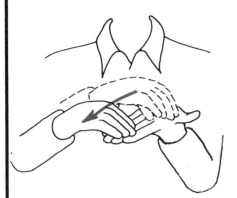

card
Open B LH palm up, tips out. C shape RH palm down. Slide off left palm.

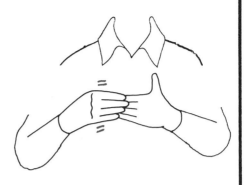

cardboard
Open B LH palm in, tips right. B shape RH palm in, tips left. Grasp left fingers with right fingers and wiggle back and forth.

care
V shape both hands palms facing, tips out. Strike index side of left V with little finger side of right V. Repeat.

careful
V shape both hands tips out, left palm right, right palm left. Place right V on left then circle forward and back.

careless
V shape RH palm left. Hold at right side of face and pass down across mouth ending palm down.

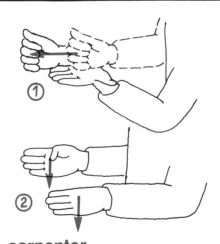

carpenter
Open B LH palm up, tips out. A shape RH. Place A on base of left palm and push forward as if planing a piece of wood. Follow with agent marker.

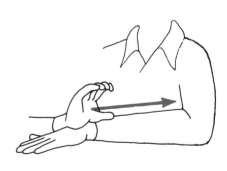

carpet
Open B LH palm down, tips out. Place base of right C on left wrist and slide up to elbow.

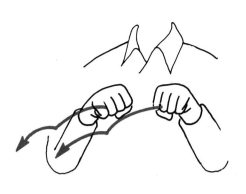

carriage
S shape both hands knuckles down. Move forward as if pushing a carriage.

carrot
Hold right S up to mouth and twist slightly as if crunching a carrot.

carry
Open 5 both hands palms up, tips slanted left. Move from left to right or vice versa in front of body.

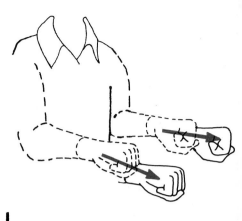

cart
S shape both hands palms down. Push straight forward.

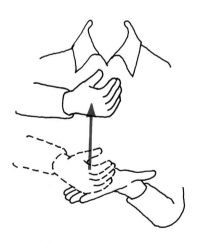

carton
Open B LH palm up, tips right. Place little finger side of right C in left palm then lift up high.

carve
C shape LH palm and tips down. B shape RH palm left. Make carving motions across left index and thumb with palm of right B.

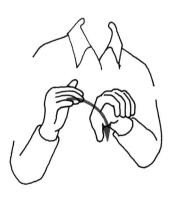

case
C shape both hands, right palm left. Arc fingers of right C into left C and hang over thumb.

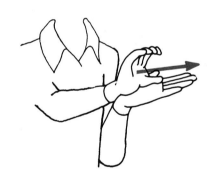

cash
Open B LH palm up, tips out. Place base of right C on base of left palm and move forward.

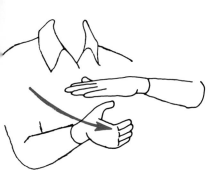

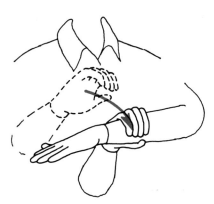

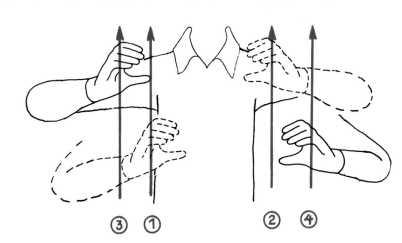

casserole

Open B LH palm down, tips right. C shape RH palm and tips left. Slide under left hand.

cast

Open B LH palm down, tips slanted right. Grasp left arm with right C.

castle

C shape both hands palms facing, left held higher than right. Move up alternately.

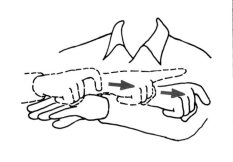

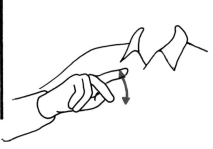

cat

Place thumb and forefinger of right 9 at side of mouth and pull away twice (indicating whiskers).

catch

Open B LH palm right, tips up. Hit middle of left palm with index and thumb of right C.

caterpillar

Open B LH palm down, tips right. Rest knuckles of right X on back of LH and make crawling movements up arm.

catsup (or ketchup)

K shape RH palm out, tips left. Shake up and down.

47

cauliflower

C shape RH. Place at right side of nose. Turn to left ending with little finger side touching face at left side of nose and palm facing right.

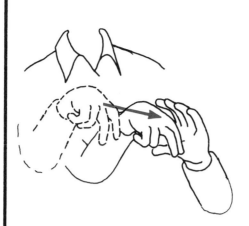

cave

C shape LH palm right. "Walk" right bent V into left C.

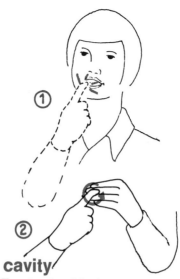

cavity

Tap teeth with right index then make circular movement on back of bent B which is held palm in.

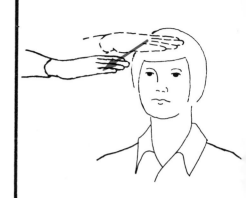

ceiling

B shape RH palm down, tips left. Place over head and move out.

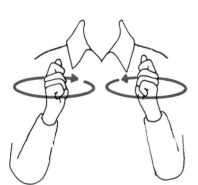

celebrate

S shape both hands knuckles facing. Circle toward one another.

celery

Bring right G up to mouth as if eating a piece of celery.

cellar

Open B LH palm down, tips right. C shape RH palm and tips left. Circle under right B counterclockwise.

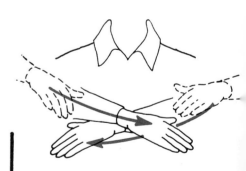

cemetery

Open B both hands palms down, left tips slanted right, right tips slanted left. Cross hands, right over left.

48

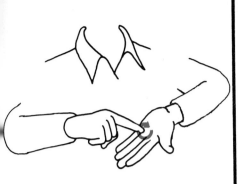

cent
Circle right index finger in left palm.

-cereal
Open B LH palm up, tips right. Place back of right C in left palm then lift to mouth.

certain
C shape RH palm and tips left. Place at mouth then move out forcefully.

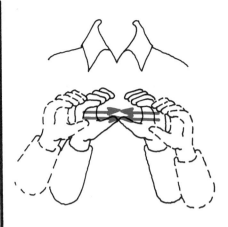

certificate
C shape both hands palms facing. Tap thumbs together.

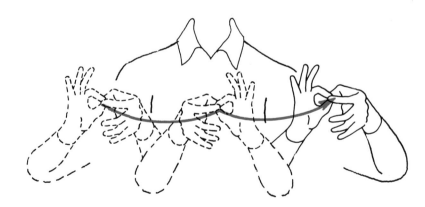

chain
Interlock index fingers and thumbs then reverse several times while moving to left.

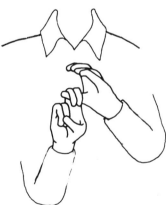

chair
C shape LH palm right. Hang right N over left thumb.

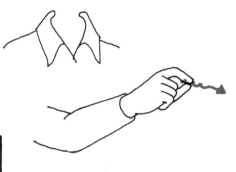

chalk
Mime writing on blackboard with chalk.

change
A shape both hands left knuckles up, right knuckles down. Place right wrist on left wrist, then reverse positions.

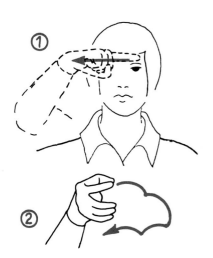

charcoal
Draw right index finger across brow from left to right and form the letter F. Move to left in short jumps and back to right as if placing coals on grill.

charge
Open B LH palm in, tips right. Strike with knuckles of right C.

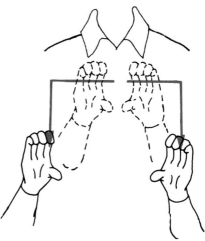

chart
C shape both hands. Hold close together then move apart and down in straight line.

chase
A shape both hands thumbs up, right A behind left. Move right A toward left in circular motion.

cheap
Open B LH palm right, tips out. B shape RH palm down, tips out. Place index side of right B on left palm and bend fingers down.

cheat
Open B LH palm right, tips out. Straddle with right middle and index fingers. Move hands up and down several times.

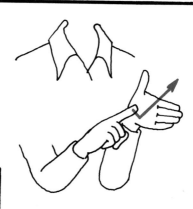

check
Open B LH palm up, tips out. Outline check mark in left palm with right index.

50

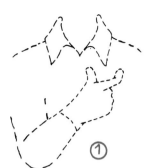 ①  ②

checkered

G shape RH palm in. Place tips on left upper chest. Then turn upside down so that index finger is on the bottom.

cheek

Make circle on right cheek with right index tip.

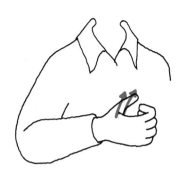

cheer

C shape RH palm and tips in. Place on chest and brush up and out twice.

cheese

Twist heel of right palm on heel of left palm.

cherry

V shape LH palm down, tips right. Twist left index then middle finger with tips of right flat O.

chest

Place tips of left bent B on upper left side of chest then move over to right side.

chew

Bent V both hands left tips up, right tips down. Circle right tips over left tips clockwise.

51

chewing gum

V shape RH palm left. Place tips on right cheek then bend up and down rapidly.

chick

Open B LH palm up, tips slanted right. Place knuckles of right G in left palm and tap index and thumb together twice.

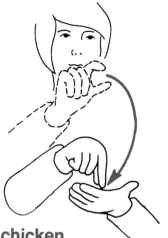

chicken

Place side of right G on mouth then place tips in left palm.

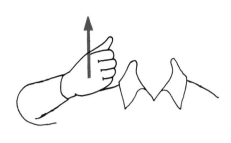

chief

A shape RH knuckles left, thumb extended. Raise up above shoulder level.

child

Open B RH palm down, tips out. Move down to the right.

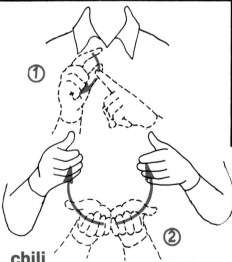

chili

One shape LH palm right, tips out. Strike once with tips of right G. Now place cupped hands together, palms up, then move apart and up outlining shape of bowl.

chill

Place right bent V on top of left bent V with thumbs touching. Rub back and forth (teeth chattering).

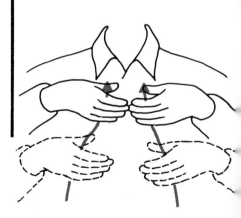

chimney

C shape both hands palms in, tips almost touching. Draw up in shape of chimney.

52

chin

Make circle on chin with index finger.

China

Place tip of right index on edge of right eye and twist forward.

chipmunk

C shape both hands palms facing, wrists touching. Tap tips together at mouth.

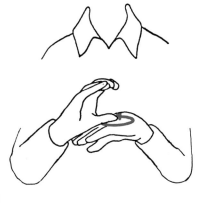

chocolate

Place thumb of right C on back of left hand and circle counterclockwise.

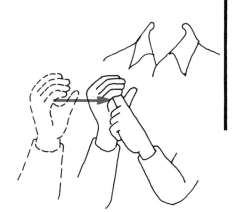

choke

One shape LH. C shape RH palm and tips left. Hit left index with right C.

choose

Right open F shape fingers spread. Move to right closing thumb and index.

chop

Open B both hands left palm up, tips slanted right; right palm and tips slanted left. "Chop" left palm with little finger of right B.

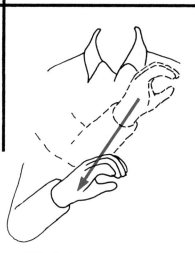

Christ

Place right C against left shoulder and move to right side of waist.

53

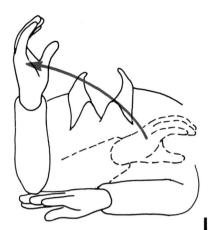

Christmas
Place elbow of right C on back of LH which is held before you tips right. Arc right C from left to right.

chubby
Place claw hands on cheeks.

church
Tap right C on back of left S twice.

cider
Place thumb of right C on right cheek and twist forward.

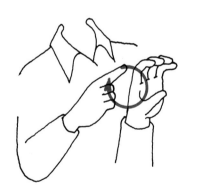

circle
C shape LH palm and tips right. Circle clockwise with right index finger without touching.

circus
Bent B LH palm down. Place tips of right bent V on back of LH and circle clockwise.

city
Open B LH, palm right, tips up. C shape RH palm left. Tap hands together twice.

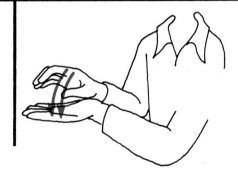

clam
Open B LH palm up, tips out. Curved open B RH palm down. Place base of right B on base of left. Lower fingers then raise. Repeat.

clap

Open B both hands palms facing. Clap together several times.

class

C shape both hands palms facing. Move down in semicircles ending with palms up.

claw

Claw shape RH palm out. Turn so that palm faces body.

clay

Put hands together and move slightly as if molding clay.

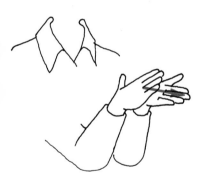

clean

Open B both hands left palm up, tips out; right palm down, tips left. Brush right palm across left as if wiping clean.

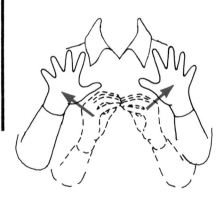

clear

Place tips of flat O's together, open into five shapes and turn out.

clever

Place tip of right middle finger on forehead then flick out.

climb

Bent V RH palm out. Move up in short movements as if climbing ladder.

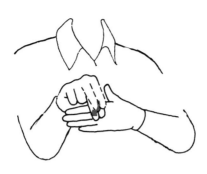

clip (noun)
Open B LH palm in, tips right. Snap right index, middle finger and thumb over left index.

clip (verb)
Flat O LH tips up. V shape RH palm down, tips left. Snip over left tips with right V.

clock
Touch back of left wrist with right index finger. Then outline clock with double C's facing one another.

close (verb)
B shape both hands palms facing, tips out. Turn toward each other so that index fingers touch.

closet
B shape both hands index fingers touching. Turn RH to right, then, hook right index over base of left and move forward.

cloth
Open B RH palm in, tips left. Rub up and down on upper right side of chest.

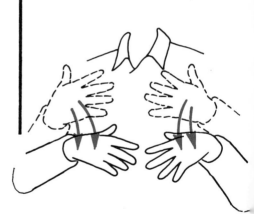

clothes
Brush open palms down chest twice ending with palms out.

clothespin
Brush open palms down chest twice then snap right index, middle finger and thumb over left index.

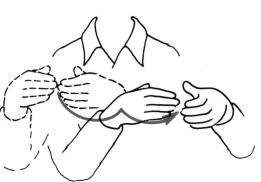

cloud
Loose C shape both hands palms facing. Drift toward left in two movements.

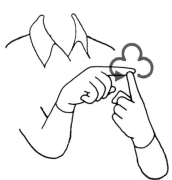

clover
One shape LH. Touch with right index and outline clover leaf.

clown
Place tips of right claw hand on nose and move back and forth several times.

club
C shape both hands palms facing, thumbs touching. Draw apart and around until little fingers touch.

coal
Draw thumb of right C across eyebrows from left to right.

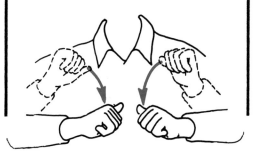

coat
A shape both hands. Trace shape of lapels with thumbs.

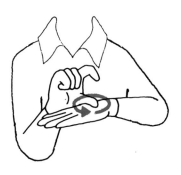

cocoa
Place thumb of right C (middle, fourth and little fingers closed) on back of left hand and circle counterclockwise.

coconut
Mime holding coconut at right side of head and shaking.

cocoon
Interlock thumbs, palms in, and close fingers.

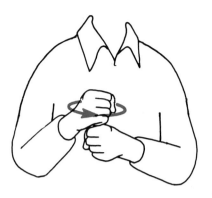

coffee
Place right S on left S and make a grinding motion counter clockwise.

coke
Hold left arm out. Stick upper arm with index finger of right L and wiggle thumb.

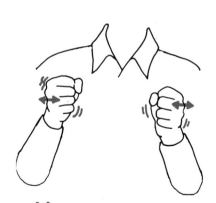

cold
S shape both hands. Draw hands close to body and "shiver".

collar
G shape both hands tips facing. Place at neck and outline collar.

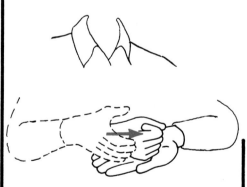

collect
Open B LH palm up, tips out. Pass right C over left palm and close into S shape.

color
Five shape, RH, palm in. Flutter fingers at chin level.

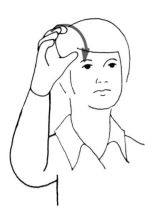

colt

Place thumb of right C against right temple and bend fingers forward twice.

comb

Brush open fingers through hair twice.

come

One shape both hands knuckles up, tips out. Bring tips up and back toward chest.

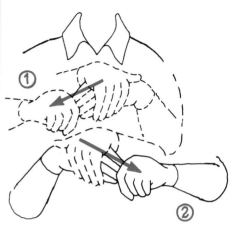

comfortable

Curved open B shape both hands palms down. Place right palm on back of LH, slide off then reverse motion.

compare

Curved open B both hands, tips out, left palm up, right palm down. Turn each over reversing positions.

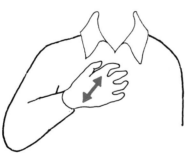

complain

Tap tips of right claw on chest.

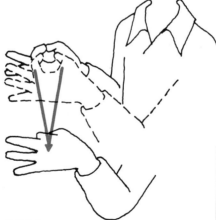

cone

F shape both hands palms facing, tips out. Drop left F down.

confuse

Curved five shapes both hands left palm up, right palm down, held over left. Circle both hands counterclockwise.

59

connect
Lock right index and thumb into left index and thumb and wiggle slightly.

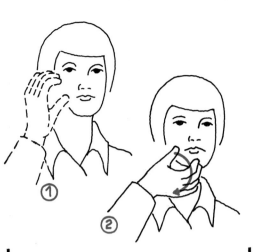

consonant
Place right C on mouth, then circle forward.

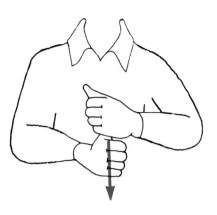

constipate
A shape both hands left palm right, right palm left, thumb extended. Place right thumb in left A and pull down once.

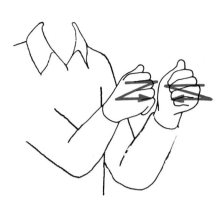

contest
A shape both hands, knuckles facing. Zig-zag back and forth.

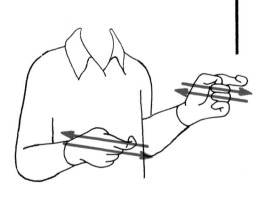

control
X shape both hands knuckles facing. Move back and forth alternately as if holding reins.

cook
Open B both hands left palm up, right palm down. Place right palm on left and flip over. (Flipping pancakes.)

cookie
Open B LH palm up, tips out. C shape RH palm down. Place tips of right C in left palm and twist as if cutting out cookies.

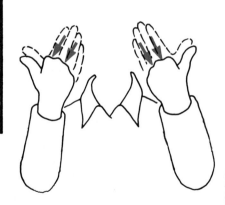

cool
Open B both hands palms in, tips up and slanted toward one another. Hold above shoulders and wave fingers backward.

cooperate
Hook right index and thumb into left index and thumb then circle counterclockwise.

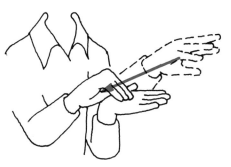

copy
Open B LH palm up, tips out. Hold right hand palm down, fingers spread, above and slightly ahead of LH. Draw back into flat O shape and place in left palm.

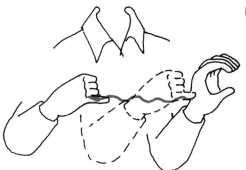

cord
C shape LH palm out. Place tip of right little finger on back of right C and draw away to right in wiggly motion.

cork
S shape LH knuckles right. Place right thumb in top of left S.

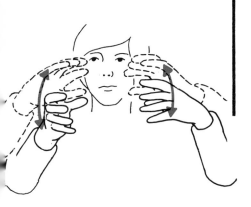

corn
Hands face each other as if holding an ear of corn. Rotate slightly.

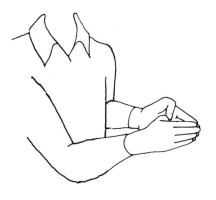

corner
B shape both hands left palm right, tips out; right palm in, tips left. Place tips together forming corner.

correct
One shape both hands tips out, left palm right, right palm left. Place right one on top of left. Repeat.

cost
Open B LH palm in, tips right. Strike with index finger of right X.

61

costume
C shape both hands, palms facing. Place thumbs on lapels, arc down and out.

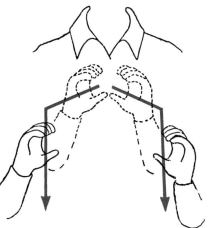

cottage
C shape both hands palms out. Outline roof and sides of cottage.

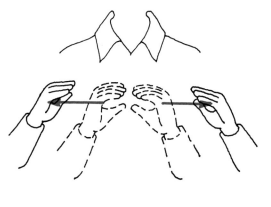

cotton
C shape both hands palms facing. Draw apart into flat O's.

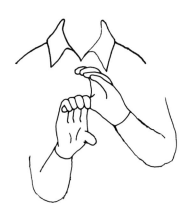

couch
C shape both hands left palm out, right palm left. Hook right C over thumb of left C.

cough
C shape RH palm in. Place under throat with index and thumb touching chest. Rock up and down.

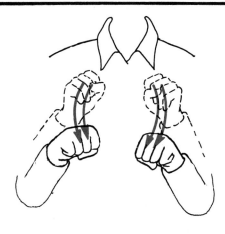

could
S shape both hands knuckles down. Move down in forceful motion. Repeat.

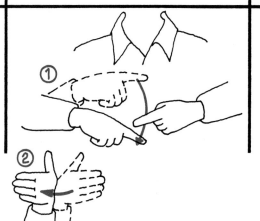

couldn't
One shape both hands palms down, tips slanted toward one another. Strike tip of left index with tip of right, then form irregular past marker.

count
Open B LH palm right, tips up. Run thumb and index finger of right nine shape up left palm.

country
Rub left elbow with palm of right open B.

cousin
Twist right C at right side of head.

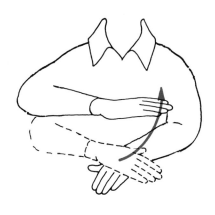

cover
Open B shape both hands palms down, tips slanted toward one another. Slide right palm over back of left hand then lift up.

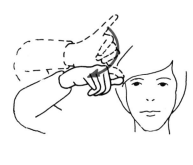

cow
Place thumb of right Y on right temple and twist forward.

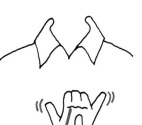

coward
One shape LH. L shape RH. Place back of right Y on back of left index and shake while moving forward.

crab
Modified L shape both hands palms facing. Snap index fingers and thumbs together twice.

cracker
Tap left elbow several times with right A.

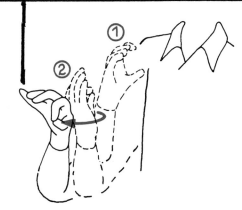

cranberry
C shape RH palm left. Twist out into nine shape.

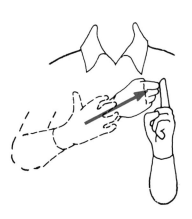

crash
One shape LH. Claw shape RH palm in. Strike against left index while closing fingers.

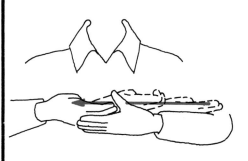

crawl
Open B LH palm up, tips right. Place back of right H on left wrist, change to bent V shape, then draw back to fingers (two movements) and change back into H shape.

crayon
Open B LH palm up, tips out. C shape RH palm left. Move right thumb forward on left palm.

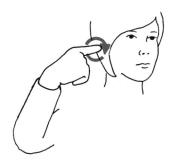

crazy
Circle right index finger around right ear.

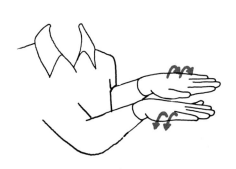

creak
Open B both hands palms down, tips out, index fingers touching. Twist hands away from each other.

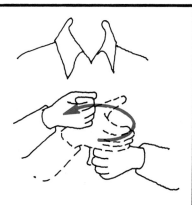

cream
S shape LH knuckles right. Pass right C over left S as if skimming cream and close into S shape.

creep
Hold left arm in front of body palm in. With right fingers "creep" up left arm from elbow to wrist.

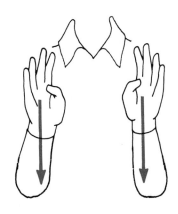

crib
Four shape both hands. Lower slightly.

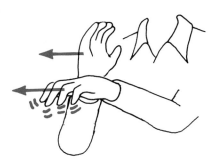

cricket

Place base of right C on back of left claw hand which is held palm down. Move left claw forward in crawling motion.

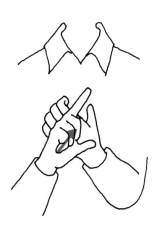

crime

C shape LH palm and tips in. Place right L against back of left C.

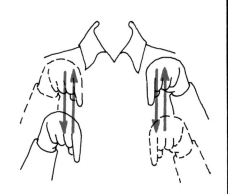

cripple

One shape both hands tips down. Move up and down alternately.

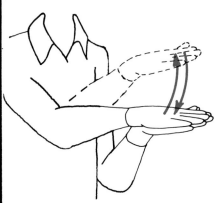

crocodile

Place right palm on left palm, tips out. Raise right hand up then drop back to original position.

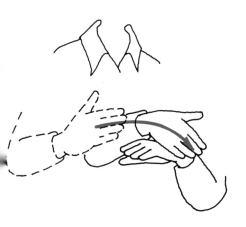

cross

Open B LH palm down, tips out. Slide little finger edge of right open B across back of LH.

crow

Place wrist of right G (tips out) on left side of chin and jerk up and down.

cruel

A shape LH knuckles right. C shape RH palm left. Place C on chin then brush past left A rapidly.

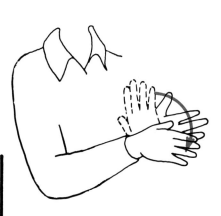

crush

Open B both hands left palm right, tips out; right palm left, tips up. Place base of right palm on base of left palm then circle forward and down.

cry
Place index tips under eyes and draw down as if tracing tears.

cub
Cross C hands on chest and tap shoulders lightly.

cube
Modified C shape RH (middle, fourth and little fingers closed) palm left. Turn over so that palm faces up.

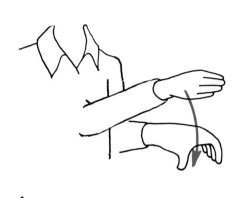

cucumber
C shape LH palm down. B shape RH palm left, tips out. Slice right B down side of left C.

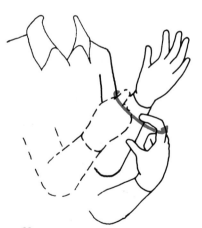

cuff
Hold LH up and outline wrist with right thumb and index (other fingers closed).

cup
Open B LH palm up, tips right. Place little finger side of right X in left palm.

cupid
C shape RH. Move back and forth toward body.

cure
Place right C on right cheek. Move upward into A shape with thumb extended.

66

curious
F shape RH palm in. Place thumb and forefinger on throat and wiggle.

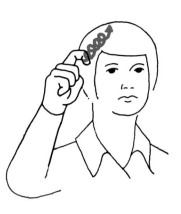

curl
With index finger of right X outline ringlets and/or curls in hair.

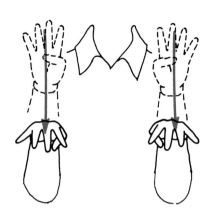

curtain
Four shape both hands. Drop forward and down ending with palms down.

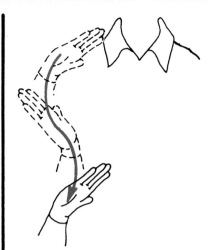

curve
Curve right C downward.

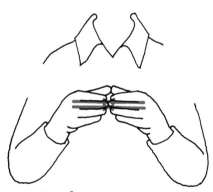

custard
C shape both hands palms facing. Place tips together. Repeat.

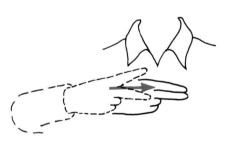

cut
V shape RH palm in, tips left. Move fingers as if snipping with scissors.

cute
Place index and middle fingers on chin. Move down closing over thumb.

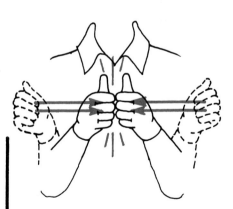

cymbal
A shape both hands knuckles facing, thumbs extended. Hit together as if banging cymbals.

D

daddy
Five shape RH palm left, tips up. Tap forehead with thumb twice.

daffodil
Place right D on right side of nose then move over to left side.

dairy
Open B LH palm up, tips out; D shape RH. Twist heel of right D on heel of left palm.

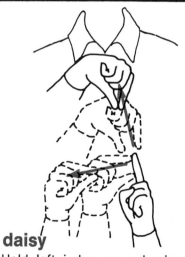

daisy
Hold left index up and mime plucking petals off with right G.

damage
A shape both hands left knuckles up, right knuckles down. Brush right knuckles over left and back once.

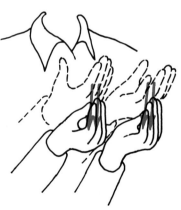

damp
Hold curved palms up then drop into flat O's. Repeat.

dance
Open B LH palm up, tips out. Sweep right V over left palm several times.

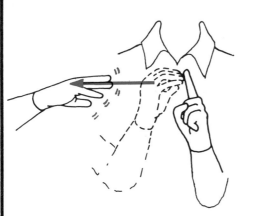

dandelion
Place tips of right flat O on left index and flutter away to right.

dangerous
A shape both hands thumbs up. Bring right A up and place wrist on back of left wrist.

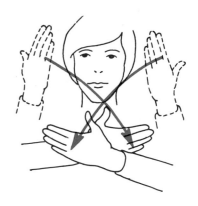

dark
Open B both hands palms in, tips up. Cross in front of eyes.

daughter
Place thumb of right A on right cheek. Change into open B palm up, tips left, and place in crook of left elbow.

day
Hold left arm before you palm down, tips right. Point right index finger up. Then rest right elbow on back of left hand and arc down to elbow.

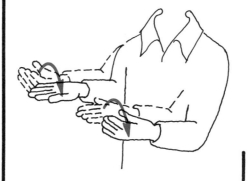

dead
Open B both hands palms facing. Turn right palm up and left palm down at same time.

deaf
Point index finger to ear. Then place index fingers of double B's together, palms down.

69

dear
D shape both hands. Cross on chest.

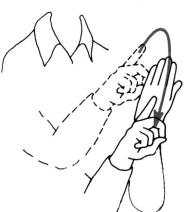

December
Open B LH palm in. Place right D against left palm, slide over fingers and down back of hand.

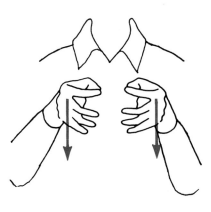

decide
F shape both hands palms facing, tips out. Lower in decisive manner.

decorate
Flat O both hands, left palm up, right palm down. Touch tips and reverse.

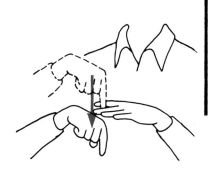

deep
Open B LH palm down, tips right. Push right index down between left middle and fourth fingers.

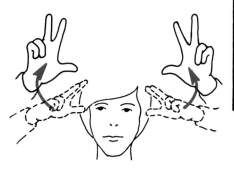

deer
Three shape both hands palms out. Place thumbs on temples and move out and up.

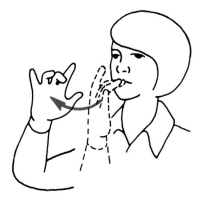

delicious
Place tip of right middle finger on lips and twist out.

deliver
Open B both hands palms in, left tips right, right tips slanted down. Place right palm on back of left hand, then move upward and out.

dentist
Tap teeth with right index finger.

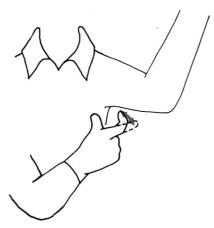

deodorant
Mime spraying deodorant under armpit.

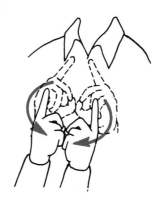

department
D shape both hands palms facing. Touch tips, move out in semi-circles and come together with little fingers together.

depend
Cross index fingers, right on top of left. Move down, then up again.

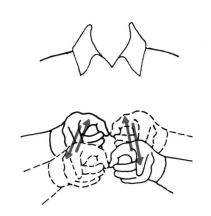

describe
D shape both hands palms facing. Move back and forth alternately.

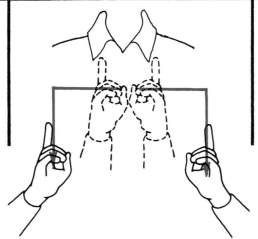

desk
D shape both hands palms facing, thumbs almost touching. Draw apart and down.

dessert
Place little finger side of right D on left palm, then raise to lips.

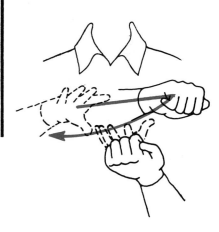

destroy
Five shape both hands tips out, left palm up, right palm down. Close into A shapes, pass right over left and back again.

detective
Place right D on upper left side of chest and circle clockwise.

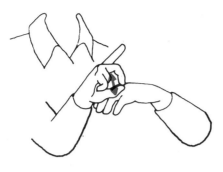

diamond
Tap left fourth finger with right D.

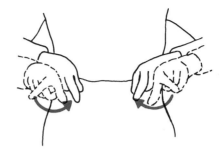

diaper
L shape both hands palms down, held at waist. Close forefingers and thumbs.

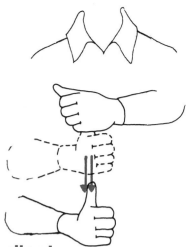

diarrhea
A shape both hands left knuckles right, right knuckles left, thumb extended. Place right thumb in bottom of left A and withdraw twice.

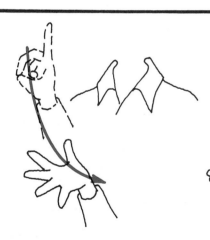

dice
D shape RH. Throw to the left opening into five shape.

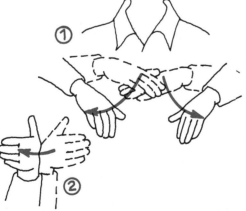

didn't
Open B both hands palms down, left tips slanted right, right tips slanted left. Place RH on LH, draw apart and use irregular past marker.

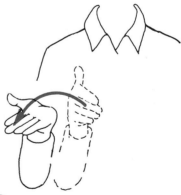

die
Open B RH hand palm left, tips out. Turn so that palm faces up.

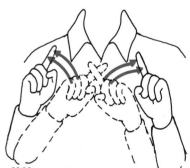

different
Cross index fingers and pull apart so that fingers point outward. Repeat.

72

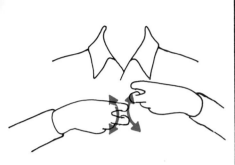

difficult
Bent V both hands knuckles facing. Strike together once or twice.

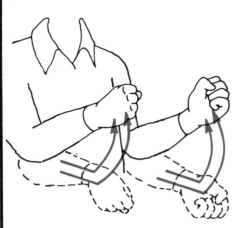

dig
S shape both hands left palm up, right palm down. Push down and up as if digging with a shovel.

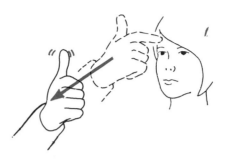

dime
Place right index finger on right temple. Bring out into ten shape and shake.

dimple
Twist tip of right index finger in right cheek.

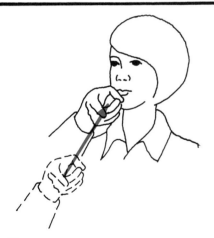

dine
D shape RH knuckles left. Bring up to mouth as if eating.

dinner
Place tips of right flat O on lips. Hold left arm in front of body palm down, tips right. Turn right flat O over into open B palm down, and droop over left wrist.

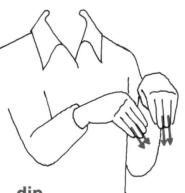

dip
Flat O both hands tips down. Dip down twice.

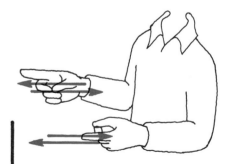

direct
D shape both hands palms facing, index tips out. Move back and forth alternately as if handling reins.

73

dirt
Place back of RH tips left under chin. Wiggle fingers.

disappear
V shape LH palm down, tips slanted right. Place right index between left V and draw down into S shape.

disappoint
Place tip of right index on chin.

disease
D shape both hands palms in, left knuckles right, right knuckles left. Place right D on forehead and left on chest.

disguise
Open B RH palm in. Hold above shoulder level, then pass down in front of face ending with tips left.

dish
Place tips of curved open B's together. Arc back so that wrists touch — outlining dish.

disobey
S shape RH palm in, knuckles up. Twist so that palm faces out.

disposal
Open B both hands left palm up, tips out; right palm in, tips left. Scrape little finger side of right B outward across left palm.

74

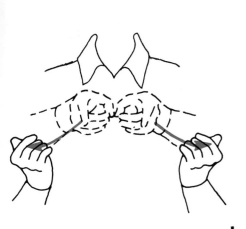

dissolve
D shape both hands palms facing, tips touching. Draw down and apart ending in A shapes, knuckles out.

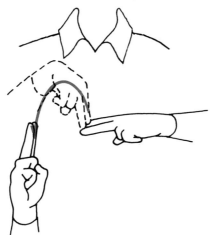

dive
H shape both hands left palm down, tips right; right palm right, tips down. Place right tips on left tips then arc up to right ending with tips up.

do
Claw shape both hands palms down. Swing back and forth.

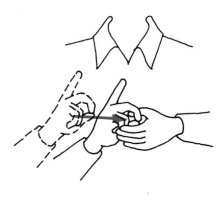

dock
C shape LH palm and tips right, little finger side down. D shape RH palm left. Slide right D into left C.

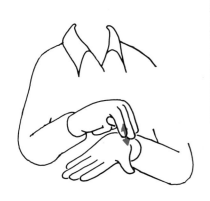

doctor
Open B LH palm up, tips out. Touch left wrist with tips of right M.

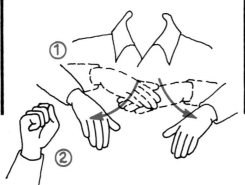

doesn't
Open B both hands palms down, left tips slanted right, right tips slanted left. Place RH on LH, draw apart and form right S.

dog
Snap thumb and middle finger twice.

doll
Brush tip of nose with right X twice.

75

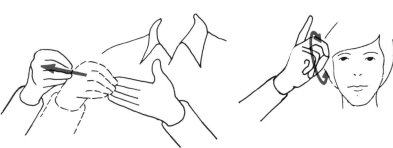
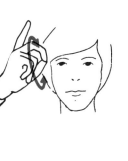
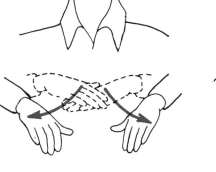

dollar
Open B LH palm in, tips right. Grasp left fingers with right fingers and thumb. Draw RH back to right.

donkey
Place tips of right D on right temple. Twist back and forth.

don't
Open B both hands palms down, left tips slanted right, right tips slanted left. Place RH on LH and draw apart.

door
B shape both hands palms out slightly, tips a little up. Place index fingers together then turn right hand to right ending with palm up.

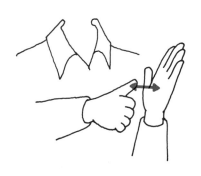
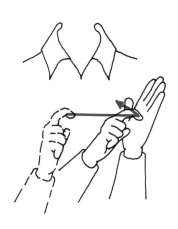

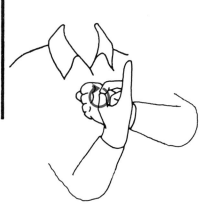

doorbell
Open B LH palm right. A shape RH knuckles left thumb extended. Punch left palm with right thumb.

dot
Open B LH palm right. Place tip of slightly bent right index in left palm.

double
Open B LH palm up tips out. Place middle finger of right V in left palm and flip over.

dough
S shape LH palm in, knuckles right. D shape RH palm right. Circle clockwise on back of left S.

doughnut
R shape both hands palms out, fingers touching. Turn over ending with R's touching, palms up.

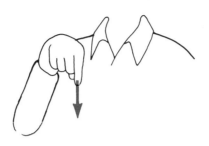

down
Point index finger down.

downstairs
Point index finger down and move up and down twice.

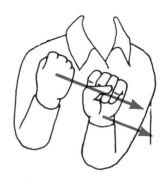

drag
S shape both hands, right held about shoulder level with knuckles in; left in front of chest. Move forward simultaneously.

draw
Open B LH palm right, tips up. Draw right little finger down left palm in wavy motion.

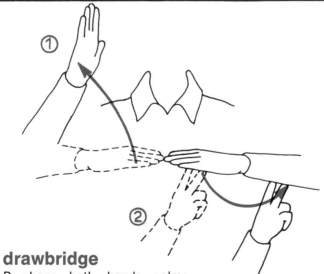

drawbridge
B shape both hands palms down, tips touching. Raise RH up. Now hold left arm in front palm down, tips right, place tips of right V under wrist and arc to elbow.

drawer
Hold cupped hands in front of body palms up then draw back as if pulling drawer open.

77

dream
Place right index finger on forehead. Move up and out crooking finger several times.

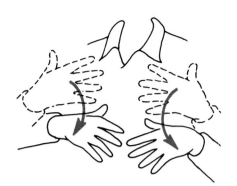

dress
Five shape both hands, palms in. Brush thumbs down chest ending with palms down, fingers out.

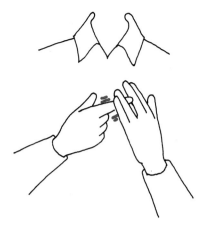

drill
Open B LH palm right, tips out. Push index finger of right L through left middle and fourth fingers in jerky motion.

drink
Place C shape on mouth as if drinking.

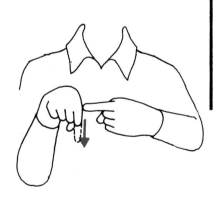

drip
One shape LH palm down, tip right. S shape RH palm down. Place left tip on base of right index then flip right index out.

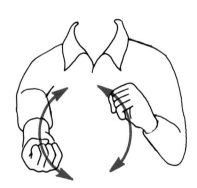

drive
A shape both hands. Move as if turning steering wheel of car.

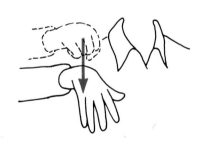

drop
Hold right S at shoulder level. Drop into 5 shape, fingers and palm down.

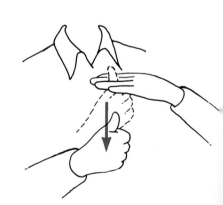

drown
Open B LH palm down, tips right. Place extended thumb of right A between left middle and fourth fingers and pull down.

78

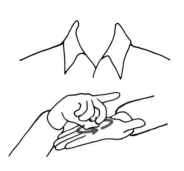

drug
Circle tips of right D on left palm.

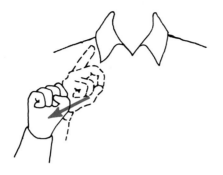

drugstore
Form the letters D and S in quick succession.

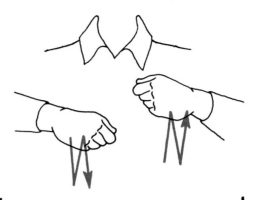

drum
Mime holding drum sticks and beating drum.

dry
Draw bent index finger from left to right across chin.

duck
Snap thumb, index and middle fingers together at mouth. (i.e., duck quacking)

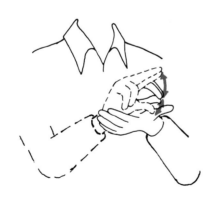

duckling
Snap thumb, index and middle fingers of RH in palm of LH.

dull
D shape RH palm in. Place on left side of chin then slide over to the right side.

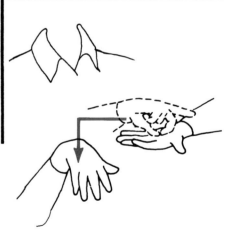

dump
Open B LH palm up, tips right. Slide right D off left palm and drop down opening into five shape palm in.

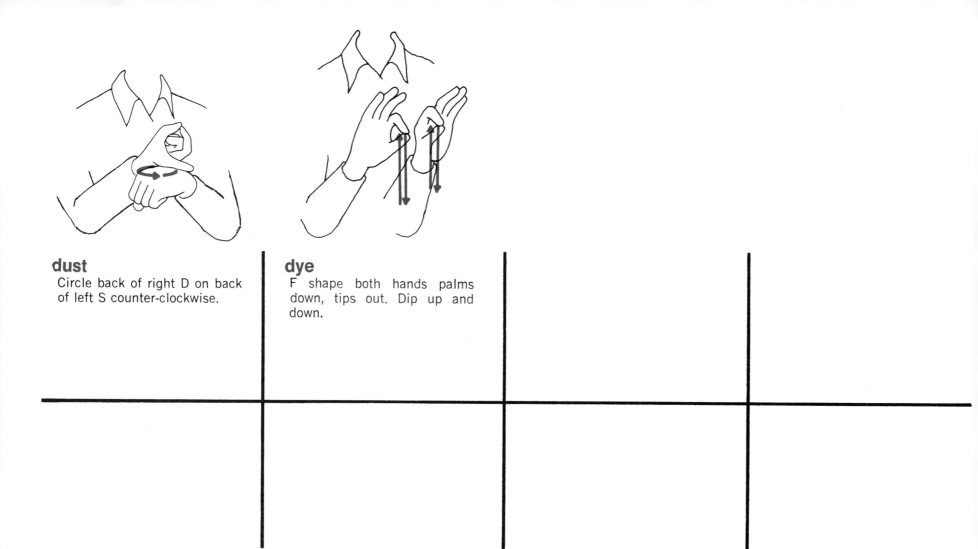

dust
Circle back of right D on back of left S counter-clockwise.

dye
F shape both hands palms down, tips out. Dip up and down.

E

each
One shape LH knuckles right. Slide knuckles of right A (thumb up) down left index finger.

eagle
Crook right X around tip of nose and turn slightly.

ear
Pinch lobe of right ear with right index and thumb, other fingers closed.

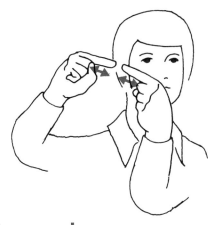

earache
Point index fingers at each other beside right ear. Repeat.

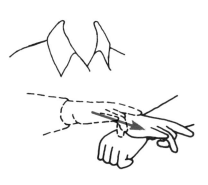

early
S shape LH palm down, knuckles out. Place tip of right middle finger on back of left S, bend down and over.

earmold
Place right index finger and thumb in right ear (other fingers spread).

81

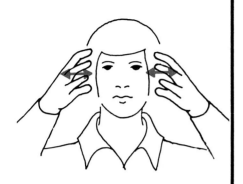

earmuff
Claw shape both hands. Tap tips over ears.

earring
Grasp tip of right ear with right thumb and index finger.

earth
S shape LH palm down. Place right thumb and middle finger on back of left hand near wrist and rock back and forth.

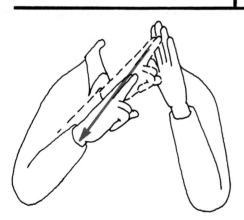

easel
Open B LH palm right. Place tips of right H on left palm then draw away and down at angle.

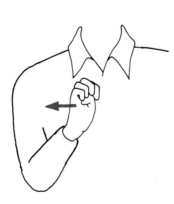

east
Hold right E a little to the left and move over to right.

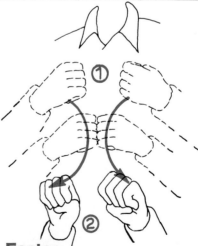

Easter
E shape both hands knuckles facing. Bring together then draw apart ending with knuckles out.

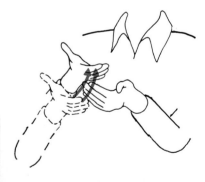

easy
Open B both hands palms up, left hand above right. Place right fingers on back of left fingers and brush up twice.

82

eat
Place tips of right flat O on lips. Repeat several times.

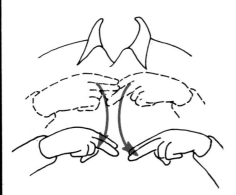

egg
H shape both hands palms facing, tips down. Hit left H with right H then draw apart.

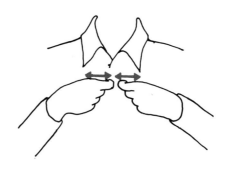

electric
X shape both hands palms in. Tap together twice.

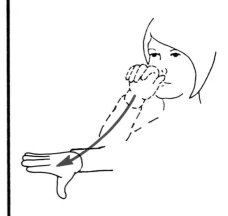

elephant
Place back of right curved B on nose and trace trunk of elephant downward.

elevator
One shape LH. E shape RH palm left, knuckles out. Slide right E up left index finger.

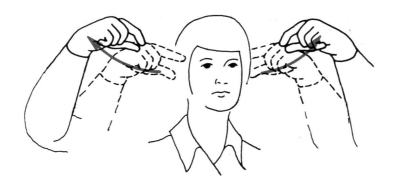

elf
G shape both hands palms facing. Place tips just in front of ears, then arc up and out closing thumbs and forefingers.

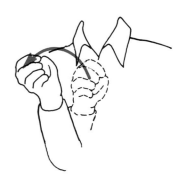

else
E shape knuckles left. Twist wrist so that knuckles face up.

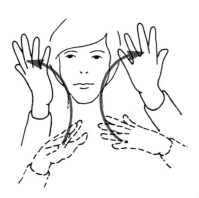

embarrass

Five shape both hands palms slightly in. Move up sides of cheeks (blush spreading).

empty

Open B LH palm down, tips out. Place right E on back of left hand and move out.

end

B shape LH palm and tips slanted right. Open B RH, palm and tips slanted left. Slide right B off end of left B and drop down.

ending

E shape both hands knuckles facing. Zig-zag up and down.

England

Open B LH palm down, tips right. Clasp with RH and draw back to body.

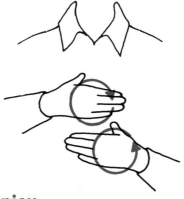

enjoy

Open B both hands palms in, left tips right, right tips left. Place on chest. Circle RH clockwise and LH counter-clockwise.

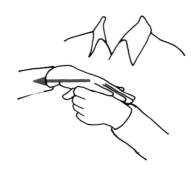

enough

S shape LH knuckles right. Brush right palm over left S away from body.

enter

Open B shape both hands palms down, left tips slanted right, right tips slanted left. Slide RH under left palm.

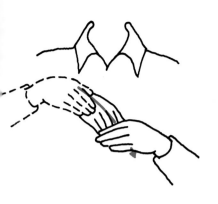

envelope

Bent B both hands left palm in, tips right; right palm and tips down. Slide right B into left.

erase

Open B LH palm right, tips out. Rub knuckles of right E back and forth on left palm once or twice.

escalator

Five shape LH palm down, tips out. Bent V RH. Place tips of bent V on left index and move both hands upward to the left.

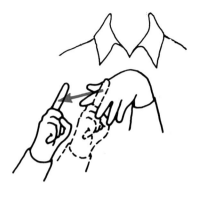

escape

Five shape LH palm down, tips slanted right. Place right index finger between left index and middle fingers then pull out to the right.

Europe

Circle right E at right temple counterclockwise.

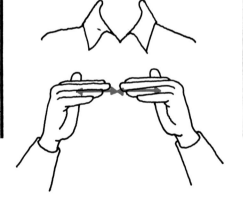

even

Bent B both hands palms down. Tap tips together.

ever

E shape RH. Circle clockwise.

every

A shape both hands thumbs up. Brush right A down left A

evil

E shape RH knuckles in. Place on chin then twist out and down ending with knuckles facing out in correct E position.

exact

Closed X shape both hands palms in, knuckles facing. Tap thumbs and forefingers together once.

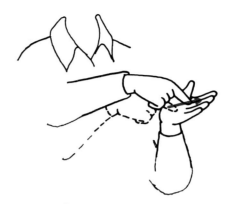

examine

Open B LH palm up, tips out. One shape RH palm down. Slide right index forward on left palm.

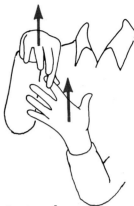

except

Five shape LH palm in, tips slightly right. Grasp left index finger with right thumb and forefinger and pull up.

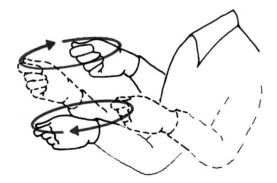

exchange

A shape both hands knuckles facing. Circle right A back over left, and left A under right reversing positions.

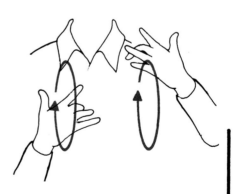

excite

Five shape both hands palms in, tips facing. Alternately brush tips of middle fingers upward on chest.

excuse

Open B LH palm up, tips out. Brush lightly with right tips.

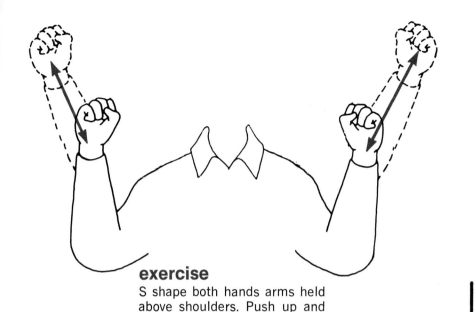

exercise

S shape both hands arms held above shoulders. Push up and out.

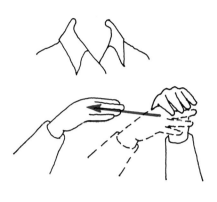

exit

Claw shape LH palm and tips down. Five shape RH palm down, tips left. Place in left claw then draw back to right ending in flat O.

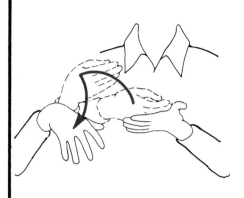

expensive

Open B LH palm up, tips right. Place back of right flat O in left palm, lift up and turn palm down.

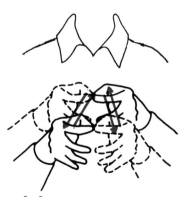

explain

F shape both hands palms facing, tips out. Move back and forth alternately.

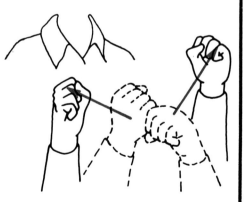

explode

S shape both hands palms in. Place right S on left. Draw apart quickly moving upward.

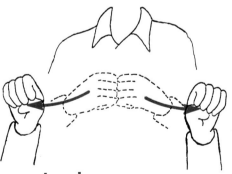

extension

E shape both hands knuckles touching. Separate and turn out into correct E position.

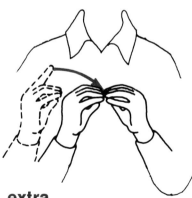

extra

Flat O shape LH palm down, tips right. One shape RH palm left. Change into flat O and touch tips of left flat O.

eye
Place tip of index finger on eye.

eyebrow
Outline eyebrow with tip of index finger.

eyelash
Four shape RH tips out, palm down and slanted in. Place thumb side against right eye then flip hand up and out.

F

face
Circle face with index finger.

factory
A shape LH knuckles down. F shape RH palm left. Place right wrist on side of left A. Slide back into Y shape, then forward.

faint
S shape both hands palms down. Drop into five shapes and bow head.

fair (adj)
F shape RH. Place thumb and index tip on chin.

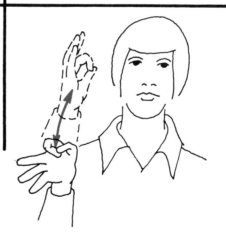

fairy
F shape RH. Dip forward as if touching something with a wand.

fall (season)
Hold left arm upright, palm in. Brush index finger of right open B palm down, tips left, against left elbow.

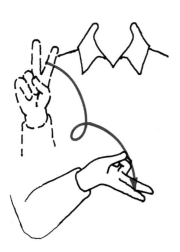

fall (verb)

Hold right V near face. Loop forward ending with palm up.

false

One shape RH palm left. Brush across nose ending with index tip pointing left.

family

F shape both hands palms out, thumbs and forefingers touching. Draw apart and around until little fingers touch.

famous

One shape both hands palms in. Place tips on chin then move up and out in small semi-circle.

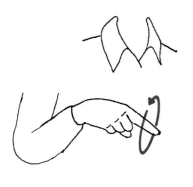

fan

One shape RH palm in, tip left. Circle rapidly.

fancy

Claw shape both hands palms and tips out. Move RH clockwise and LH counterclockwise.

fang

G shape both hands palms in, tips up. Place index fingers on sides of mouth. Bring down and apart closing forefingers and thumbs.

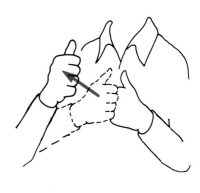

far

A shape both hands thumbs up, knuckles touching. Move right A forward.

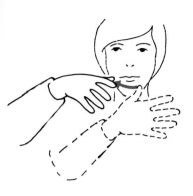

farm
Five shape RH palm in, tips left. Place thumb on left side of chin and draw across to right side.

fast
L shape both hands palms facing, index tips out. Draw back quickly into S shapes.

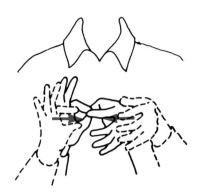

fasten
F shape both hands slightly open. Bring together hooking thumbs and forefingers.

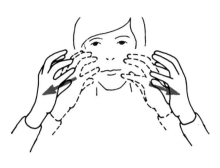

fat
Hold claw hands on cheeks, then move away (puffy, fat face).

father
Five shape RH palm left. Place thumb on forehead and wiggle fingers.

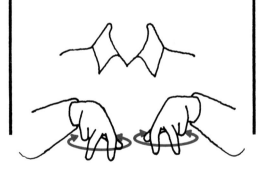

faucet
Mime turning faucets with thumbs, index and middle fingers.

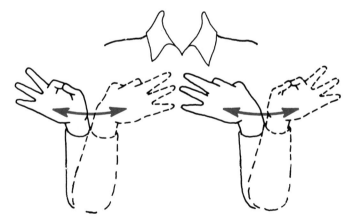

favor
F shape both hands (fingers spread) left palm out, tips left, right palm in, tips left. Swing in and out alternately.

favorite
Five shape RH palm in. Tap middle finger on chin twice.

feather
Pluck at left index finger with right G as if plucking feathers from a fowl.

February
Open B LH palm in. Place right F on left palm, slide over fingers and down.

feed
O shape both hands, left in front of body, right on lips. Move right O down toward left O and shake both hands slightly.

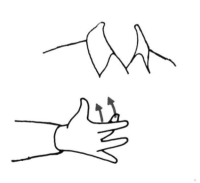

feel
Place right middle finger on chest and move up and down once or twice.

female
Place thumb and index finger of right F on right cheek and slide down.

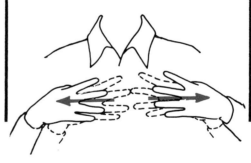

fence
Four shape both hands palms in, tips facing. Place tips of middle fingers together then draw apart.

fever
Open B RH palm out, tips left. Place back of hand on forehead.

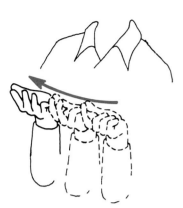

few

"Loose" A shape RH palm up. Pass thumb along first three fingers while opening them up slightly.

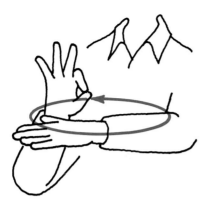

field

Open B LH palm down, tips slightly right. Place right F on left wrist, circle counter clockwise over elbow and return to original position.

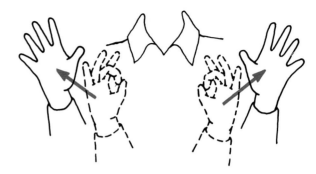

fierce

Eight shape both hands. Open quickly into five shapes while moving apart.

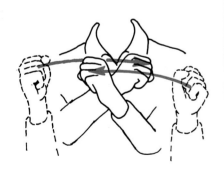

fight

S shape both hands (fist) knuckles facing. Cross hands in front of body once or twice.

fill

C shape LH palm right, little finger side down. B shape RH palm down. Starting at bottom of left C move right B up to top.

film

Open B LH palm and tips slanted right. Place base of right F in left palm and flick back and forth.

final

I shape both hands left palm in, tip right; right palm left, tip out. Bring right I up in semicircle then down striking tip of left little finger.

93

find
Five shape RH palm down, tips out. Close thumb and forefinger and raise hand as if picking up something.

fine
Five shape RH palm left. Place thumb on chest and move slightly up and out.

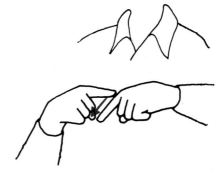

finger
One shape both hands palms down, left tip out, right tip left. Slide right tip forward on side of left index.

fingernail
Tap nail of left index finger with tip of right index finger.

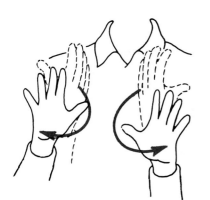

finish
Five shape both hands palms in. Turn suddenly so that palms and tips face out.

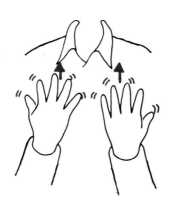

fire
Claw shape both hands palms up. Move up, fluttering fingers.

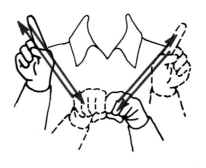

firework
S shape both hands knuckles down, index fingers touching. Pop index fingers out and to the sides alternately.

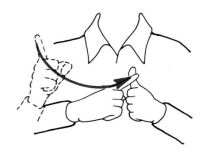

first
A shape LH knuckles right, thumb up. Strike left thumb with tip of right index.

94

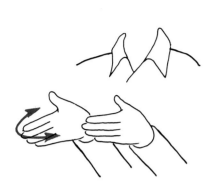

fish

Open B both hands left palm in, tips right; right palm left, tips out. Place left tips on right wrist. Flutter right hand while moving forward.

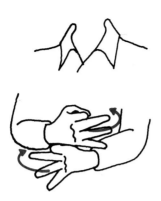

fix

F shape both hands left palm right, tips out; right palm in, tips left. Place right F on left F and twist.

flag

Place right elbow on back of left hand which is held before you. Wave right hand back and forth.

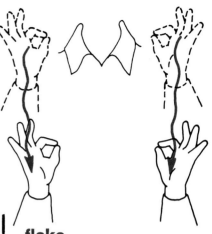

flake

F shape both hands. Shake RH down, then left.

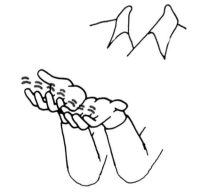

flame

Hold cupped hands in front of body palms up, little fingers touching. Flutter fingers.

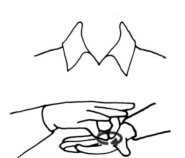

flannel

Open B LH palm up tips right. Circle tips of right F in left palm clockwise.

flash

Flat O RH palm down tips out. Place left index under RH then open right fingers quickly.

95

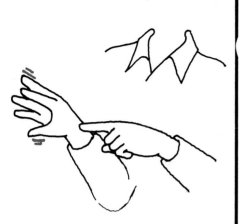

flashlight
Five shape RH palm down fingers slightly bent. Place tips of left index on right wrist and move hands around as if searching with a flashlight.

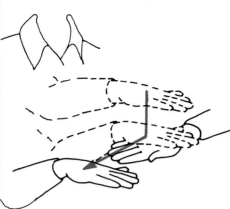

flatten
Open B both hands left palm up tips slanted right; right palm down tips slanted left. Slap right hand on left palm and slide off to right.

float
Place little finger side of right A on back of left hand. Move in floating motion.

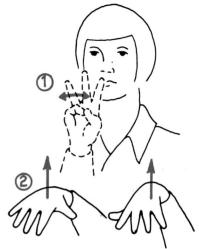

flood
Tap lips twice with index finger of right W. Now, hold hands in front of body palms down, then raise up.

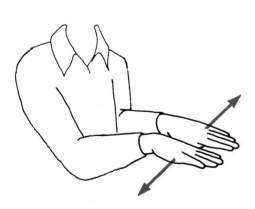

floor
B shape both hands palms down tips out, index fingers touching. Move apart.

flour
S shape LH palm in knuckles right. Place index and thumb of right F on back of left S and circle clockwise.

flower
Flat O shape RH. Place tips on right side of nose and move to left.

flu
F shape RH palm in. Place thumb and index in middle of forehead.

flute
Mime holding flute to mouth and playing.

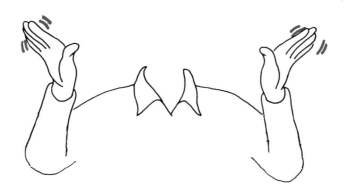

fly
Open B both hands palms out, held at shoulders. Flap from wrists two or three times closing fingers.

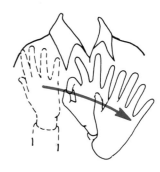

fog
F shape LH. Five shape RH palm in. Brush across thumb and forefinger of left F.

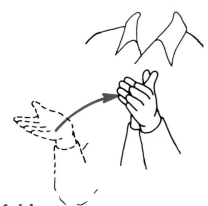

fold
Open B both hands left palm right tips out; right palm up tips out. Bring right hand up and place against left.

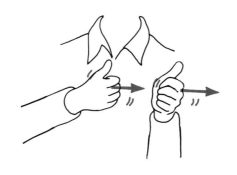

follow
A shape both hands thumbs up, left slightly ahead of right. Move both forward in parallel action.

food
Place tips of flat O on mouth.

fool
Y shape RH palm left. Shake at right temple.

foolish

Y shape RH palm left. Place at right cheek and arc down to left.

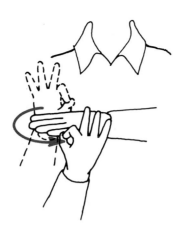

foot

B shape LH palm down tips out. Outline with thumb and index finger of right F ending with right palm facing right.

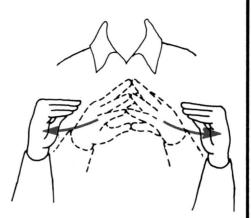

football

Five shape both hands palms facing, tips touching. Draw apart into flat O's.

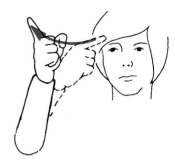

for

One shape RH palm in. Place tip on forehead, twist wrist and point tip forward.

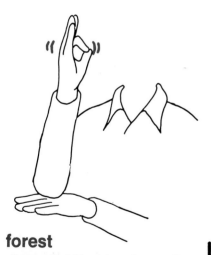

forest

Open B LH palm down, tips right. Place right elbow on left hand, form F and shake.

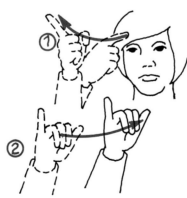

forever

Place index finger on forehead, twist out into Y shape and move forward.

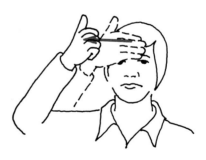

forget

Open B RH palm in, tips right. Draw tips across forehead from left to right ending in A shape.

forgive

Open B LH palm up, tips out. Brush with right tips in strong, sweeping movement. Repeat.

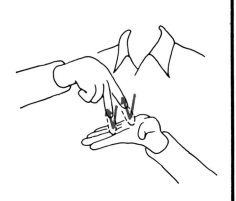

fork

Open B LH palm up, tips right. Tap left palm with tips of right V .

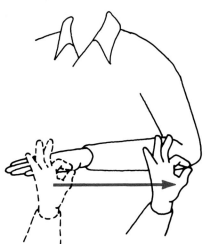

fort

Extend left arm before you palm down. Place index side of right F on left little finger and slide up to elbow.

fountain

Mime turning on water fountain.

fox

Enclose tip of nose with index and thumb of right F. Wave to left and back to right.

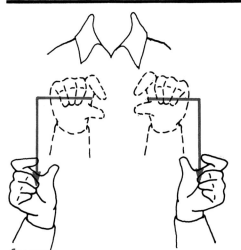

frame

G shape both hands palms out, hands held close together. Draw apart and down ending with palms facing.

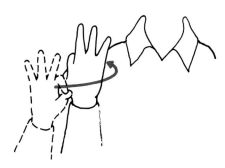

France

F shape RH. Twist inward.

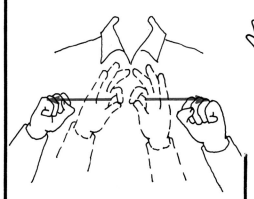

frankfurter

F shape both hands almost touching. Draw apart in S shapes.

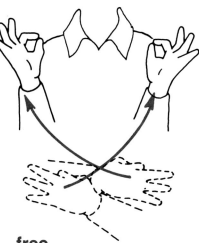

free

F shape both hands palms in tips opposite, wrists crossed. Draw apart and up ending with palms out.

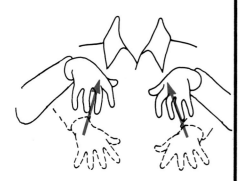

freeze
Five shape both hands palms down, tips out. Bring up into claw shapes.

freight
B shape LH palm down tips out. Slide right F, palm left, forward on index side of left hand.

French fries
F shape RH palm down, tips out. Move to right.

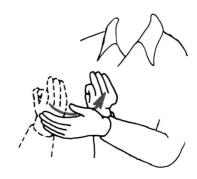

fresh
Open B LH palm up tips out. Brush back of right F across left palm from right to left.

Friday
Make small circle with right F.

friend
Hook right X over left X which is turned up, then reverse.

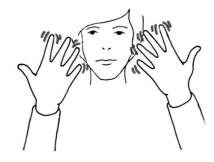

friendly
Five shape both hands palms facing body at shoulder level. Wiggle fingers slightly.

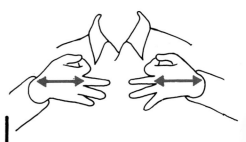

fright
F shape both hands palms in. Move back and forth toward one another as if shaking.

frisbee
A shape RH palm up. Move quickly to the right opening into five shape.

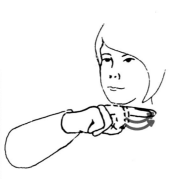

frog
Place right S under chin and flick index and middle fingers out twice.

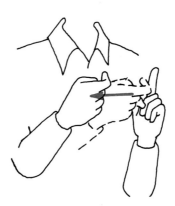

from
One shape LH palm right. Place index finger of right X against left index and draw back to body.

frost
Open B LH palm up tips right. G shape RH knuckles down, tips left. Circle in left palm counterclockwise.

fruit
Nine shape RH. Place thumb and forefinger on right cheek and move to chin.

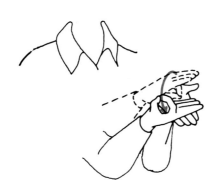

fry
Open B LH palm up tips out. Place thumb and index of right F in left palm and flip over.

fudge
B shape LH palm down tips out. Circle right F counterclockwise over left hand.

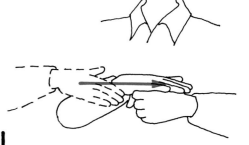

full
S shape LH knuckles right. Brush right palm across left S toward body.

fun

H shape both hands, left palm down. Place right H on nose then place on back of left H.

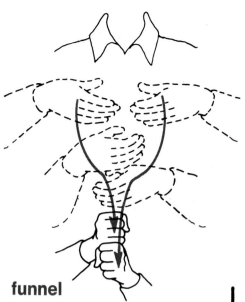

funnel

Curved open B both hands palms in, tips facing. Outline funnel shape while moving down ending in S shapes, right on top of left.

funny

Brush tip of nose with tips of right N twice.

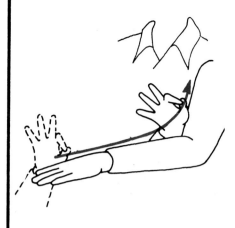

fur

Extend left arm before you palm down. Run right F all the way up left arm to shoulder.

furnace

C shape LH palm and tips in. Move up while fluttering fingers of right five underneath.

furniture

F shape RH. Move briskly back and forth sidewise.

fuss

L shape RH palm left, little finger extended. Place index on lip and move back and forth quickly.

future

F shape RH palm left. Place at right side of face and move forward in semi-circle ending with tips out.

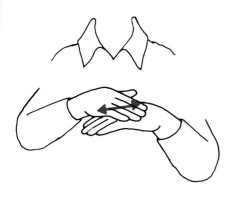

fuzz
Open B both hands palms down, left tips slanted right, right tips slanted left. Rub back of left hand with right tips.

G

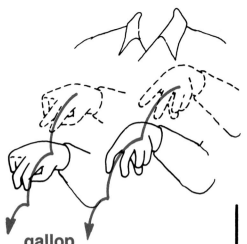

gallop
V shape both hands palms down, tips out. Jump forward several times bending V fingers.

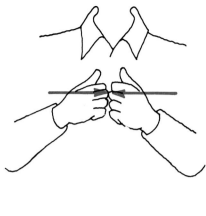

game
A shape both hands palms in, thumbs up. Hit knuckles together once.

garage
Open B LH palm down, tips out. Slide right 3 (palm in) under left hand.

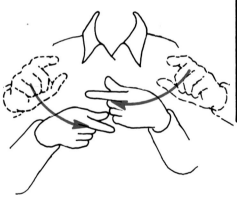

garden
G shape both hands. Move right G in front of left G turning right tips left and left tips right.

gasoline
S shape LH knuckles right. A shape RH knuckles left, thumb extended. Arc right A up over left S and turn down as if pouring gasoline into tank.

gate
Four shape both hands palms in, middle fingers touching Move right hand out so that tips face out and palm faces left.

gentle

G shape both hands crossed at chin. Separate and move down ending with G's facing each other.

gentleman

Place thumb of right A on forehead. Bring down to chest changing to open five palm left.

gerbil

G shape both hands palms facing. Place tips on cheeks, arc down and twist up slightly.

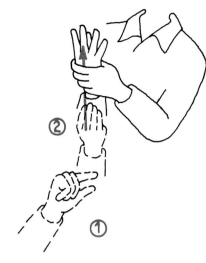

germ

C shape LH palm and tips right, little finger side down. Form right G, change into flat O and pass up through left C while spreading fingers.

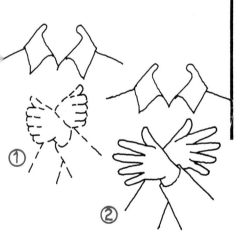

Germany

A shape both hands palms in. Cross at wrists and snap sharply into five shapes.

get

C shape both hands palms facing. Place right C on left and close both as if grasping something.

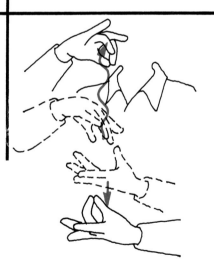

ghost

Open 8 shape both hands left palm up, right palm down. Close right thumb and middle finger around left thumb and middle finger. Now, slip right hand up in wavy motion ending in 8 shape.

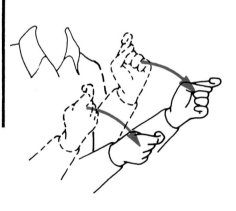

gift

X shape both hands knuckles facing. Arc both hands forward.

giraffe
Place right C on side of neck. Raise up indicating long neck.

girl
A shape RH. Place thumb on cheek and move down twice.

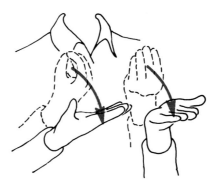

give
O shape both hands, palms up, left a little ahead of right. Move out opening fingers.

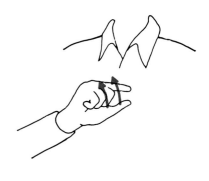

glad
Place index finger and thumb of right G on chest and brush upward twice.

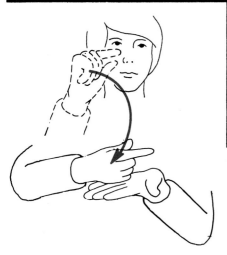

glass
Open B LH palm up, tips right. Place tips of right G on upper cheek then place little finger side of G in left palm.

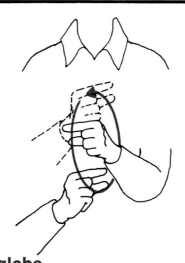

globe
G shape both hands knuckles facing. Place right G on left, circle forward and under returning to original position.

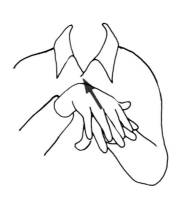

glove
Five shape both hands palms down, tips out. Draw right fingers back over left fingers.

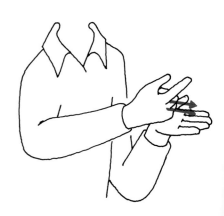

glue
Open B LH palm up, tips out. Rub right G forward on left palm. Repeat.

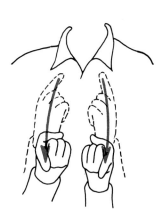

go
One shape both hands knuckles in. Point fingers out ending with knuckles up.

goat
Flick tips of right bent V on chin, then on forehead.

gobble
Flat O shape both hands tips up. Place tips on mouth alternately as if eating very fast.

God
B shape RH palm left, tips slanted out. Arc up, back and down ending with tips up.

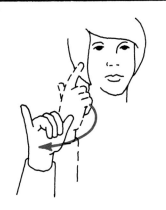

gold
Point right index finger to right ear then twist out ending in Y shape.

good
Open B both hands palms in, tips slanted up. Place right tips on mouth then move out and down placing back of hand in left palm.

goose
Open B LH palm down, tips right. G shape RH palm and tips out. Rest right elbow on back of left hand.

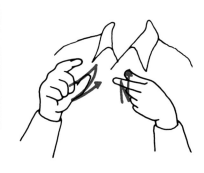

gorilla
G shape both hands knuckles facing. Hit chest with tips alternately.

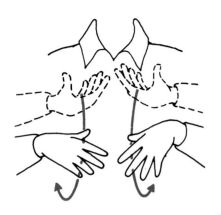

gown
Bent open B shape both hands palms in, tips touching upper chest. Brush down and out ending with palms down.

grab
C shape RH palm down, fingers slightly spread. Bring hand down and close into S shape.

grace
Hold right G up, palm in, then arc down to left shoulder.

grand
G shape both hands, tips facing. Change into D shapes.

grandchild
G shape RH palm down, tips left. Place on forehead then move to chin. Now, change to open B, palm down, and move to right.

granddaughter
G shape RH palm down, tips left. Place on forehead, then move to chin. Form right A, place thumb on right cheek, change into open B palm up, tips left, and place in crook of left elbow.

grandfather
Five shape both hands, left palm right, right palm left. Place right thumb on forehead and left thumb on edge of right hand. Move out in two short jumps.

108

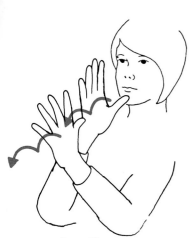

grandmother
Five shape both hands, left palm right, right palm left. Place right thumb on chin and left thumb on edge of right hand. Move out in two short jumps.

grandson
G shape RH palm down, tips left. Place on forehead, then move to chin. Now, place thumb side of right flat O on forehead, arc down and place in crook of left elbow.

grape
Hop curved right fingers across back of LH.

grass
B shape LH palm down, tips right. G shape RH. Outline left hand with right G.

grasshopper
Place right G on back of left bent V, palm down. Hop forward twice.

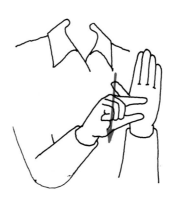

graveyard
Open B LH palm right. Place right G against left fingers and lower to base of palm.

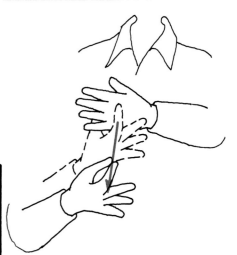

gravy
Open B LH palm in, tips right. Grasp bottom of palm with right index finger and thumb, then slip right fingers off into 9 shape.

gray
Five shape both hands palms in, tips facing. Move right fingers back and forth between left fingers.

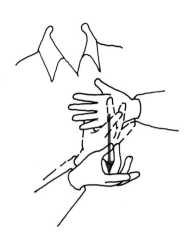

grease
Open B LH palm in, tips right. Grasp bottom of palm with right middle finger and thumb, then slip right fingers off into 8 shape.

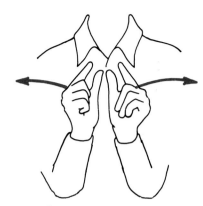

great
G shape both hands knuckles out, tips up. Draw hands apart.

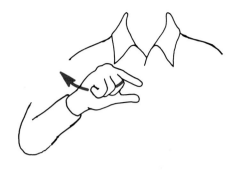

green
G shape RH palm in, tips left. Rock up and down.

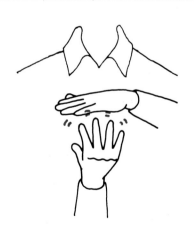

grill
Open B LH palm down, tips right. Flutter fingers of right five, palm in, underneath left B.

grin
G shape both hands knuckles and tips facing. Place tips on sides of lips and arc up slightly.

grocery
Circle right G up and out from mouth.

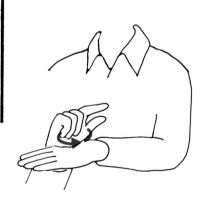

ground
Open B LH palm down, tips right. Place base of right G on back of LH and move in circle counterclockwise.

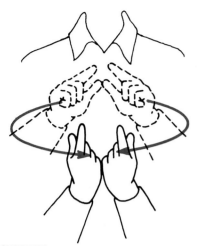

group
G shape both hands palms facing, thumbs touching. Draw apart and around to front ending with little fingers touching.

grow
Hold left C before body. Pass right O up through left C spreading fingers as hand emerges.

growl
Grab throat with cupped hand.

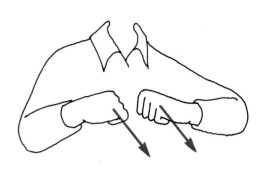

guard
S shape both hands palms down, knuckles facing. Push forward forcibly.

guess
C shape RH palm left. Move to left in front of face closing into S shape.

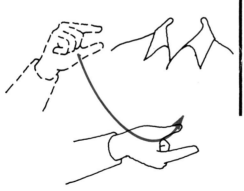

guest
G shape RH palm up. Make sweeping motion to the left.

guinea pig
G shape RH tips left. Brush nose twice. Then, place back of RH under chin and drop fingers twice.

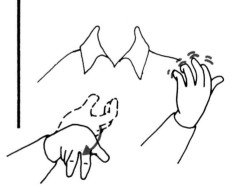

guitar
Mime holding, fingering and strumming a guitar.

gull
Open B LH palm down, tips right. G shape RH palm and tips out. Rest right elbow on back of LH and dip fingers down. Repeat.

gum
G shape RH knuckles and tips left. Place on left side of cheek and slide to right side outlining gum.

gun
L shape RH palm left, index finger out. Crook thumb down.

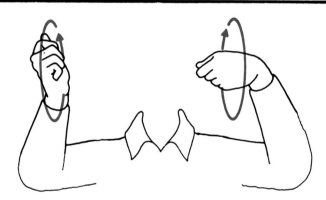

gym
A shape both hands knuckles facing. Hold above shoulders and move forward in circular movements alternately.

H

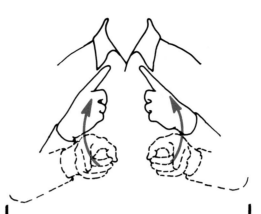

had
D shape both hands palms up, index tips out. Draw up and back to chest.

hair
Place right thumb and forefinger on hair.

half
Form the number one and drop down into the number two.

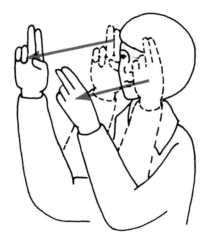

hall
H shape both hands palms facing. Place at sides of temples then move out in straight line.

Halloween
H shape both hands palms in, tips up. Place thumbs on mouth and move to ears.

ham
H shape LH palm and tips slanted right. Grasp left hand between thumb and index finger with right thumb and index and shake.

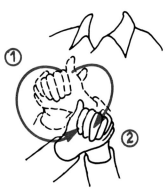

hamburger
Clasp hands together and move as if making hamburger patty.

hammer
S shape LH knuckles right. A shape RH. Move right A toward left S as if hitting nail.

hamper
S shape LH palm down, arm extended. H shape RH palm in, tips left. Place against left wrist and arc down and up to elbow.

hamster
H shape both hands, left palm and tips slanted right, right palm and tips slanted left. Place tips on cheeks, move down and turn palms up.

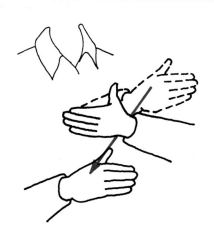

hand
Open B both hands left palm up, tips slanted right; right palm left, tips out. Draw little finger side of right B across left wrist.

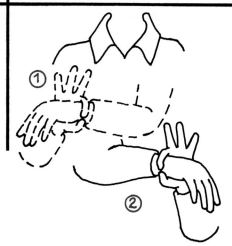

handcuff
Circle left wrist with right thumb and index finger, then circle right wrist with left thumb and index finger.

handkerchief
Place thumb and index finger on nose and draw down.

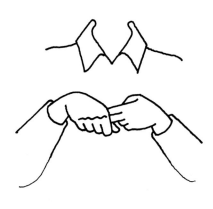

handle
H shape LH palm in, tips right. Grasp and hold with right S.

114

handsome
Circle face with right index then brush right palm across left palm.

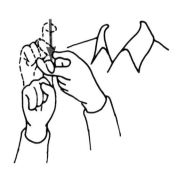

hang
X shape both hands. Hook right X over left X.

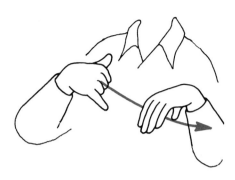

hangar
C shape LH palm down. Y shape RH palm down, tips left. Pass under left C.

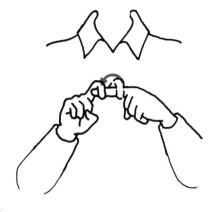

hanger
One shape LH palm in, tips right. Hook right index over base of left and move forward.

happen
One shape both hands palms up, tips out. Twist toward each other ending with palms down.

happy
Place open B on chest and brush up and out twice.

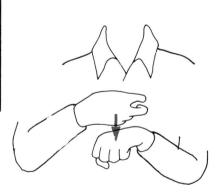

hard
S shape LH knuckles down. Hit back of left S with side of right bent V.

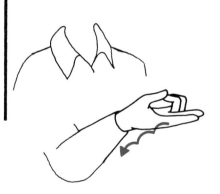

hardware
H shape RH palm up, tips out. Move toward right in short jumps.

harmonica
Mime holding and playing a harmonica.

harp
Mime plucking and strumming a harp with both hands.

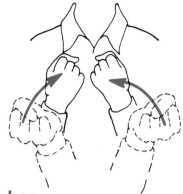

has
S shape both hands knuckles up. Draw up and back to chest.

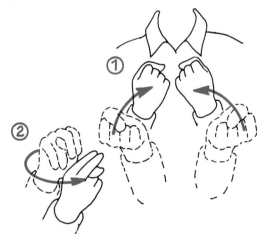

hasn't
S shape both hands knuckles up. Draw up and back to chest. Then form right N and twist in.

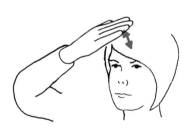

hat
Pat top of head with palm of RH.

hatchet
B shape LH palm and tips slanted right. H shape RH palm and tips slanted left. Chop left index with right H backwards, then forward.

116

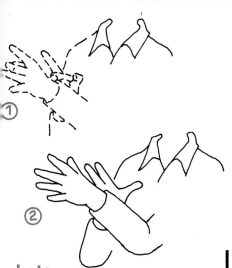

hate
Eight shape both hands palms facing, tips out, left slightly in front of right. Flick middle fingers from thumbs.

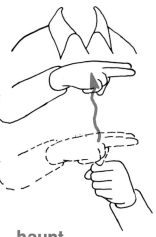

haunt
S shape LH knuckles right. H shape RH palm in, tips left. Place on left S then wave upward.

have
V shape both hands palms up tips slanted out. Draw back to chest.

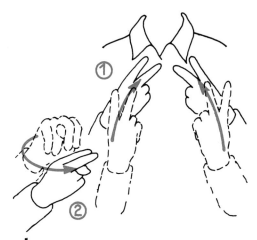

haven't
V shape both hands palms up, tips slanted out. Draw back to chest, then form right N twist in.

hay
Tap base of right claw hand (palm up) on chin twice.

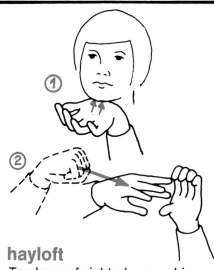

hayloft
Tap base of right claw on chin. Now, form left C and right S. Place right S in left C, then open into five shape.

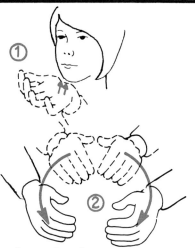

haystack
Tap base of right claw hand (palm up), on chin. Then with both claw hands palms down, outline shape of haystack.

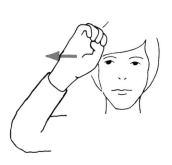

he
E shape RH. Place on right temple, then move out.

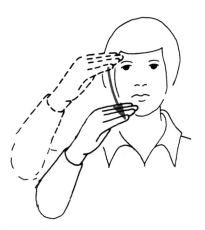

head
Bent B RH palm down, tips left. Place tips on right temple then on chin.

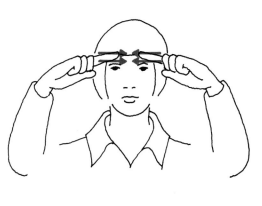

headache
One shape both hands palms in, tips facing. Move back and forth in front of forehead.

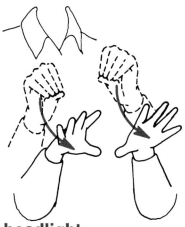

headlight
Flat O both hands palms and tips out. Swing forward opening into five shapes.

headphone
Claw shape both hands palms facing. Place tips on sides of head covering ears.

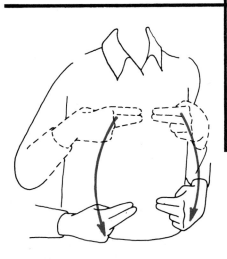

health
H shape both hands palms in, tips facing. Place tips on upper chest then move down to stomach.

hear
Point index finger to ear.

heart
Touch "heart" with right middle finger.

heat
Claw shape RH palm in. Place tips on mouth, then twist wrist quickly so that palm faces down. Repeat.

118

Heaven
Open B shape both hands palms facing. Move up in semi-circles passing right B under left.

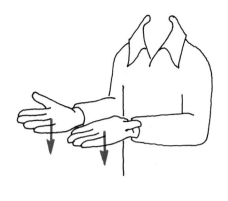

heavy
Open B both hands palms up, tips out. Lower slowly.

heel
Open B LH palm down, tips out. G shape RH palm up, tips out. Place under base of left palm.

helicopter
Support open right palm with left index finger and shake right fingers.

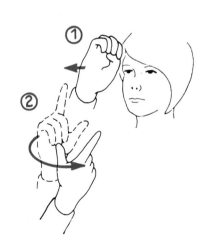

he'll
E shape RH. Place on temple, then form right L and turn inward.

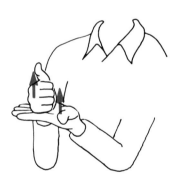

help
Place little finger side of right A, thumb up, in left palm. Raise left palm up.

hen
Three shape RH palm left, tips out. Tap thumb on chin.

her
R shape RH. Place on right cheek, then move out.

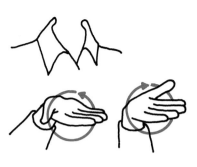

here
Open B both hands palms up, tips out. Circle toward one another and back.

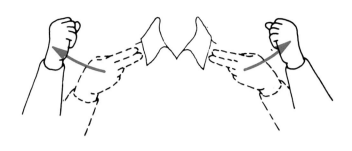

hero
H shape both hands palms in, tips facing. Place on upper chest, then move apart and up ending in S shapes.

he's
E shape RH. Place on right temple. Move out, form S and twist in.

hi
Wave open palm from left to right.

hide
Bent B shape LH palm down. Place thumb of right A on lips then move down and under LH.

high
H shape RH palm in, tips left. Move up several inches.

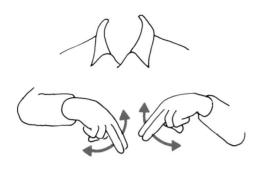

highway
V shape both hands left palm in, right palm out, tips up. Move back and forth alternately. (traffic flowing)

hike
H shape both hands palms in, tips down. Move forward alternately.

hill
Open B RH palm down, tips left. Dip down and up outlining shape of hill.

him
M shape RH palm down, tips out. Place just above right eye and move out about four inches.

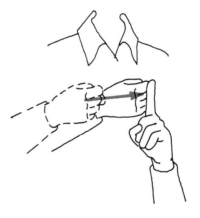

hippopotamus
Y shape both hands , left tips up, right tips down. Place right tips on left. Open wide and close again.

his
Place right S on right temple. Move out slightly toward right.

hit
One shape LH palm right. Strike with right fist.

hoe
Open B LH palm up, tips out. Bent open B RH palm in, tips down. Scrape left palm with right tips.

121

hog

H shape RH palm down, tips left. Place under chin and drop fingers twice.

hold

S shape both hands. Place right on top of left as if grasping rope.

hole

C shape LH palm and tips right, little finger side down. Circle with right index which is pointed down.

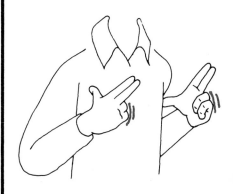

holiday

H shape both hands palms facing, tips out, thumbs extended. Tap thumbs on upper chest several times.

hollow

C shape LH palm and tips right. Circle with right middle finger, other fingers spread.

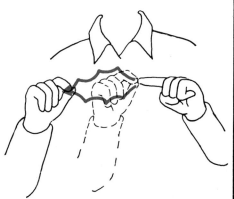

holly

Point left index finger right, palm in. Touch with right thumb and forefinger then draw right hand away snapping thumb and forefinger.

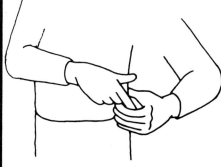

holster

C shape LH palm and tips right. Place on left hip. Stick index finger of right L into left C.

home

Place tips of right flat O to edge of mouth and move to upper cheek.

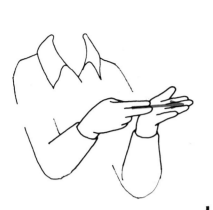

honest
Open B LH palm up, tips out. H shape RH palm left, tips out. Slide forward on left palm.

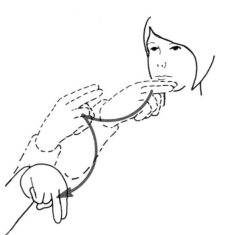

honey
Draw index finger of right H across chin, then flick wrist out and down.

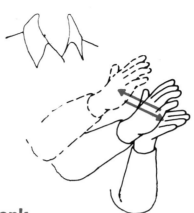

honk
Hit base of upturned left palm with base of right palm.

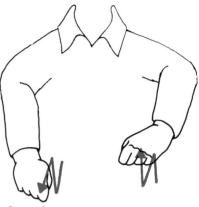

hoof
S shape both hands. Move up and down alternately (horse clopping along).

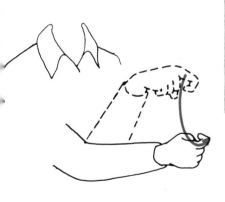

hook
X shape RH palm down. Drop down then turn up.

hoop
G shape both hands palms out. Draw apart and down in circular motion outlining hoop.

hop
Open B LH palm up, tips out. Place middle finger of right P on left palm then hop forward once.

hope
Open B LH palm right, tips up. Place right index finger on forehead, form right open B palm left, tips up. Now, bend fingers of both hands toward one another.

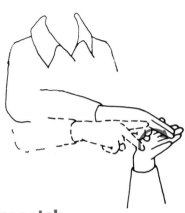

hopscotch
Open B LH palm up, tips out. Place middle finger of right P on base of left palm then hop forward changing into H shape.

horn
C shape LH palm and tips right. S shape RH palm left. Hold at mouth and blow.

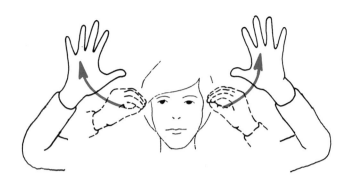

horrible
Flat O both hands tips touching temples. Bring both hands forward suddenly ending in five shape palms out, tips up.

horse
H shape RH thumb extended. Place thumb on right temple. Move H fingers forward twice.

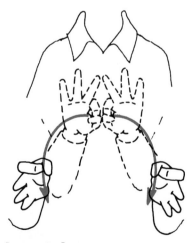

horseshoe
F shape both hands palms out, thumbs and index fingers touching. Circle apart and down in shape of horseshoe.

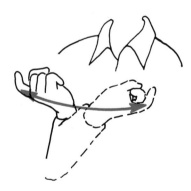

hose
X shape RH palm up, thumb out. Move from left to right as if watering plants or grass.

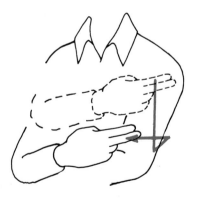

hospital
H shape RH. Make cross on upper left arm.

124

hot
Place tips of right claw on mouth. Twist wrist quickly so that palm faces down.

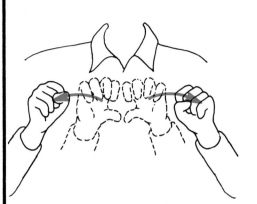

hot dog
Claw shape both hands palms down, index fingers almost touching. Draw apart and Close into S shapes twice.

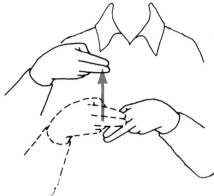

hotel
H shape both hands left palm right, tips out; right palm in, tips left. Place right H on left H, then move up several inches.

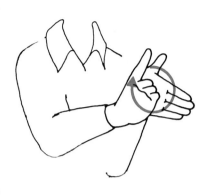

hour
Open B LH palm right, tips out. Place knuckles of RH, index finger extended, in left palm and describe a circle.

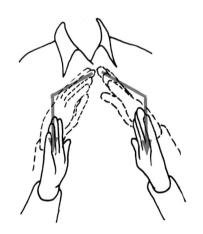

house
Place tips of both hands together to form roof. Move apart and down to form sides of house.

how
Hold backs of fingers together palms down. Turn in and up,

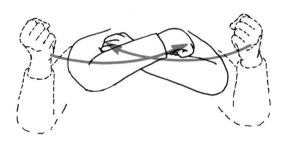

hug
S shape both hands. Cross arms on chest as if hugging something.

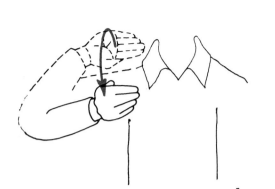

hump
B shape RH palm out, tips left, held at shoulder. Move up and down in shape of hump ending with palm in.

hungry
Draw tips of claw hand down upper chest.

hunt
L shape both hands palms facing, index tips out. Shake up and down.

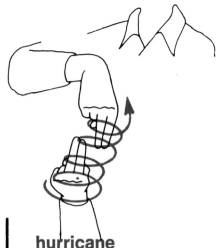

hurricane
H shape both hands palms in, left tips up, right tips down. Circle around each other quickly.

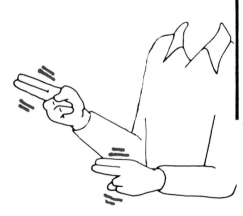

hurry
H shape both hands palms facing, tips out. Shake up and down rapidly.

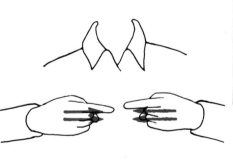

hurt
One shape both hands palms in, tips facing. Move back and forth toward one another.

husband
Place right C at right temple. Move down and clasp LH which is held palm up.

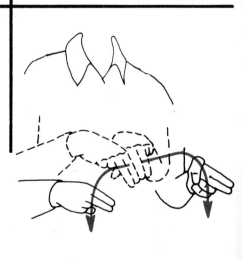

hut
H shape both hands palms down, index fingers touching. Move apart and down outlining shape of hut.

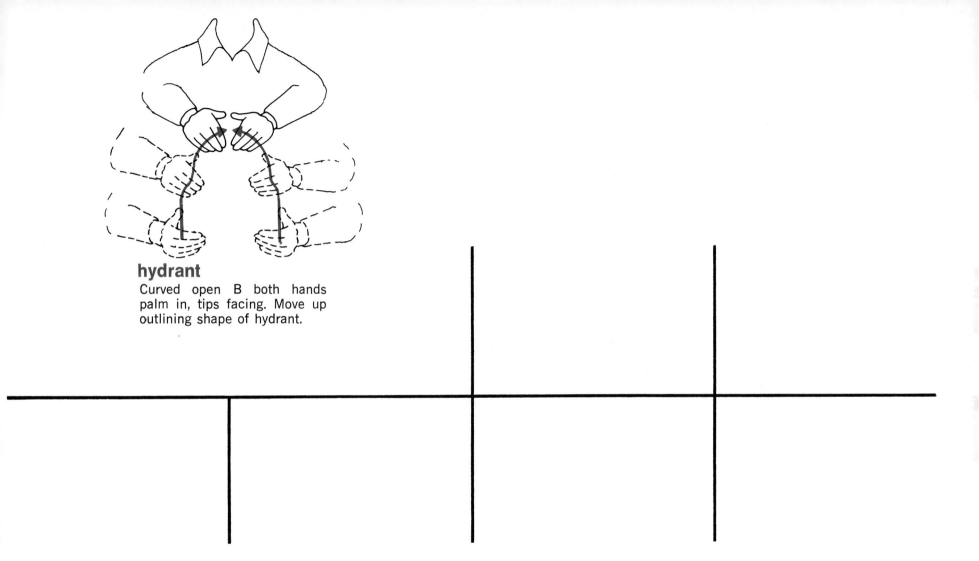

hydrant

Curved open B both hands palm in, tips facing. Move up outlining shape of hydrant.

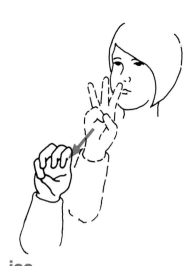

I
I shape RH palm left. Place thumb side on chest.

ice
Place right W at mouth. Move out. into bent W.

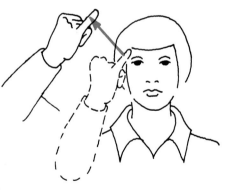

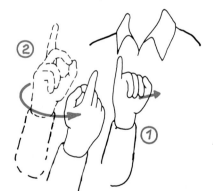

ice cream
Mime eating ice cream cone (S shape holding cone).

ice-skate
X shape both hands palms up. Swing back and forth alternately.

idea
I shape RH palm in. Place little finger tip on right temple then move out.

I'd
I shape RH palm left, thumb side touching chest. Move out, form D shape and turn in.

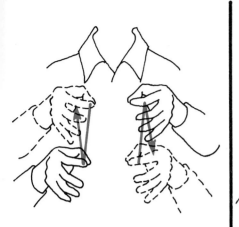

if
F shape both hands palms facing, tips out. Move up and down alternately.

igloo
I shape both hands. Curve down outlining shape of igloo.

ill
Five shape both hands palms in. Tap forehead with right middle finger and stomach with left middle finger. Repeat.

I'll
I shape RH palm left, thumb on chest. Move out, form L and turn in.

I'm
I shape RH palm left, thumb on chest. Move out, form M and twist in.

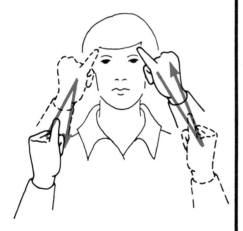

imagine
I shape both hands palms in. Place tips of little fingers on temples alternately.

important
F shape both hands palms facing up, tips out. Draw up in semi-circle toward center until forefingers and thumbs touch.

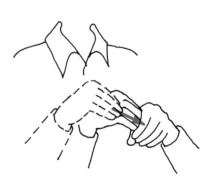

in
C shape LH palm right. Place tips of right flat O into left C.

Indian

Place index finger and thumb of right F on tip of nose. Move up and rest on right temple.

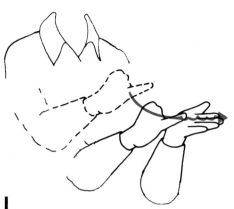

ink

Open B LH palm up, tips out. Place little finger tip of right I in left palm and move forward as if writing.

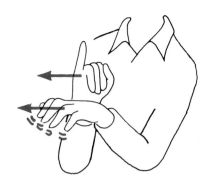

insect

Place base of left I on back of left claw hand which is held palm down. Move LH forward in crawling motion.

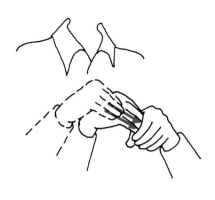

inside

C shape LH palm right. Place tips of RH in left C twice.

instead

F shape both hands palms facing, tips out. Hold right above left and move under and out, reversing positions.

instrument

Open B LH palm up, tips out. I shape RH palm up, tip left. Place tip on base of left palm and move forward in short jumps.

interest

Eight shape both hands palms in, tips facing. Place tips of middle fingers and thumbs on chest then move out.

interrupt

Open B both hands left palm right, tips out; right palm in, tips left. Strike LH between thumb and index with little finger side of right B.

130

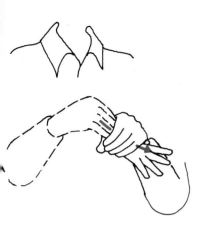

into

C shape LH palm right. Place tips of right flat O in left C and push through and forward.

invite

Open B RH palm and tips slanted left. Arc down and up toward body ending with palm up.

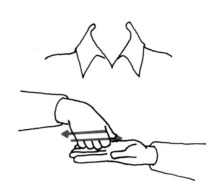

iron

Mime ironing clothes.

is

Place little finger of right I on lips and move out.

island

A shape LH palm down. Describe circle counterclockwise on back of left A with tip of right little finger.

isn't

Place little finger of right I on lips. Move out, form N and twist in.

it

Open B LH palm right, tips out. Place tip of right little finger in palm of LH.

itch

Claw shape both hands palms in, tips opposite. Scratch back of LH with right tips.

131

it's
Open B LH palm right, tips out. Place tip of right little finger in palm of LH, move out into S shape and twist in.

I've
I shape RH palm left, thumb side on chest. Move out, form V and twist in.

ivy
Hold left forearm up palm right. Form right I shape, change into five shape and slide up left arm from elbow to wrist in wavy motion.

J

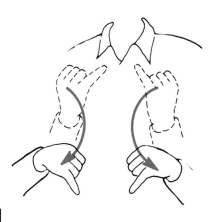

jacket
I shape both hands palms in. Place fingers on chest and move down outlining shape of lapels.

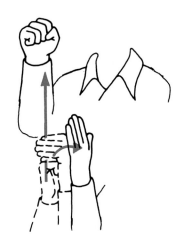

jack-in-the-box
Place knuckles of right S in palm of left bent B. Jerk up suddenly while opening left bent B.

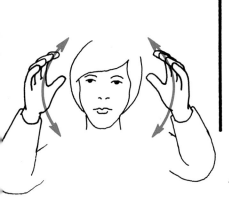

jack-o-lantern
C shape both hands palms facing. Move up and down sides of cheeks.

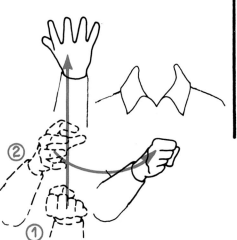

jackstone(s)
S shape RH knuckles up. Throw up into five shape, come back down, close into S shape and twist to left.

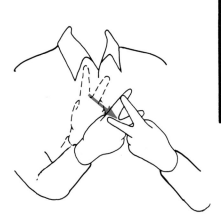

jail
V shape both hands palms in, tips slanted toward each other. Place back of right V against left V.

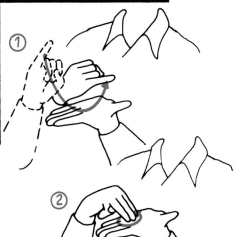

jam
Open B LH palm up, tips out. Make right J over left palm, turn into M shape and make circle in left palm with right tips.

January

Open B LH palm in. Make upside down J with RH over left hand.

jar

C shape both hands palms and tips facing. Raise up outlining jar, then twist right C, palm down, on left C as if screwing on top.

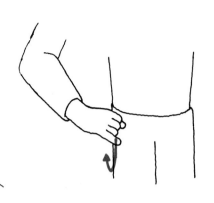

jeans

Place right little finger on right hip and form a J.

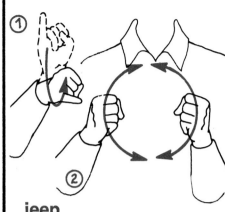

jeep

Make a right J. Now, form A shapes both hands. Move as if turning steering wheel of car.

jello

Open B LH palm up, tips slightly right. C shape RH palm down. Wiggle right fingers over left palm and draw up into O shape.

jelly

Dip right J shape into upturned palm of LH.

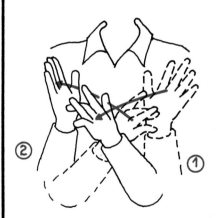

Jesus

Open B both hands palms facing, tips out. Place tip of right middle finger on left palm then place tip of left middle finger on right palm.

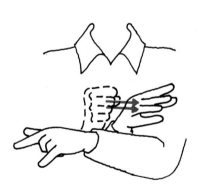

jet

Y shape LH palm down, index finger extended. Place base of right S on left wrist and open into five shape several times.

134

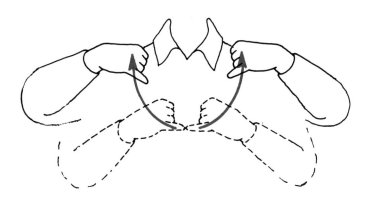

jewel
I shape both hands palms in, tips touching. Circle toward neck outlining necklace.

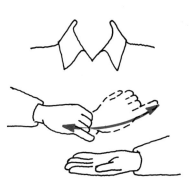

jingle
Open B LH palm up, tips out. Swing right J over LH up to elbow and back. Repeat.

join
Nine shape LH palm right, tips out. Open 9 shape RH palm left. Move to left and hook thumb and index in left thumb and index.

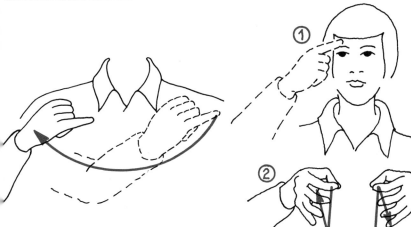

Joseph
Place little finger of right J on left shoulder and draw across to right shoulder.

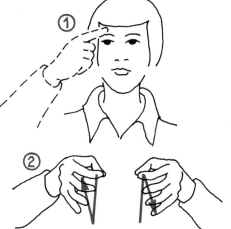

judge
Tap forehead with right index then form F shapes both hands palms facing, tips out, fingers spread. Move up and down alternately.

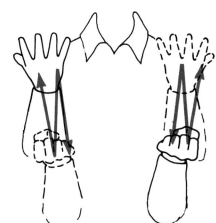

juggle
S shape both hands knuckles up. Juggle up and down alternately opening into five shapes palms in.

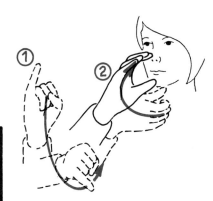

juice
Form letter J then raise cupped hand to mouth as if drinking.

July
Open B LH palm in. Outline J on left palm with RH, skip over fingers and form Y shape.

jump
Open B LH palm up, tips out. Place tips of right bent V in left palm and lift up quickly straightening V.

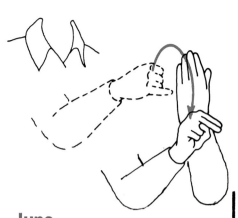

June
Open B LH palm in. Outline J on left palm with RH, skip over fingers and form N shape.

jungle
Open B LH palm down, tips right, I shape RH. Place right elbow on left hand and shake right I.

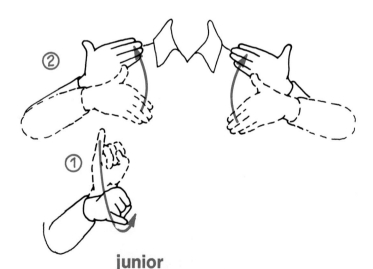

junior
Form right J, then bent B shapes both hands palms in, thumbs up. Place tips on shoulders and move up.

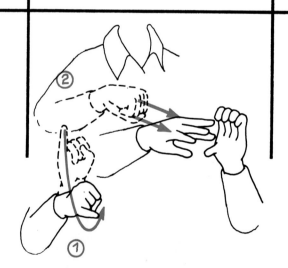

junk
C shape LH. Make J with RH then close into S shape. Now open into five shape several times in left C.

just
Open B LH palm right, tips up. Trace J on left palm with right little finger.

136

K

kangaroo
Curved open B both hands palms down. Place left wrist just above right elbow and hop forward twice.

keep
V shape both hands palms facing, tips out. Place right V on left V.

kettle
S shape LH. Place right K on left S then circle forward and under so the left S rests on right K.

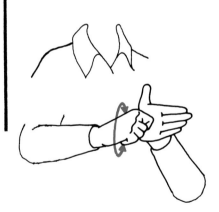

key
Open B LH palm right, tips out. Twist knuckle of right index in left palm.

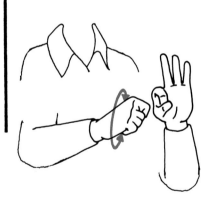

keyhole
F shape LH. Twist knuckle of right index at side of left F.

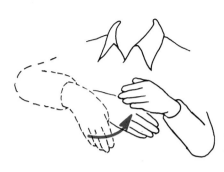

kick
Open B LH palm right, tips out. B shape RH palm in, tips left. Hit little finger side of left B with index side of right B.

kid (goat)
Place right K on chin, then on forehead.

kill
Open B LH palm slanted right, tips up. Slide right index finger under and out of left palm.

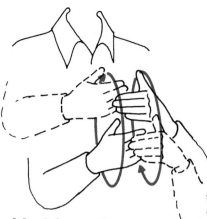

kind (good)
Open B both hands palms in, left tips right, right tips left. Circle around one another.

kind (type)
K shape both hands palms facing, middle tips touching. Circle out and around ending with palms in, little fingers touching.

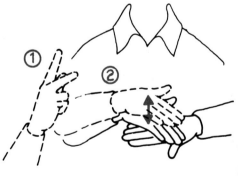

kindergarten
Open B LH palm up, tips out. K shape RH. Change into open B palm down, then clap hands together.

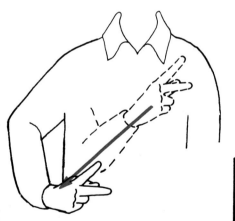

king
Place right K on left shoulder then move down to right side of waist.

kiss
Place tips of right open B on mouth and move back to cheek.

138

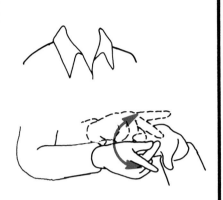

kit
Open B LH palm up, tips out. Place right K, palm down, tips left, in left palm then turn over (i.e., open kit).

kitchen
Shake right K.

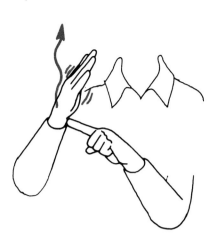

kite
B shape RH palm left. Place tip of left index on right wrist then wiggle right B upward.

kitten
Brush side of right cheek with middle finger of right K twice.

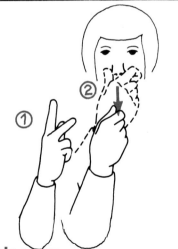

kleenex
Form right K, then place right thumb and index on nose and draw down.

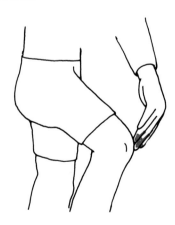

knee
Raise right knee and touch with tips of right hand.

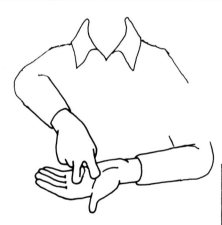

kneel
Place knuckles of bent right V in left palm.

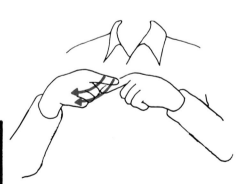

knife
Strike right index against left index and move out sharply twice.

139

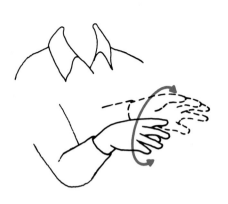

knob
Mime turning doorknob.

knock
Open B LH palm right. Knock knuckles of right A against left palm twice.

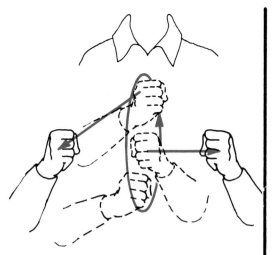

knot
S shape both hands knuckles facing. Make motion of tying knot and pulling tight.

know
Open B RH palm in, tips up. Pat forehead with tips.

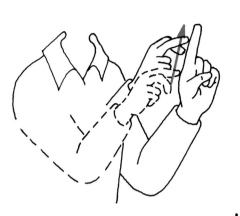

ladder
One shape LH. Make motion of climbing up left index with right index and middle fingers.

lady
L shape RH palm left, tips up. Place thumb on chin and arc to chest.

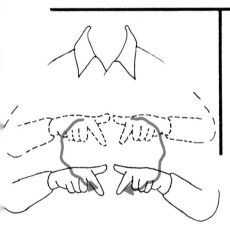

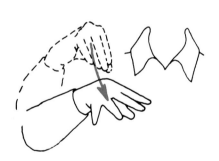

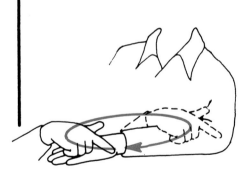

lake
L shape both hands thumbs touching. Shake forward in circle ending with thumbs together again.

lamb
Chip left forearm with right L twice (shearing wool).

lamp
Flat O RH tips down. Drop into five shape palm down.

land
B shape LH palm down, tips out. L shape RH palm down. Circle right L over left hand up to elbow and back.

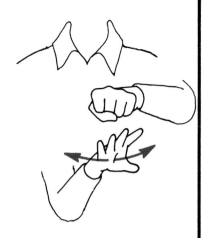

lantern
S shape LH knuckles down. Five shape RH palm down, tips out. Swing under left S.

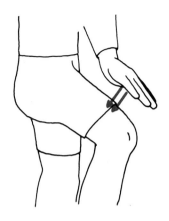

lap
Raise right knee and pat thigh with right palm several times.

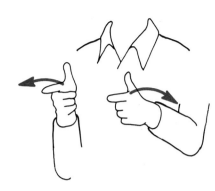

large
L shape both hands palms facing, thumbs up. Move hands away from each other.

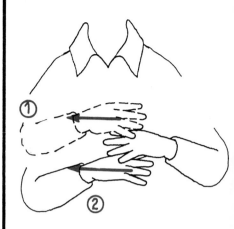

lasagna
Four shape both hands palms down, tips opposite. Place right 4 over left, draw back to right, then place under left hand and draw back to right again (i.e., layers).

last
I shape LH knuckles right, tip slanted out. Strike left little finger with right index.

late
Hold right open B down by side. Wave back and forth twice.

later
L shape RH palm left, index tip up. Move up and forward in semi-circle ending with tip out.

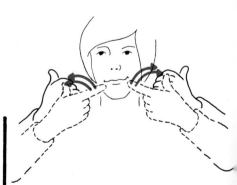

laugh
Place index fingers on sides of mouth and move up into A shapes twice.

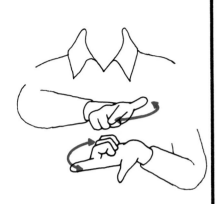

laundry
L shape both hands left palm up, tips slanted right; right palm down, tips slanted left. Twist hands back and forth.

law
Open B LH palm right. Place right L, palm out, against left palm.

lawn
B shape LH palm down, tips right. L shape RH. Outline LH with right L.

lay
Open B LH palm up, tips out. Lay back of right V in left palm.

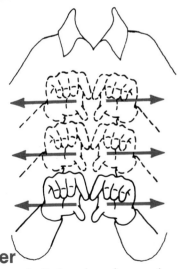

layer
G shape both hands palms and tips out. Move apart and back three times lowering the hands a little each time.

lazy
L shape RH palm in. Place just below left shoulder. Repeat.

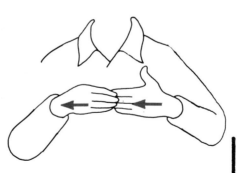

lead
Open B LH palm in, tips right. Grasp with fingers and thumb of RH and pull to right.

leaf
One shape LH palm in, tip right. Place right wrist over left index and move hand back and forth.

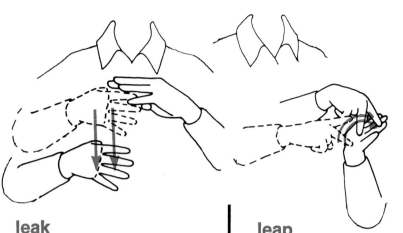

leak
Four shape both hands left palm down, tips right; right palm in, tips left. Place under left palm and drop down twice.

leap
Open B LH palm up, tips out. Place middle finger of right P on base of left palm, then place tip of index on fingers. Repeat.

leapfrog
Bent V both hands palms down. Leap forward alternately.

learn
Open B LH palm up, fingers spread. Drop fingers of right 5 into left palm and move to forehead ending in flat O.

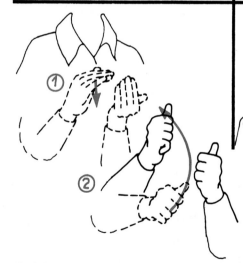

least
Bent B both hands left palm up, tips right; right palm down, tips left. Lower right hand. Now form A shape both hands knuckles facing, thumbs up, left A slightly higher than right. Bring right A up brushing left in passing.

leave
Five shape both hands palms down, tips slanted left, left hand in front of right. Draw back into O shapes.

left
Move right L to the left.

leg
B shape LH palm down, arm extended. Place palm of right L on left fingers then slide up to shoulder.

lemon

shape RH palm left, thumb
n. Tap chin with thumb.

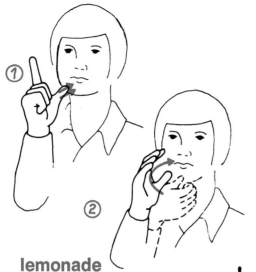

lemonade
Tap chin with thumb of right
L. Change into C shape and
move to mouth as if drinking.

lend
V shape both hands left palm
and tips slanted right; right
palm and tips slanted left.
Place right V on left and move
both hands forward.

less
Bent B both hands left palm
up, right palm down, tips left.
Lower RH.

let
L shape both hands palms facing, index tips pointed slightly
down. Bring to upright position.

letter
Place thumb of right A on
mouth and then on upturned
left palm.

lettuce
Tap base of right L against
right temple twice.

library
L shape RH. Circle in front of
body.

lick
Open B LH palm and tips slightly up. Place tips of right H on left palm and brush forward twice.

lid
O shape LH palm in, tips right. Bent B RH tips left. Place on left O then straighten into regular B shape.

lie (recline)
Open B LH palm up tips out. Draw back of right V across left palm.

lie (falsehood)
Push right index finger across chin from right to left.

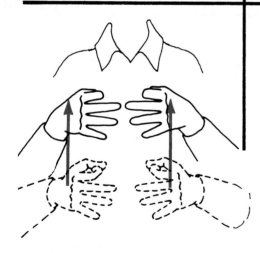

life
F shape both hands palms in, tips facing. Move up sides of body.

lift
L shape both hands palms up, index tips out. Lift up.

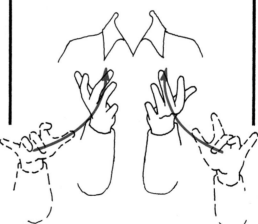

light (weight)
Five shape both hands palms down, tips out, middle fingers bent down. Twist in and up.

light
Flat O's both hands fingers back to back. Bring up and spread fingers wide, palms in.

lightning
Hold right index finger up and zig-zag down.

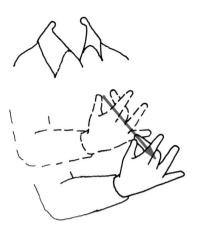

like (verb)
Place right middle finger and thumb on upper chest, then draw out and close fingers.

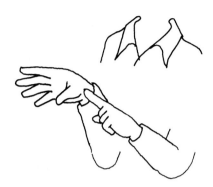

lily
Five shape RH bent at wrist, palm and thumb down, tips out. Place left index tip on side of right wrist.

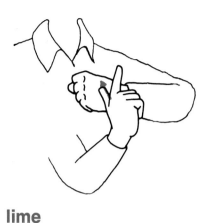

lime
S shape LH knuckles right, palm in. Tap thumb of right L on back of left S.

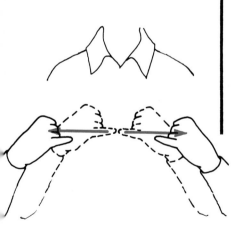

line
I shape both hands palms in, tips touching. Draw apart in straight line.

lion
C shape RH palm and tips down, fingers slightly separated. Place on head and move back.

lip
Rub lips with right index finger.

lipread
Bent V RH palm and tips in. Describe circle around lips.

lipstick
Mime applying lipstick to lips.

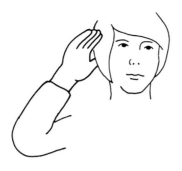

listen
Cup hand over ear.

little
L shape both hands palms facing, index tips out. Move close together.

live
L shape both hands palms in, thumbs up. Move up sides of body.

lizard
Open B LH palm right, tips up. Run right L up left palm in wiggly motion.

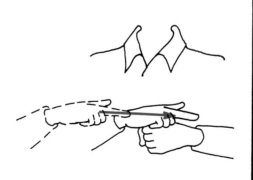

load
S shape LH knuckles right. L shape RH palm down, index tip left. Pass over left S toward body.

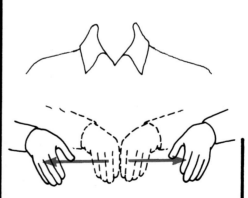

loaf (bread)
Bent B both hands palms and tips down, index fingers touching. Draw apart.

loaf (verb)
L shape both hands palms facing, thumbs up. Draw back and place thumbs on upper chest.

148

lobster
V shape both hands palms facing, tips slanted toward one another. Snap V fingers together.

lock
S shape both hands palms down. Turn right S over and rest on back of left S.

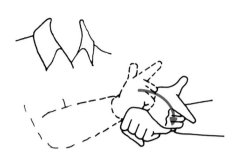

log
S shape LH knuckles down. See-saw right L, palm left, over left wrist.

lollipop
L shape RH palm left. Place index tip on mouth several times.

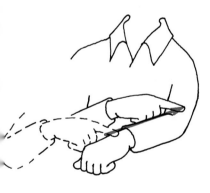

long
A shape LH knuckles down, arm extended. Run right index finger up left arm.

look
Point to eyes with tips of right V, then twist and point out.

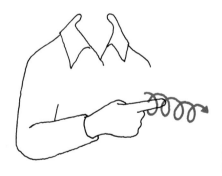

loop
One shape RH palm in, tip left. Loop forward.

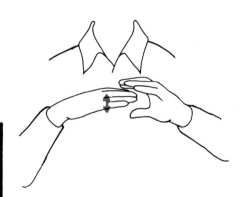

loose
C shape LH palm right. B shape RH palm down, tips left. Move up and down in left C.

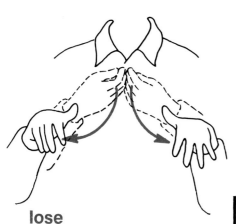

lose
Flat O shape both hands backs of fingers touching. Drop into 5 shapes, palms down.

lotion
Open B LH palm up, tips out. Dip thumb of right L into left palm (i.e., pouring).

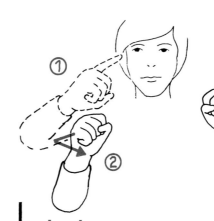

loud
Place right index finger in right ear. Form S's and shake in front of body.

love
S shape both hands. Cross arms on chest.

low
L shape RH. Lower.

luck
Place right middle finger on chin then twist out into Y shape, index finger extended.

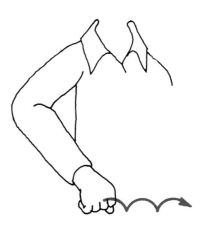

luggage
A shape RH knuckles down. Mime carrying suitcase.

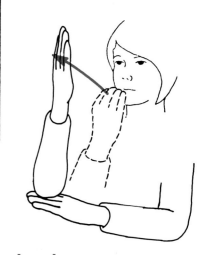

lunch
Place tips of right flat O on lips. Move out into B shape palm in, tips out, and rest elbow on back of left hand which is held before body.

M

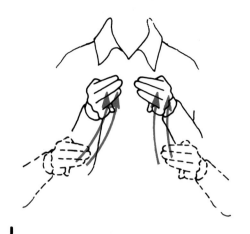

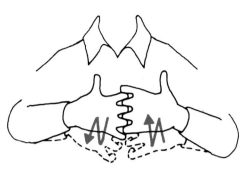

macaroni
M shape both hands palms in, tips facing. Move up and down as if draining macaroni.

machine
Interlock fingers, palms in, and move up and down.

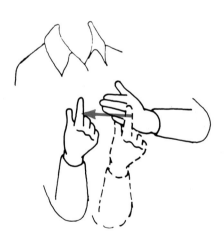

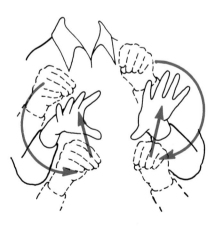

mad
Claw shape RH palm in. Hold in front of face and move out.

magazine
Open B LH palm in, tips right. Grasp bottom of LH with right index and thumb and slide RH to right.

magic
Flat O shape both hands tips out. Move away in semi-circle opening into five shapes palms out, tips up.

magnet
Open B LH palm right, tips out. Five shape RH palm left. Close rapidly into flat O and "stick" to left palm.

maid
Brush right cheek with tips of right M once or twice.

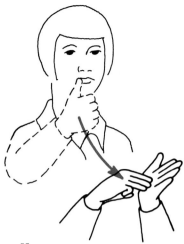

mail
Place thumb of right A on mouth. Change to M shape and place tips in upturned left palm.

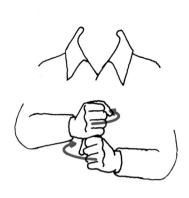

make
Twist right fist on top of left fist.

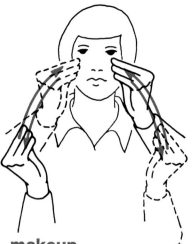

makeup
Flat O both hands palms and tips facing. Place tips on cheeks alternately.

male
M shape RH palm down, tips left. Place index side on forehead.

man
Open B RH palm left. Touch thumb to forehead then arc down to chest.

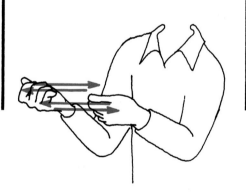

manage
"Loose" A shape both hands palms up, thumbs out. Move back and forth alternately as if handling reins.

mane
Place tips of right M on hair and draw back over head.

manger
Open B both hands tips down, left palm out, right palm in. Hold at left side of body then slide to right.

many
O shape both hands tips up. Snap open quickly into five shapes palms up.

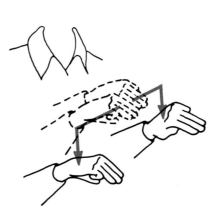

map
M shape both hands palms down, tips out, index fingers touching. Move apart and down.

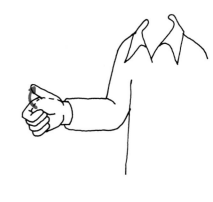

marble
A shape RH with thumb tucked under index. Flick thumb out as if shooting a marble.

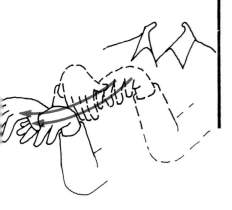

march (verb)
Five shape both hands palms in, tips down. LH in front of right. Swing fingers back and forth while moving both hands forward.

March (month)
Open B LH palm in, tips up. M shape RH palm down, tips left. Place against left palm, slide over fingers and down.

mark
Open B LH palm right. X shape RH. Draw tip of right X down left palm.

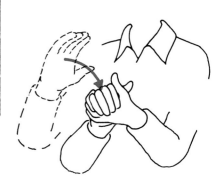

marry
Clasp hands together.

marshmallow
C shape LH palm and tips right, little finger side down. Open and close right fingers in left C.

Mary
Place right M just above left shoulder. Circle over head to right shoulder.

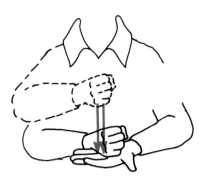

mash
Open B LH palm up, tips right. S shape RH. Strike left palm with right S.

mask
M shape both hands palms in, tips up. Place tips on bridge of nose and move to temples ending with palms out.

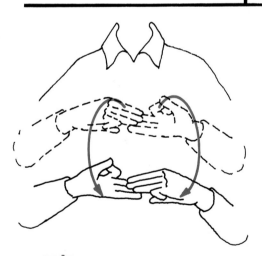

mate
M shape both hands left palm up, tips slanted right; right palm down, tips slanted left. Place right fingers on left, then reverse positions.

matter
Open B both hands palms in, tips facing. Flip back and forth.

may
M shape both hands palms down, tips out. Move down.

May (month)
Open B LH palm in, tips up. M shape RH palm down, tips left. Place against left palm, slide over fingers and down changing into Y shape.

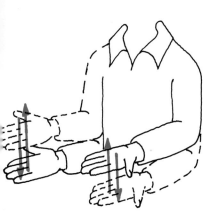

maybe
Open B both hands palms up, tips out. Move up and down alternately.

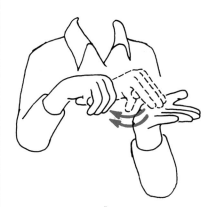

mayonnaise
Brush fingers of right M across heel of upturned left palm twice.

me
Touch chest with index finger.

meadow
Place tips of right M on back of left wrist. Circle counter clockwise over elbow and return to original position.

meal
Open B LH palm and tips slanted right. Place tips of right M in left palm, then move up to mouth.

mean (verb)
Open B LH palm right, tips out. V shape RH palm in, tips left. Place tips on left palm and reverse.

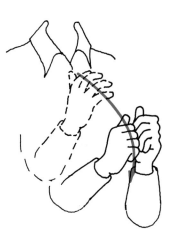

mean
Claw shape both hands palms facing. Change to A shapes and brush right A down against left A.

measles
Claw shape both hands. Tap tips on cheeks several times (indicating spots).

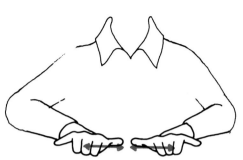

measure
Y shape both hands palms down, thumbs facing. Move back and forth toward one another.

meat
Open B LH palm in, tips right. Grasp left hand between thumb and index with right thumb and index.

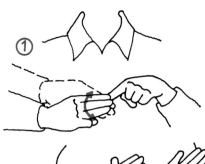

mechanic
One shape LH palm down, tips out. M shape RH palm in, tips left. Place over tip of left index and twist back and forth. Follow with agent marker.

medicine
Stir right middle finger in left upturned palm.

meet
One shape both hands palms facing. Bring together.

melon
S shape LH palm down. Thump with right middle finger.

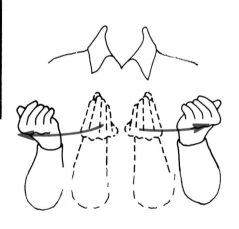

melt
Flat O shape both hands palms in, tips up. Draw apart and slightly down ending in A shapes.

mend
M shape both hands left tips up, right tips down. Circle right tips around left tips.

merry
Open B both hands palms in, tips facing. Brush up chest twice.

merry-go-round
Bent V shape both hands palms down. Circle down and up alternately.

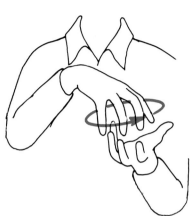

mess
Claw shape both hands left palm up, right palm down. Stir right claw over left counterclockwise.

microphone
S shape RH palm in. Hold in front of mouth as if holding a microphone.

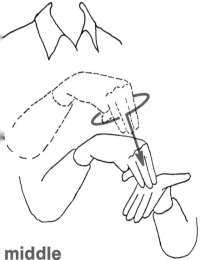

middle
Open B LH palm up, tips out. Place tips of right M in middle of left palm.

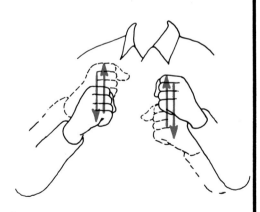

milk
S shape both hands. Mime milking cow.

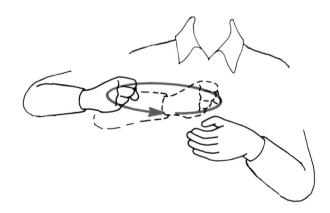

mill
C shape LH palm right, index and thumb side up. S shape RH. Move right S over left C clockwise in grinding motion.

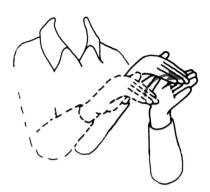

million

Open B LH palm up, tips slanted left. Place right tips on base of left palm then hop to fingers.

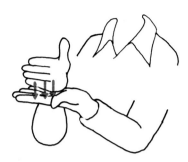

mince

Open B both hands, left palm up, tips out; right palm in, tips left. Chop left palm with little finger of right B.

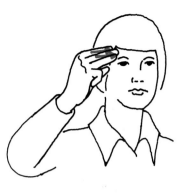

mind

Tap right temple with tips of right M.

minute

Open B LH palm right, tips up. Place knuckles of right one against left palm and move forward slightly.

mirror

Open B RH palm in. Hold before face and twist slightly to the right.

miss (verb)

One shape LH, knuckles right. Make sweeping pass by left index with right claw shape ending in S.

Miss

M shape RH palm down, tips left. Place on right side of chin then move out.

mistake

Tap chin with knuckles of right Y several times.

158

mitten
Open B LH palm right, tips up. Outline with right fingers.

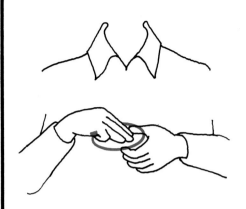

mix
C shape LH palm and tips right, little finger side down. Stir right M over left C.

mommy
Five shape RH palm left, tips up. Tap chin with thumb twice.

Monday
M shape RH. Move in small clockwise circle.

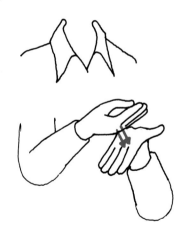

money
Open B LH palm up, tips out. Tap left palm with back of right flat O twice.

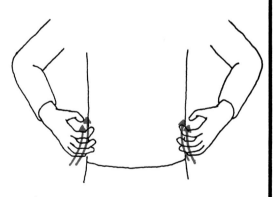

monkey
Claw shapes both hands. Scratch sides of body with tips.

monster
Claw shape both hands palm down. Hold at shoulder level and shake back and forth.

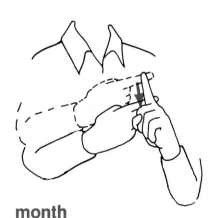

month
One shape both hands left palm right, right palm in, tip left. Place right index against left and slide down.

moon
Circle right eye with right index and thumb (other fingers closed).

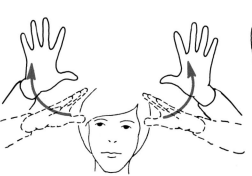

moose
Five shape both hands palms out, tips up. Place thumbs on temples and move up.

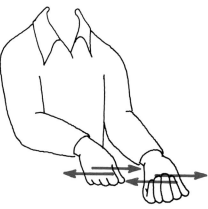

mop
A shape both hands. Mime holding and pushing a mop back and forth.

more
Flat O shape both hands palms and tips facing. Tap tips together once or twice.

morning
Hold right arm out palm up. Place little finger side of left open B palm in, tips right, on inside of right elbow. Bring right arm up slightly.

mosquito
Place thumb and index finger of right F on right cheek. Move away into B shape palm slightly left, tips up, then brush right cheek lightly.

most
A shape both hands knuckles facing, thumbs up, left A slightly higher than right. Bring right A up brushing left as it passes.

mother
Open B RH palm left. Place thumb on chin and flutter fingers.

160

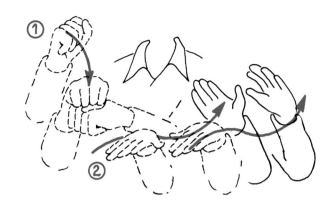

motor
M shape both hands palms down, right tips left, left tips right. Place right M in front of left and move hands up and down alternately.

motorcycle
Hold hands in front of body as if grasping large handlebars. Vibrate slightly.

mountain
Rest knuckles of right S on back of left S. Separate into open B's raising left above right. Move both hands up twice.

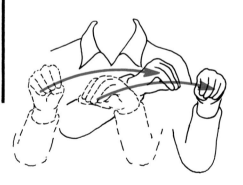

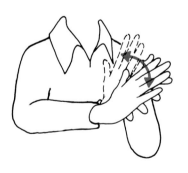

mouse
Strike tip of nose with right index finger.

mouth
Outline mouth with right index finger.

move
O shape both hands palms down. Move from right to left or vice versa.

movie
Five shape both hands, left palm right, right palm left. Flick right palm in left (flickers).

mow
S shape both hands thumbs down. Push forward and up.

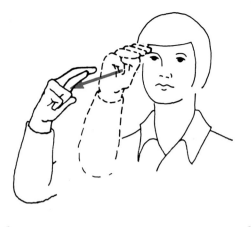

Mr.
M shape RH palm down, tips left. Place on forehead then move out ending in R shape.

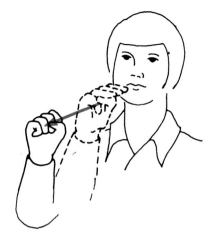

Mrs.
M shape RH palm down, tips left. Place on right side of chin then move out ending in S shape.

much
Claw shape both hands palms facing. Place tips together and draw apart.

mud
Open B LH palm down, tips right. Place fingers of right M between left middle and fourth fingers and push through.

muffin
Open B LH palm up, tips right. Place right tips in left palm then draw up into claw shape.

mug
Open B LH palm up, tips left. S shape RH knuckles left. Place in left palm then arc up to mouth.

mule
B shape RH palm out, tips up. Place knuckle of right thumb on right temple and bend fingers forward twice.

162

mumps
Claw shape both hands palms facing. Hold at sides of neck indicating swollen glands.

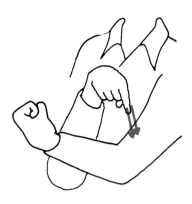

muscle
Hold LH in tight S palm up. Tap upper arm with right index.

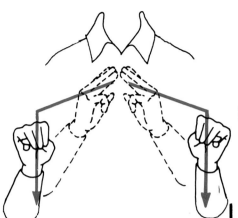

museum
M shape both hands palms facing, tips touching. Draw apart and down closing fingers over thumbs.

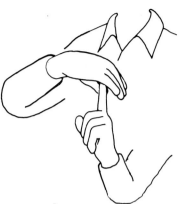

mushroom
C shape RH palm down, fingers left. Support with left index tip.

music
Open B LH palm up, tips slightly right. Swing right M back and forth over left palm without touching.

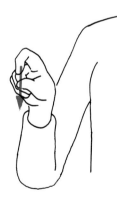

must
X shape RH knuckles down. Move down.

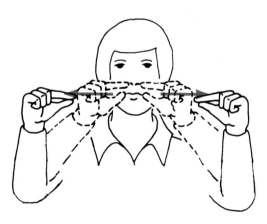

mustache
G shape both hands knuckles and tips facing. Place under nose then draw apart closing thumbs and index fingers.

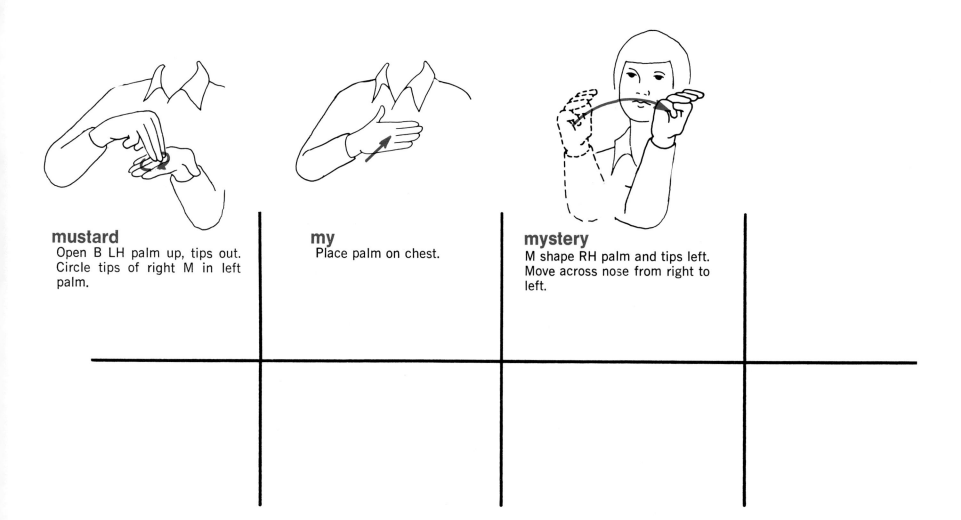

mustard
Open B LH palm up, tips out.
Circle tips of right M in left
palm.

my
Place palm on chest.

mystery
M shape RH palm and tips left.
Move across nose from right to
left.

N

nail
A shape LH knuckles right, thumb extended. Strike with tips of right G.

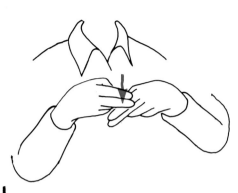

name
H shape both hands left palm right, right palm in. Hit left H with right H.

napkin
Place tips of right fingers on mouth and make small circle clockwise.

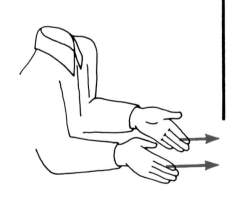

narrow
Open B both hands palms facing, tips slanted down. Hold close together and move forward.

naughty
N shape RH. Place tips on chin and twist out.

near
Open B both hands palms in, thumbs up. Place back of right hand against palm of left.

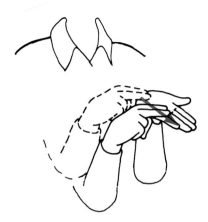

neat

Open B LH palm up, tips out. Place tips of right N in left palm and slide forward.

neck

Bent open B RH palm down, tips left. Tap right side of neck with tips.

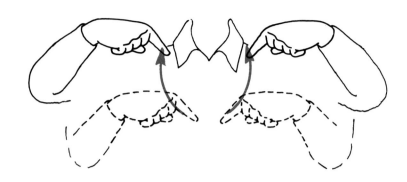

necklace

One shape both hands palms down, tips facing. Place on upper chest and slide up to shoulder outlining shape of necklace.

need

Right N moves down and up again.

needle

One shape LH, nine shape RH. Mime threading needle.

neighbor

Open B both hands palms in, tips opposite. Place right B on back of left, then arc up and out.

nephew

Move right N back and forth beside right temple.

nervous

Five shape both hands palms facing, tips out. Shake in nervous fashion.

nest

C shape LH palm up. Place right N in left palm.

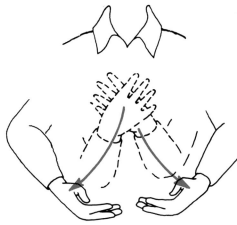

net

Four shape both hands palms in, left tips slanted right; right tips slanted left. Place RH on back of left. Draw hands down and apart ending in cupped shapes palms up.

never

B shape RH palm left, tips up. Move down in wavy motion.

new

Open B LH palm up, tips out. Brush back of right open B across left palm from right to left.

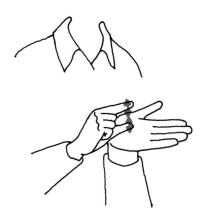

newspaper

Open B LH palm up, tips out. Place thumb of right G in left palm and snap index finger down once or twice.

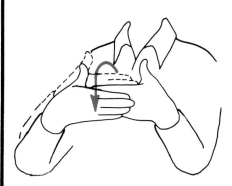

next

Open B both hands palms in, right tips left, left tips right. Place back of right fingers against left palm, then place on back of left hand.

nibble

Make nibbling motion at mouth with right thumb, index and middle fingers.

167

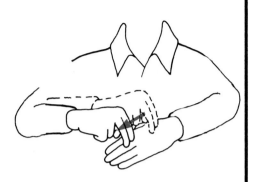

nice
B shape LH palm and tips slanted right. Slide right N forward over left index finger.

nickel
Touch forehead with middle finger of right 5 then move hand out.

niece
Move right N back and forth beside right cheek.

night
Hold left arm before you palm and tips slanted down. Open B RH palm in, tips down. Place on left wrist.

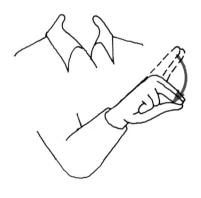

no
Snap middle finger, index and thumb together quickly (like an abbreviated n and o).

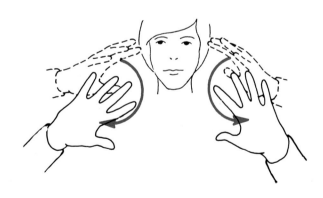

noise
Five shape both hands index fingers held at ears. Flick hands out.

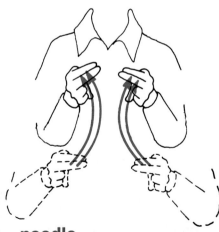

noodle
N shape both hands palms in, tips facing. Move up and down as if mixing noodles.

noon
Hold right arm straight up palm left, open B shape. Rest elbow on left open B, palm down, tips right.

north
Move right N upward.

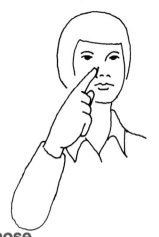

nose
Point to right side of nose with right index finger.

not
A shape RH knuckles left, thumb extended. Place thumb under chin and move out.

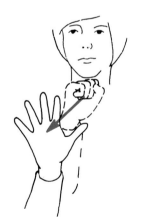

nothing
S shape RH. Place knuckles under chin and flick out into 5 shape palm out, tips up.

November
Open B LH palm in. Place right N in left palm, slide over tips and down.

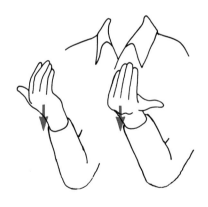

now
Bent open B both hands palms up. Lower slightly.

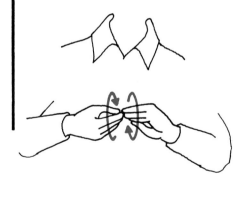

number
Flat O shape both hands left palm in, right down, tips touching. Reverse positions.

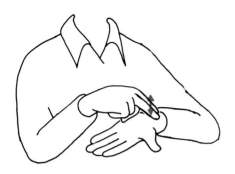

nurse
Open B LH palm up, tips out.
Tap left wrist with tips of right
N.

nut
Flip thumb out from under
teeth. Repeat.

170

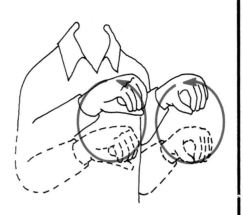

oar
O shape both hands. Mime holding oars and rowing.

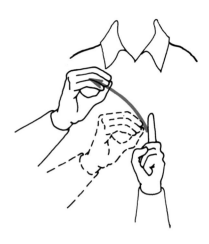

oat
One shape LH. Flat O RH. Place right tips on left index then move up and away to right.

obey
Flat O shape RH palm in, tips on forehead. Move forward opening into open B shape palm up, tips out.

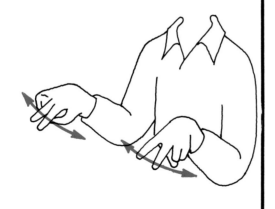

observe
V shape both hands palms down, tips out. Swing back and forth from left to right.

ocean
O shape both hands. Open into 5's and dip forward in wavy motion.

171

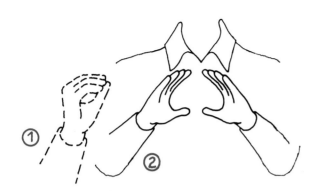

o'clock
Form right O, then, C shape both hands palms facing as if outlining a round clock.

October
Open B LH palm in. Place tips of right O on left palm, slide over fingers and down back of hand.

of
Form letters O and F in quick succession as if one movement.

of course
Shake Y up and down.

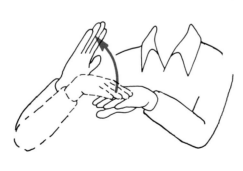

off
Open B both hands palms down. Place right palm on back of left hand and lift off.

office
O shape both hands tips facing. Move right O around in front of left O.

oh
Form the letters O and H in quick succession as if one movement.

172

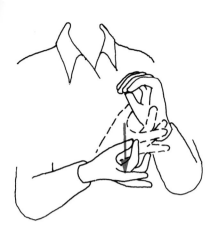

oil
O shape LH palm and tips right. Grasp base of left thumb with right thumb and middle finger and pull down.

OK
Form the letters O and K in quick succession as if one movement.

old
Place right S under chin then move down in wavy motion.

on
Open B both hands palms down, left tips out, right tips left. Place right palm on back of left palm.

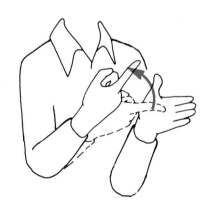

once
Open B LH palm right, tips out. Strike middle of left palm with index tip once.

onion
Twist X at corner of eye.

only
Hold index finger up palm out. Describe semi-circle counter clockwise, ending with palm in.

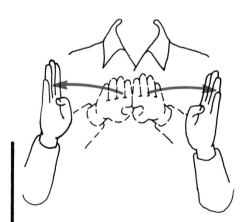

open
Open B both hands palms down, tips out, index fingers touching. Draw apart and turn so that palms face each other.

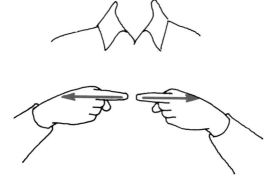

opposite
One shape both hands palms in, tips facing. Draw apart.

or
Form the letters O and R in quick succession as if one movement.

orange
Place right C at mouth and "squeeze" into S shape.

orchard
Open B LH palm down, tips right. Place right elbow on left hand, form the letter O and shake.

orchestra
Flat O both hands palms down, tips facing. Swing back and forth as if conducting an orchestra.

order
Place tip of right index on lips, then move out forcibly turning down slightly.

ornament
C shape both hands palms facing. Bring together until tips touch.

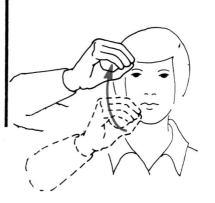

orphan
O shape RH palm and tips left. Place tips at right side of chin then move up to forehead.

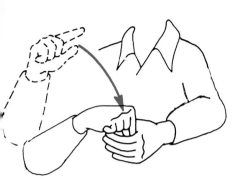

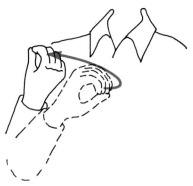

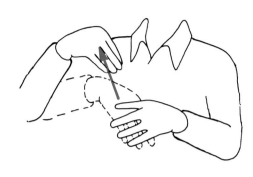

ostrich
O shape LH palm and tips right, little finger side down. G shape RH palm and tips left. Place tips of right G in left O.

other
O shape RH tips left. Turn so that tips face up.

our
C shape RH palm left. Place thumb just under right shoulder. Circle to left ending with little finger resting just below left shoulder.

out
C shape left hand palm right. Place fingers of right flat O in left C, and pull out.

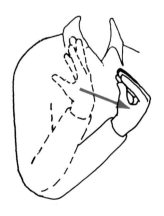

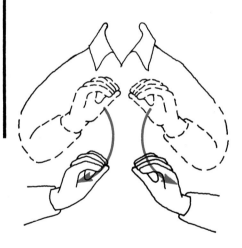

outdoor
Five shape RH palm and tips in. Move out into flat O.

outfit
Flat O shape both hands palms in. Place tips on chest and draw down.

outside
C shape LH palm right. Place tips of right flat O in left C and draw out. Repeat.

oven
Open B LH palm down, tips right. O shape RH palm and tips left. Slide under left open B.

175

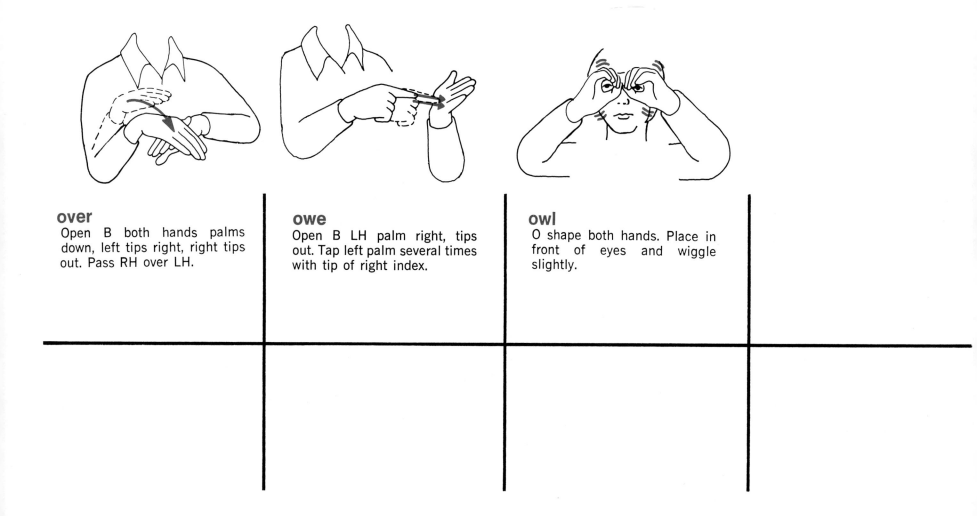

over
Open B both hands palms down, left tips right, right tips out. Pass RH over LH.

owe
Open B LH palm right, tips out. Tap left palm several times with tip of right index.

owl
O shape both hands. Place in front of eyes and wiggle slightly.

P

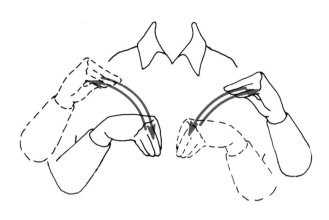

pack
Flat O both hands palms and tips down. Move down and up alternately as if putting things in suitcase or box.

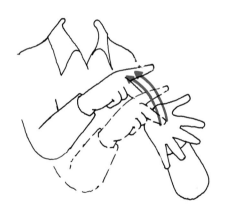

package
P shape both hands palms down, tips out. Swing left behind right and right in front of left outlining shape of package.

pad
Open B LH palm up, tips out. Brush middle finger of right P across base of left palm toward body twice.

page
Open B LH palm up, tips out. Place middle finger tip of right P on base of left palm and flip over as if turning a page.

pail
S shape LH knuckles down. One shape RH palm down, tip out. Place right index against left thumb and index, dip under and place on left little finger.

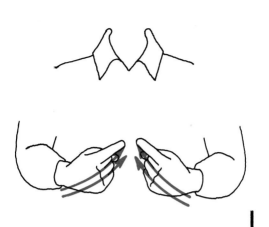

pain
One shape both hands palms in, tips slanted down. Move toward one another curling up. Repeat.

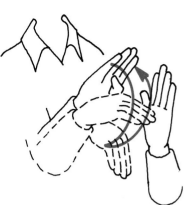

paint
Open B LH palm right, tips up. Brush fingers of right open B up and down left palm.

pajamas
Draw right fingers down over face ending in flat O. Now, form five shapes both hands, place on upper chest, then move down.

pan
Use right A as if holding pot handle while shaking back and forth.

pancake
Place back of right hand in left palm and flip over (i.e. flipping pancake).

panda
P shape both hands palms in, tips up. Circle eyes, left fingers to the left, right fingers to the right.

pansy
P shape RH palm left. Place middle finger on right side of nose, then move to left side.

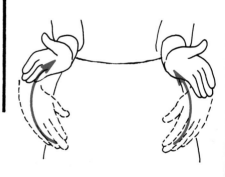

panties
Place tips of bent B's on hips (palms up). Curve up slightly so that wrists rest on waist.

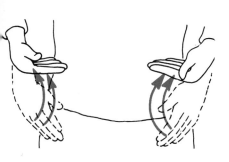

pants
Open B both hands. Place palms on hips and brush up toward waist twice.

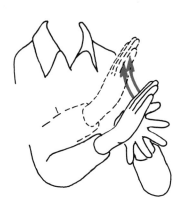

paper
Open B both hands left palm up, tips out; right palm down, tips left. Brush base of right palm across base of left palm toward body twice.

parachute
One shape LH palm in. Claw shape RH palm down. Place right claw over left index and lower.

parade
Four shape both hands palms out, tips up, RH slightly back of LH. Move forward in little dips.

parakeet
Snap right index and thumb at right side of mouth.

parent
P shape RH palm in. Place middle finger tip on forehead then on chin.

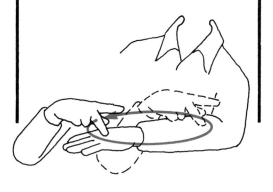

park
Open B LH palm down, tips out. Circle back of hand counter-clockwise with right P.

parrot
Snap right thumb, middle and index fingers together at right side of mouth.

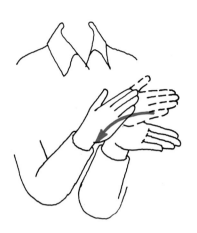

part
Open B both hands left palm up, tips out; right palm and tips left. Slice across left palm toward body.

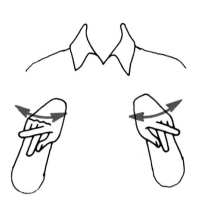

party
P shape both hands. Swing back and forth.

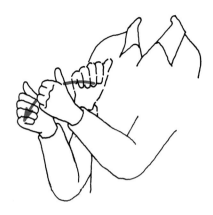

pass
A shape both hands knuckles facing. Brush right A past left A.

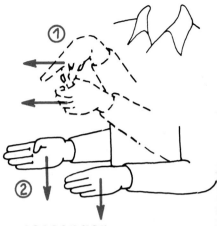

passenger
O shape LH palm and knuckles right. Place middle finger of right P in left O and move both hands forward. Follow with agent marker.

past
Open B RH palm in, tips up. Flip back and touch right shoulder.

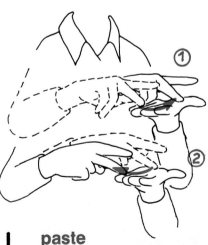

paste
Open B LH palm up, tips out. Place middle finger of right P on left fingers, draw back over palm, turn over and move back to fingers.

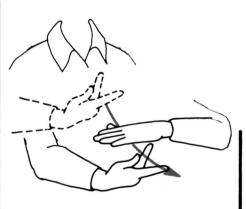

pastry
B shape LH palm down, tips right. P shape RH palm up. Slide under left hand.

pat
Pat left shoulder with right palm.

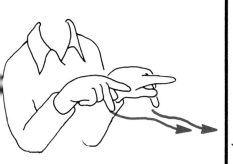

path
P shape both hands palms facing. Move forward as if following path.

pavement
B shape LH palm down, tips right, P shape RH. Circle right P counterclockwise over left hand and elbow.

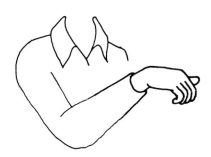

paw
C shape RH palm and tips down. Hold in front of body.

pay
Open B LH palm up, tips out. Place middle finger of right P on left palm and flick out.

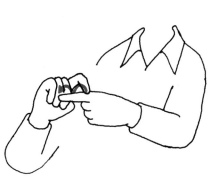

pea
One shape LH palm in, tip right. Tap from base to tip with right X.

peach
Claw shape RH palm left. Place tips on right cheek and thumb under chin. Stroke cheek ending in flat O.

peacock
Five shape LH. G shape RH palm and tips slanted left. Place against base of left palm.

peanut
Twist thumb of right A on lower lip and move out.

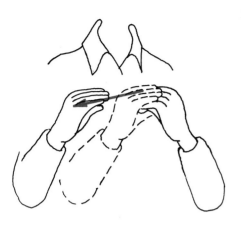

pear
Flat O left hand palm in, tips right. Grasp with right fingers and slide RH back indicating shape of pear.

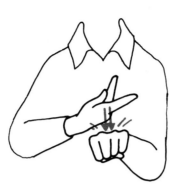

pebble
A shape LH knuckles down. Tap with back of right P.

peek
P shape RH knuckles left. Hold against right eye.

peel
Open B LH palm down, tips out. F shape RH. Place tips on back of left hand and move away as if peeling a piece of fruit.

peep
Hold left B palm right, in front of left eye and right P, knuckles left, in front of right eye.

pen
Open B LH palm up, tips out. "Write" in palm with middle tip of right P.

pencil
Place right thumb and fore-finger on mouth then slide across upturned left palm.

penguin
Open B LH palm down, tips right. P shape RH. Place right elbow on back of LH and move P from right to left.

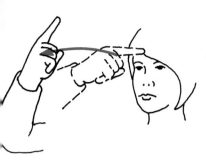

penny
Place right index on right temple then move hand out.

people
P shape both hands palms facing. Move up and down alternately in circular motion.

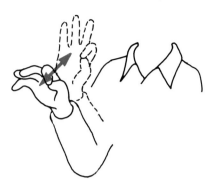

pepper
F shape RH. Mime shaking pepper shaker.

peppermint
P shape RH knuckles left. Place middle finger on chin, then move out forming M shape, tips left.

perfect
P shape both hands palms in. Drop right P in circular motion, bring back up and place middle tips together.

perfume
A shape RH knuckles left, thumb extended. Draw back to right side of neck.

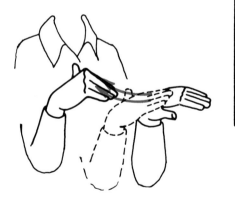

pet
Open B both hand palms down, tips out. Rub back of LH with right tips.

petal
One shape LH. Place right index and thumb close to left index then draw away to right.

183

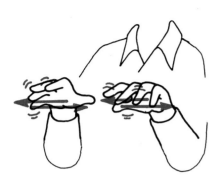

piano
Mime playing piano.

pick
G shape RH. Move up bringing index finger and thumb together.

pickle
One shape LH palm right, tips out. Place right index on mouth then move down to left index.

picnic
Place left palm on right palm. Lift both hands up until tips touch mouth.

picture
Open B LH palm right, tips up. Place thumb and index finger of right C against right eye then move down to left palm.

pie
Mime cutting slice of pie using left palm as pie and edge of right little finger as knife.

pig
Place back of RH under chin tips left. Drop fingers down twice.

pigeon
Snap right index and thumb on right cheek.

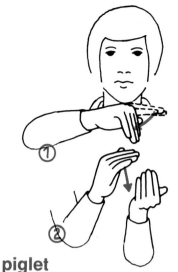

piglet
Place back of RH under chin, drop fingers down and move back up once. Now, form bent B's both hands left palm and tips up, right palm down, tips left. Hold right palm just above left.

pilgrim
Place middle finger of right P on heart. Twist so that tip points out.

pill
Mime plopping pill in mouth with thumb and forefinger.

pillow
Open B both hands palms facing, tips slanted right. Hold at side of right cheek and tilt head to right.

pilot
Zoom right Y to left, then use marker for agent.

pin
Mime sticking pin in dress or shirt with right thumb and forefinger.

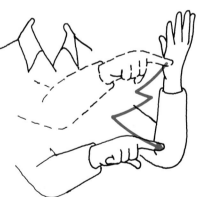

pine
Five shape LH palm right. Place right index on little finger side of LH, then zig-zag down to elbow outlining shape of pine tree.

185

pineapple
Twist middle finger of right P on right cheek.

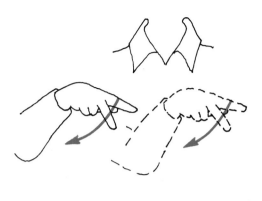

Ping-Pong
P shape RH palm in, tips left. Swing back to right. Repeat.

pink
Place middle finger of right P just above upper lip and bring down to chin.

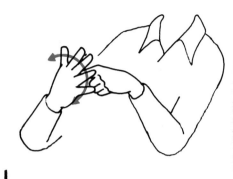

pinwheel
Five shape RH palm and tips slanted left. Place tip of left index against right palm, then twist RH down and back.

pipe
Place thumb of right Y on mouth.

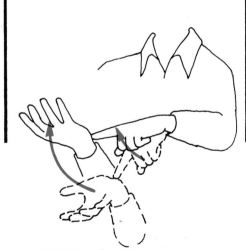

pitchfork
Place left index finger on base of RH which is held palm up with fingers spread and tips out. Now, lift right hand forward and up.

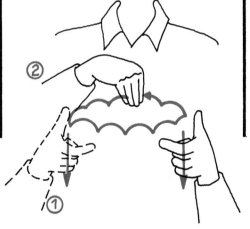

pizza
Curved L shape both hands palms facing, thumbs up. Drop down. Now form right flat O and move in circular motion over left L as if putting ingredients in a pizza.

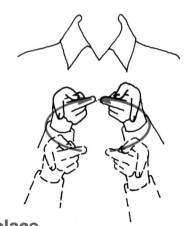

place
P shape both hands. Touch tips of middle fingers, circle back to body and touch again.

plain
Open B LH palm up, tips slanted right. Place right index on lips, change to open B, palm down, and brush across left palm.

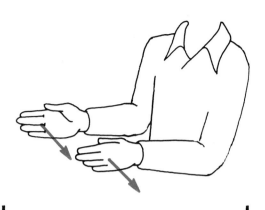

plan
Open B both hands palms facing, tips out. Move to left or right.

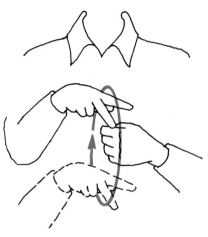

planet
S shape LH knuckles right. Place middle finger of right P on top of left S. Circle forward and under returning to original position.

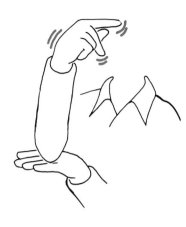

plant
Open B LH palm down, tips right. P shape RH. Place right elbow on back of LH and shake P.

plastic
Rub right P up and down on right cheek.

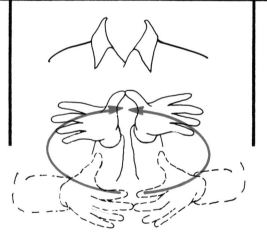

plate
Five shape both hands palms in, middle fingers touching. Circle back toward body ending with thumbs touching.

play
Y shape both hands palms in. Twist back and forth.

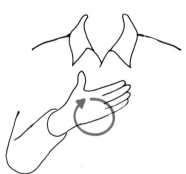

please
Rotate palm on upper chest.

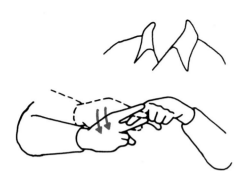

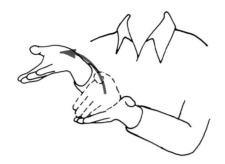

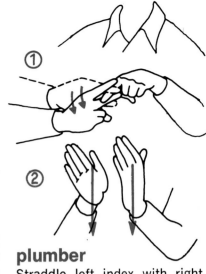

pliers

Straddle left index with right index and middle fingers. Now twist right fingers forward and back twice.

plow

Open B LH palm up, tips out. Move little finger side of right open B, palm left, tips out, across left palm and turn palm up.

plum

Stroke right cheek with right thumb, middle and index fingers. Draw away closing fingers.

plumber

Straddle left index with right index and middle fingers. Twist right fingers forward and back and follow with agent marker.

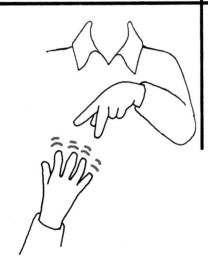

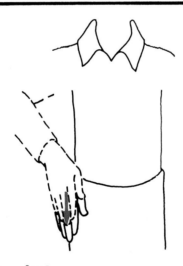

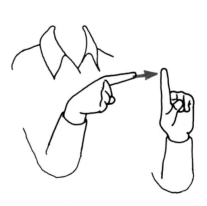

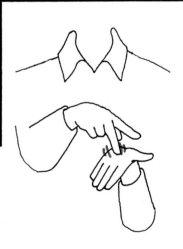

poach

P shape LH. Flutter fingers of RH beneath left P.

pocket

Mime placing hand in side pocket.

point

One shape both hands right palm in, tip left. Move toward and touch left index.

poison

Open B LH palm up, tips out. Press middle finger of right P into left palm and quiver.

polar bear
P shape both hands palms in, tips up. Cross wrists in front of chest and shake P's.

pole
C shape both hands palms in, left tips right, right tips left. Place right C on left and then lift straight up.

police
Tap right C just below left shoulder (indicating badge).

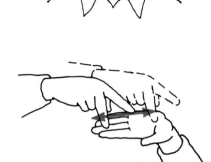

polish
Open B LH palm up, tips out. Slide middle finger tip of right P back and forth on left palm.

polite
Five shape RH palm left. Tap chest with thumb. Repeat.

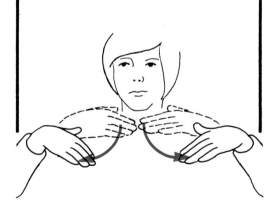

poncho
Place fingertips together at neck, palms down. Move down.

pond
P shape both hands middle fingers touching. Shake forward in a circle and touch again.

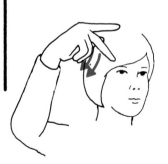

pony
P shape RH. Place thumb on right temple and move finger forward and down twice.

189

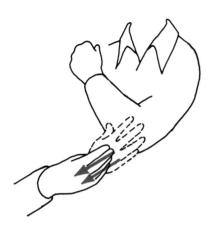

poor
Stroke left elbow with right fingers twice.

pop
O shape LH palm and tips right. Put right thumb and index finger in left O, pull out, then slap right palm on left O.

popcorn
S shape both hands palms in, knuckles up. Snap index finger up alternately.

popsicle
V shape RH palm in. Draw down over mouth and chin. Repeat.

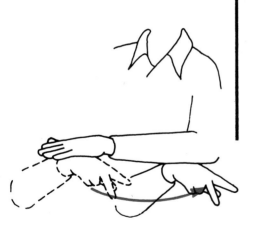

porch
B shape LH palm down, tips right. Place back of right P under LH and swing back to left elbow.

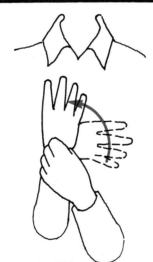

porcupine
S shape LH knuckles right. Four shape RH palm in, tips left. Place back of RH against left thumb and raise right fingers upright.

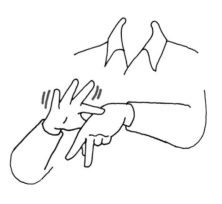

pork
P shape LH. Grasp left P with right thumb and forefinger and shake.

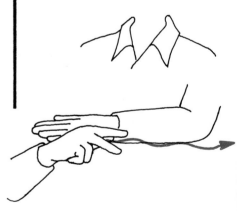

porpoise
Hold left arm before body palm down, tips right. Move right P up outside of left arm to elbow in wavy motion.

190

post
Open B LH palm up, tips slanted right. Place middle finger of right P on lips then place on left palm.

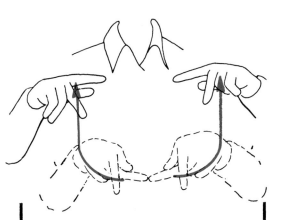

pot
P shape both hands palms in, middle fingers touching. Arc out and up in shape of pot.

potato
Tap back of LH with right bent V.

pouch
Open B shape both hands left palm in, tips right; right palm in, tips down. Slide right B down against left palm.

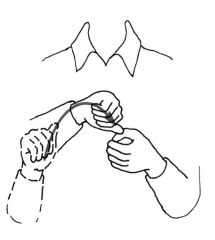

pour
O shape LH tips right, little finger side down. A shape RH thumb extended. Dip right A into left O.

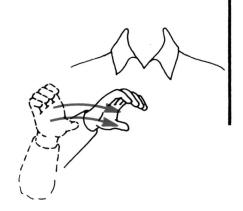

powder
C shape RH palm left. Shake toward chest twice.

pox
Curve right index finger inside right thumb, then tap right cheek in several places indicating spots.

practice
One shape LH palm right, tip out. Rub knuckles of right A back and forth on left index.

pray

Place palms together tips slanted up. Rotate toward body.

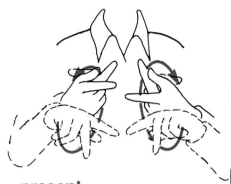

present

P shape both hands. Bring up and turn out.

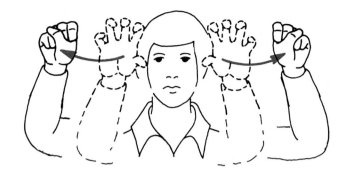

president

Claw shape both hands palms out. Place at temples, then move away ending in S shapes.

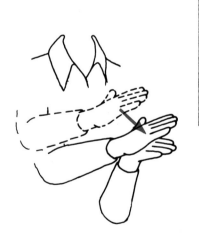

press

Open B both hands left palm up, tips out; right palm down, tips left. Press hands together.

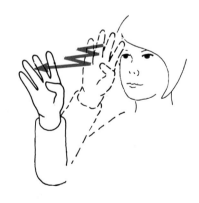

pretend

Four shape RH palm left. Place index finger against forehead then jump hand forward in three short movements.

pretty

Five shape RH palm in, tips up. Circle face from right to left ending in flat O.

pretzel

X shape both hands left palm in, right palm down. Hook X's together.

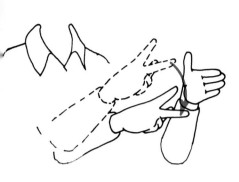

price
Open B LH palm right, tips out.
Slice middle finger tip of right
P down across left palm.

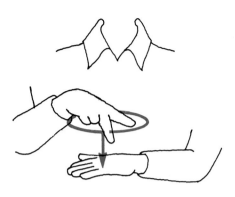

principal
Open B LH palm down, tips
out. Circle right P over back of
left B, then place middle finger
tip on back of left hand.

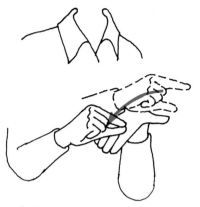

print
G shape RH tips left. Hold over
left palm, then draw back and
snap in palm twice.

prison
Five shape both hands palms
in, right tips up, left tips right.
Place right fingers against left
palm.

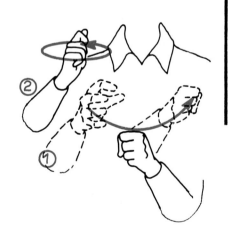

prize
S shape LH knuckles right. Claw
shape RH palm left. Swing over
left S closing into S shape.
Change to A shape and circle in
front of right shoulder.

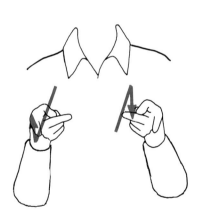

probable
P shape both hands palms up.
Move up and down alternately.

projector
S shape LH, five shape RH palm
down, tips out. Place left S
against base of right thumb and
flicker right fingers.

promise
S shape LH palm down. Place
right index finger on lips, move
out into five shape and place
against left S.

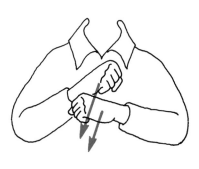

protect

S shape both hands left facing right, right facing left. Place right S slightly behind left S and push forward.

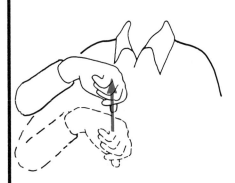

proud

A shape RH palm out, thumb down. Place on lower chest and draw up slowly.

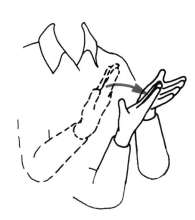

prove

Open B both hands palms up, left tips out, right tips slanted left. Place back of right B in palm of left B.

prune

Place middle finger tip of right P on left cheek, then circle back to right cheek.

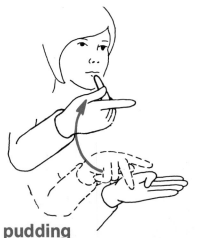

pudding

Open B LH palm up, tips out. Place middle finger of right P in left palm then move up to mouth.

puddle

Open B LH palm down, tips out. Circle right P counterclockwise over back of left B in wavy motion.

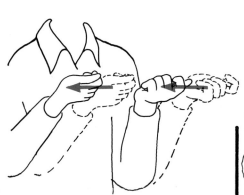

pull

A shape both hands knuckles up, left ahead of right. Pull toward body in quick motion as if pulling a rope.

pump

Mime pumping handle of old fashioned water pump.

194

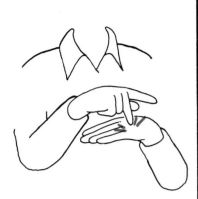

pumpkin
Thumb back of LH with middle finger of right P.

punch (beverage)
P shape RH palm down, tips left. Change to C shape palm and tips left, and move up to mouth as if drinking.

punch (verb)
One shape LH. P shape RH palm in, tips left. Punch left index with middle finger of right P.

punish
Hold left arm in front of body fist clenched. Now, strike left elbow with right X.

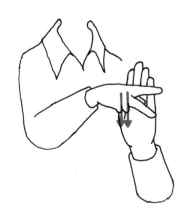

pupil (person)
Open B LH palm right. Place right P on left fingers and slide down to base of palm. Repeat.

pupil (eye)
Place middle finger of right P at corner of right eye.

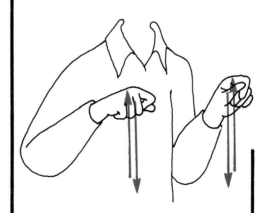

puppet
A shape both hands palms down. Move up and down alternately as if pulling strings.

puppy
Bent B LH palm up. Shake right P up and down over left palm.

195

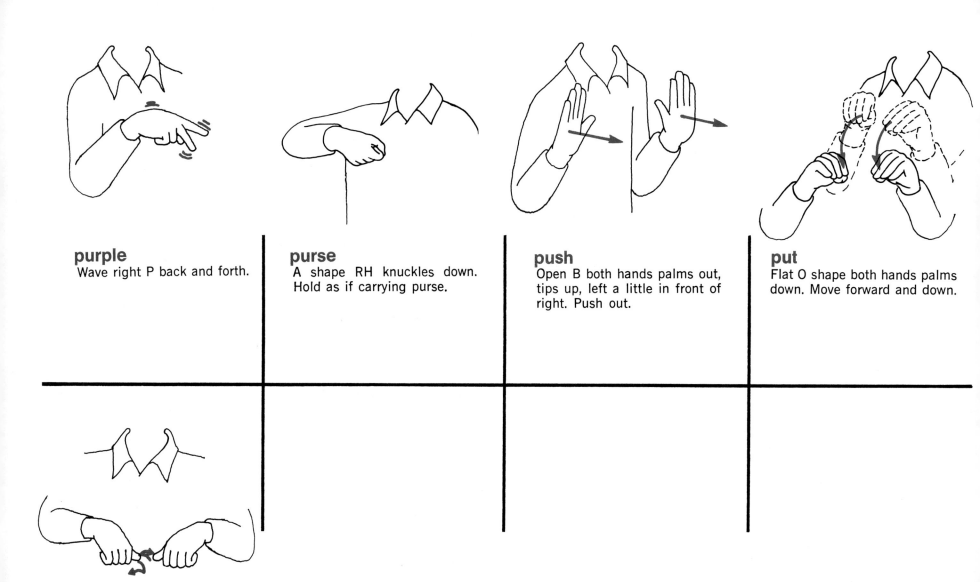

purple
Wave right P back and forth.

purse
A shape RH knuckles down.
Hold as if carrying purse.

push
Open B both hands palms out,
tips up, left a little in front of
right. Push out.

put
Flat O shape both hands palms
down. Move forward and down.

puzzle
A shape both hands thumbs
down. Make motion of fitting
together.

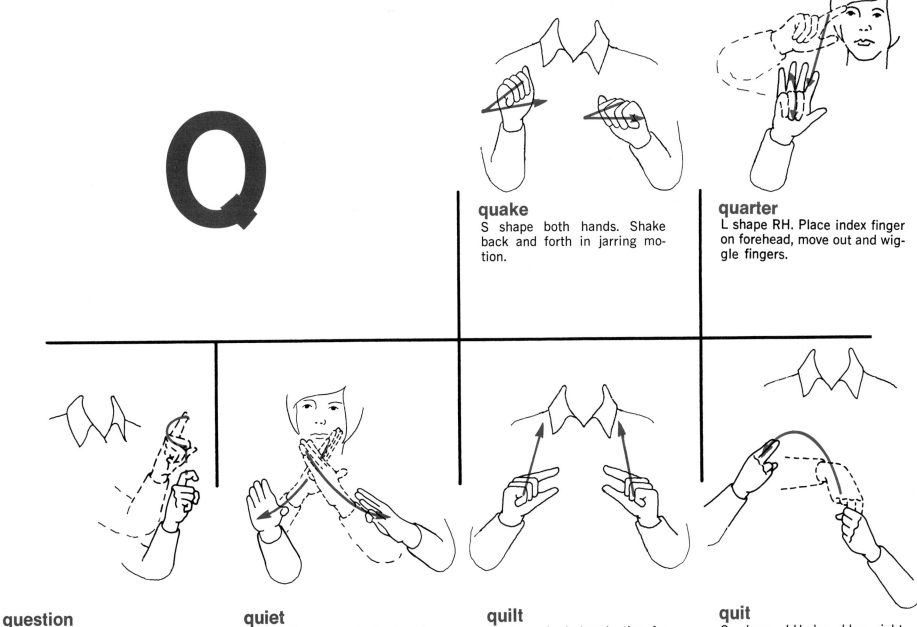

Q

quake
S shape both hands. Shake back and forth in jarring motion.

quarter
L shape RH. Place index finger on forehead, move out and wiggle fingers.

question
Outline question mark in air with right index finger.

quiet
Open B shape both hands. Cross at mouth with right index finger on lips. Draw apart ending with palms down.

quilt
Q shape both hands tips facing. Draw toward body as if pulling up quilt.

quit
S shape LH knuckles right. Place right middle and index fingers in left S, then pull out to the right.

R

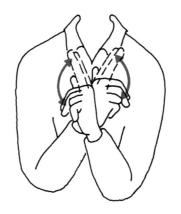

rabbit
H shape both hands palms in, right tips left, left tips right. Cross wrists and flick H's toward body.

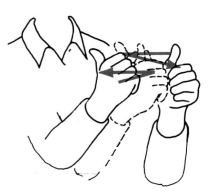

race
A shape both hands thumbs up, knuckles facing. Twist back and forth alternately.

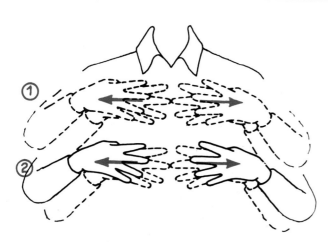

rack
Four shape both hands palms in, tips facing. Draw apart, lower, then draw apart again.

radio
Place right thumb, middle and index fingers on right ear.

radish
R shape RH palm in. Place on lips then twist out into F shape.

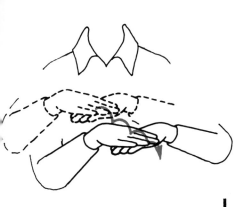

raft
B shape both hands palms down, left tips slanted right; right tips slanted left. Place RH on back of left then move both hands forward in wavy motion.

rag
R shape RH palm in. Place just below right shoulder and make a small circle.

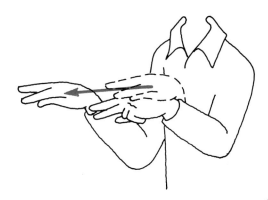

rail
V shape both hands palms down, tips out. Slide right V forward over back of left V.

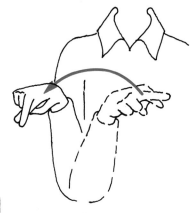

railroad
R shape RH palm down, tips slanted left. Move to right.

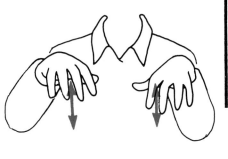

rain
Claw shape both hands palms down. Move up and down.

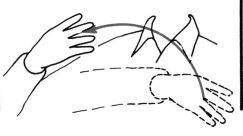

rainbow
Four shape RH palm in, tips down. Arc from left to right outlining rainbow.

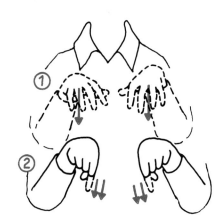

raindrop
Claw shape both hands palms down. Change to S shapes and snap index fingers down alternately.

raise
Open B's both hands palms up, tips out. Raise up several inches.

raisin
Open B LH palm in, tips right. "Hop" right R across back of left B from left to right.

rake
Rake fingers of right claw hand across upturned left palm.

rash
Flat O shape both hands palms in, tips up. Move up to cheeks opening into five shapes.

raspberry
Place right index finger on lower lip and flick out into 9 shape.

rat
R shape RH. Move across tip of nose to left.

rattle
R shape RH. Shake back and forth.

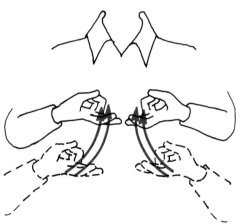

ravioli
R shape both hands palms up, tips facing. Move up and down alternately.

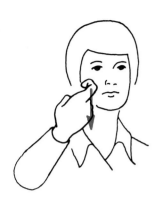

razor
X shape RH knuckles left. Scrape down right cheek.

reach
Claw shape RH palm out. Raise up and close into S shape.

read
Open B LH palm right, tips up. Brush right V down palm of LH.

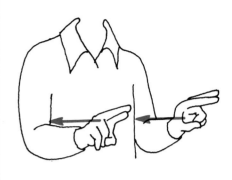

ready
R shape both hands palms down, tips out. Move from left to right.

real
One shape RH palm left. Place finger on lips and move up and out.

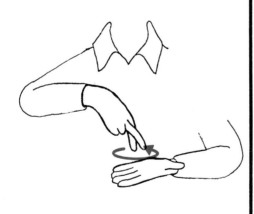

record
Open B LH palm up, tips out. Circle tips of right R clockwise over left palm.

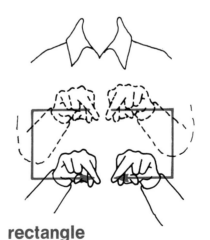

rectangle
R shape both hands palms down, tips out. Outline shape of rectangle.

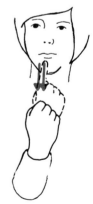

red
Brush chin with right index finger twice.

201

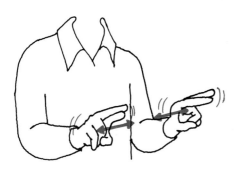

refrigerator
R shape both hands palms facing, tips out. Shiver up and down.

refuse
S shape RH knuckles left. Jerk back over right shoulder.

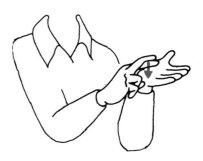

register
Open B LH palm up, tips out. R shape RH palm down, tips left. Place in left palm.

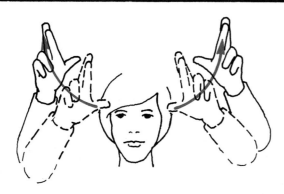

reindeer
R shape both hands thumbs extended. Place thumbs on temples and move up and out.

relative
R shape both hands left palm up, right palm down. Place right R on left, then turn both hands over, reversing positions.

remember
A shape RH knuckles left, thumb extended. Place thumb on forehead and twist wrist to the left.

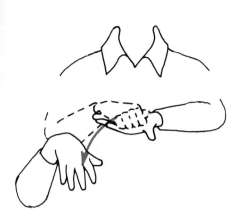

remove
Open B LH palm up, tips right. Place knuckles of right A in left palm, lift up, then drop into five shape palm in, tips down.

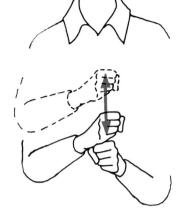

repair
S shape both hands left knuckles right, right knuckles left. Place right S on left S, move up, then down again.

rest
Fold arms across upper chest resting RH on left shoulder and LH on right shoulder.

restaurant
R shape RH palm left. Place on right side of mouth and move to left side.

return
R shape both hands palms in. Move back toward body.

rhinoceros
C shape RH palm left. Place on nose and move out ending in S shape.

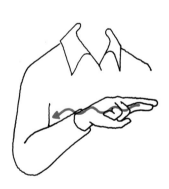

rhythm
R shape RH palm down, tips out. Move in rhythmic motion to the right.

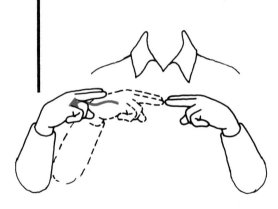

ribbon
H shape both hands palms down, tips touching. Draw right H away from left in wavy motion.

rice
Open B LH palm up, tips right. Place back of right R in left palm then move up to mouth.

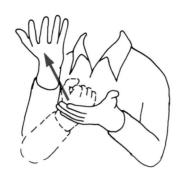

rich
Place back of right S in left palm then lift up spreading fingers.

ride
O shape LH palm right. Place fingers of right H in left O and move forward.

rifle
Open B LH palm up, fingers curved. Point index finger of right L at LH.

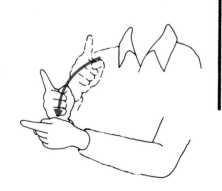

right (correct)
One shape both hands, left palm right, right palm left, tips out. Place RH on top of LH.

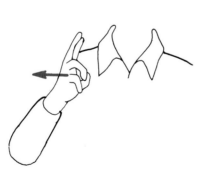

right (direction)
R shape RH. Move to right.

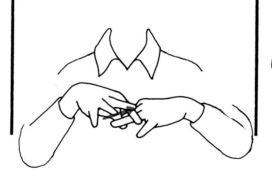

ring (noun)
Place right index and thumb around left fourth finger and slide back and forth.

ring (verb)
Open B LH palm and tips slanted right. Hit left palm with right R several times.

204

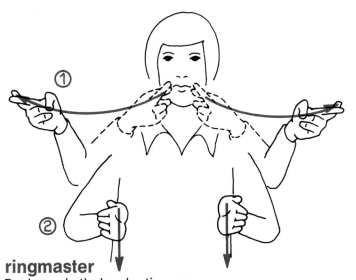

ringmaster
R shape both hands tips on either side of mouth. Swing out to side then form agent marker.

rink
Open B LH palm down, tips slanted right. R shape RH palm down, tips left. Circle right R over left hand up to elbow and back.

rinse
Flat O both hands palms in, tips down. Move up and down as if rinsing something.

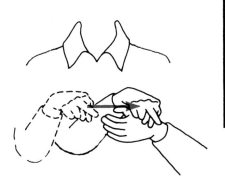

ripe
C shape LH palm and tips right, little finger side down. R shape RH palm down, tips left. Brush right R over left C toward wrist.

rise
Open B LH palm up, tips out. R shape RH palm down, tips left. Place in left palm then raise up.

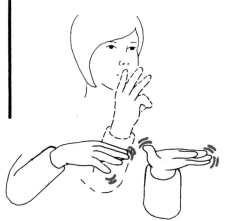

river
Place index finger of right W on mouth. Then move both hands forward, palms down, in rippling motion.

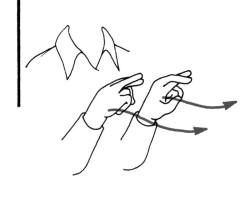

road
R shape both hands palms down, tips out. Move forward.

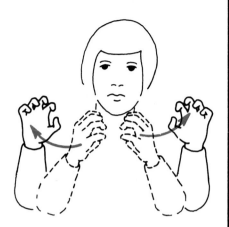

roar

Claw shape both hands palms and tips facing. Hold at throat then swing out ending with palms out.

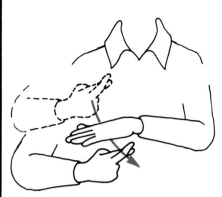

roast

Open B LH palm down, tips slanted right. R shape RH palm in, tips left. Slide under left hand.

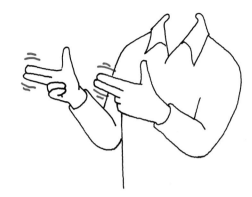

rob

L shape both hands middle fingers extended, palms facing, tips out. Shake up and down.

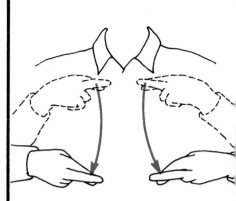

robe

R shape both hands palms in, tips facing. Brush down chest.

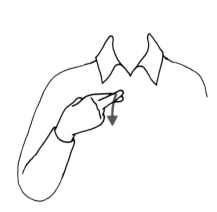

robin

R shape RH palm in, tips left. Place on chest and slide down.

robot

Open B RH palm left, tips out, elbow held at side. Walk forward, drop RH, then raise left open B in like motion.

rock (noun)

S shape LH, knuckles down. Tap back of left S with back of right R.

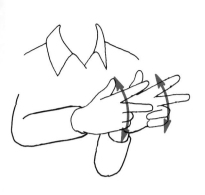

rock (verb)
Three shape both hands palms facing, tips out. Rock back and forth.

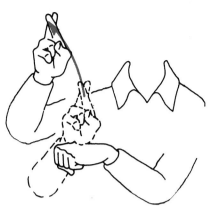

rocket
S shape LH palm and knuckles down. Place base of right R on back of left S then raise up suddenly.

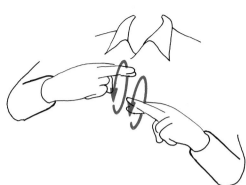

roll
R shape both hands tips facing. Roll around each other.

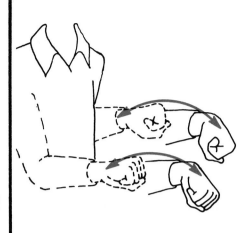

rolling pin
S shape both hands knuckles down. Mime using a rolling pin.

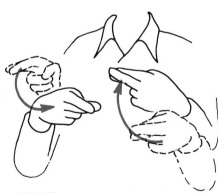

room
R shape both hands palms facing, tips out. Move right in front of left with tips facing left and left tips facing right.

rooster
Three shape RH palm left. Tap forehead with thumb twice.

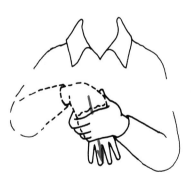

root
C shape LH palm and tips right. Push RH through left C until fingers show underneath.

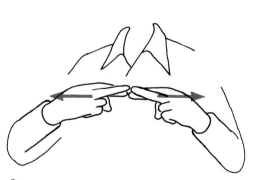

rope
R shape both hands palms in, tips touching. Draw apart.

rose

R shape RH palm left. Place against right side of nose then move to left side.

rough

Place fingers of right claw hand on left palm and push out.

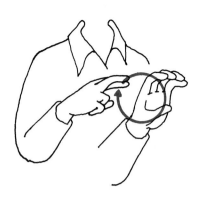

round

C shape LH palm and tips out. R shape RH palm in, tips left. Circle left C with right R.

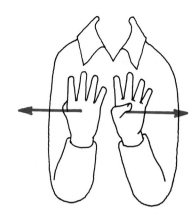

row (noun)

Four shape both hands, right palm in. Hold hands in front of body then draw apart.

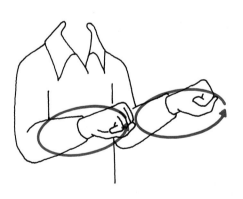

row (verb)

S shape both hands. Mime grasping oars and rowing.

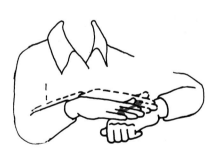

rub

A shape LH knuckles down. Open B RH palm down, tips left. Place on back of left A and rub back and forth.

rubber

X shape RH. Rub up and down on right cheek.

rude

R shape LH palm down, tips out. Place right C on left R and slide forward.

208

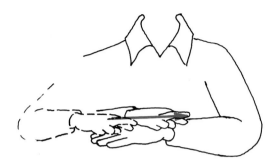

rug

B shape LH palm down, tips right. R shape RH palm down, tips out. Place on back of left fingers and slide to wrist.

ruin

X shape both hands left palm and tips right, little finger side down; right palm and tip left. Place right X on top of left then move off to right.

rule

Open B LH palm right. R shape RH palm left. Tap fingers then base of left hand with tips of right R.

ruler

R shape both hands thumbs extended. Tap thumbs together.

run

L shape both hands palms facing, LH a little ahead of right. Hook right index finger around left thumb and wiggle both index fingers forward.

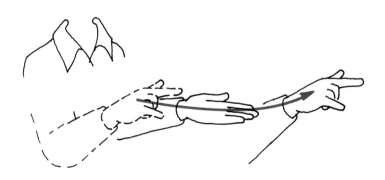

runway

Open B LH palm up, tips out. Y shape RH index finger extended, palm down and tips out. Slide into left palm.

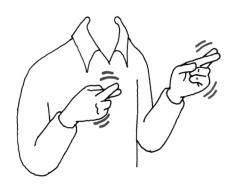

rush

R shape both hands palms facing, tips out. Shake up and down rapidly.

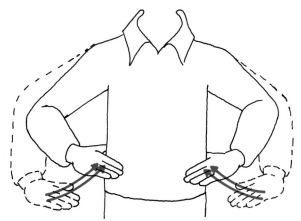

Russia

Open B both hands palms down, left tips right, right tips left. Tap against sides of waist several times.

S

sad
Five shape both hands palms up, fingers slightly curved, LH a little below RH. Hold in front of face and drop slowly.

saddle
Open B LH palm and tips slanted right. Close RH over left.

safe
S shape both hands knuckles in, wrists crossed. Break apart turning knuckles out.

safety
S shape both hands knuckles in, wrists crossed. Break apart turning knuckles out, then form right Y.

sail
Open B LH palm up, tips out. Place right 3 in left palm and move forward in wavy motion.

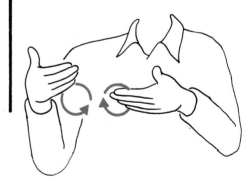

salad
Open B both hands, palms up, fingers curved. Mime tossing salad.

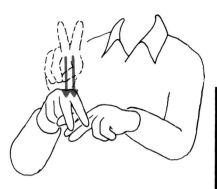

salt
Tap right V on back of left V twice.

same
One shape both hands palms down, tips out. Bring index fingers together.

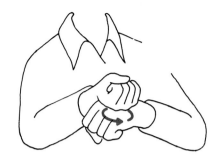

sand
S shape both hands, left S down, right S up. Place right S on back of left S and move in small circle counter-clockwise.

sandal
Five shape LH palm down, tips slanted right. Slide right index finger, pointed down, between left middle and fourth fingers.

sandwich
Open B both hands palms up, left tips right, right tips out. Slide right B into left palm and close left thumb.

Santa Claus
C shape RH palm in. Place index finger on chin and arc down to chest.

satisfy
Open B both hands palms down, left tips right; right tips left, held above left hand. Draw both hands back to chest.

Saturday
Move right S in small clockwise circle.

sauce
Open B LH palm up, tips right. Circle right A, thumb down, over left palm as in pouring.

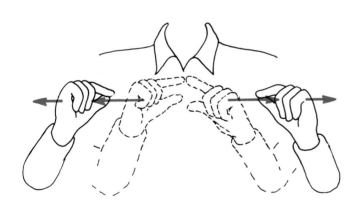

sausage
G shape both hands palms and tips out, index fingers touching. Draw apart snapping fingers twice (indicating links).

save
S shape LH knuckles right, little finger side down. V shape RH palm up, tips left. Place under left S.

say
One shape RH palm in, tip left. Hold at mouth and make small circle forward.

213

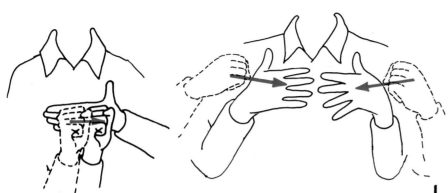

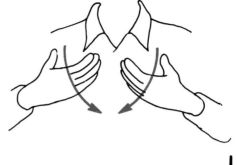

scale (weighing)
Open B LH palm in, tips right. S shape RH palm down. Slide thumb side of right S across back of left B from right to left.

scare
S shape both hands, knuckles facing. Open into 5 shapes and move toward one another.

scarf
C shape both hands palms and tips in. Place tips on shoulders then draw down and together outlining scarf.

school
Open B both hands, left palm up, tips out; right palm down, tips left. Clap together.

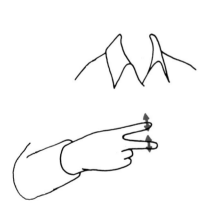

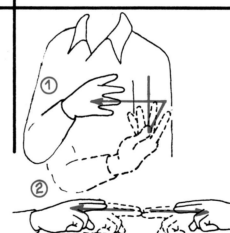

scissors
V shape RH palm in, tips left. Open and close fingers like scissor blades.

scooter
S shape both hands knuckles down. Hold as if holding handle of scooter and twist up and down.

Scotch tape
Four shape RH palm right. Place on upper left arm and make a cross. Now, form H shapes both hands palms down, fingers touching. Draw apart in straight line.

Scotland
Four shape RH palm right. Place on upper left arm and make a cross (i.e., plaid).

scout
B shape LH palm down, tips right. Place on forehead. V shape RH palm down, tips out. Wave from left to right beneath left B.

scramble
Claw shape LH palm up. S shape RH knuckles down. Circle over left palm.

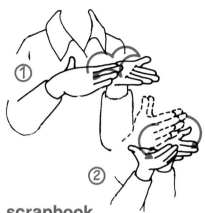

scrapbook
Open B both hands tips out, left palm up, right palm down. Place right tips on base of left palm, arc up and down several times, as if pasting pictures, then place palms together, thumbs up, and open.

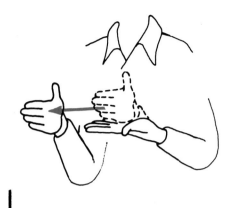

scrape
Open B both hands left palm up, tips right; right palm left, tips out. Slide little finger side of right B off left palm to the right.

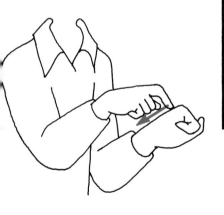

scratch
Scratch back of LH with right index finger.

scream
C shape both hands, palms in. Hold under chin then move up and out.

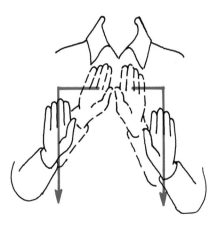

screen
Hold hands together in front of body, palms out, tips up. Draw apart, then down, outlining screen.

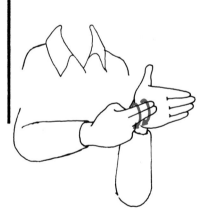

screw
B shape LH palm right, tips out. H shape RH palm in, tips left. Turn tips of right H in left palm twice.

215

scribble

Open B LH palm up, tips out. Move right thumb and index tip forward on left palm in scribbling motion.

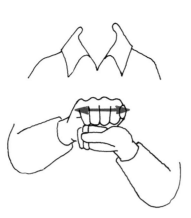

scrub

A shape both hands left knuckles up, right knuckles down. Rub right knuckles back and forth across left knuckles in scrubbing motion.

sea

S shape both hands knuckles down. Open into 5's and dip forward in wavy motion.

seal

S shape LH, knuckles down. Place right open B on top of left S and wave fingers down twice.

seat

S shape LH knuckles right, thumb side up. Bent V RH palm and tips down. Place on top of left S.

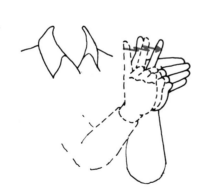

second (time)

Open B LH palm right, tips out. Place knuckles of right one against left palm and move back and forth in small movements.

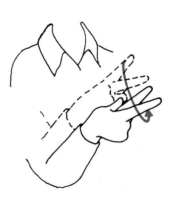

second

Two shape RH palm in, tips left. Twist so that palm faces in.

secretary

Open B LH palm up, tips out. K shape RH. Place middle finger on right cheek, then move down to left palm and slide forward.

216

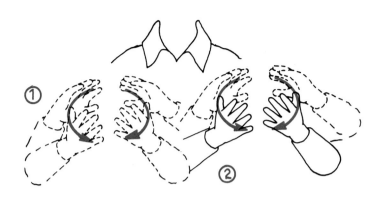

section
Open B both hands, palms and tips facing. Twist down and up, move to left and repeat.

see
V shape RH palm in. Point tips at eyes, then draw back.

seed
Flat O shape RH palm down. Punch thumb out as if pushing seed in ground.

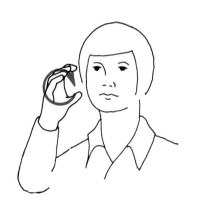

seek
C shape RH palm and tips left. Circle clockwise in front of right eye.

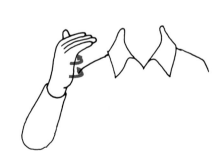

seem
Bent B RH palm and tips left. Twist inward twice.

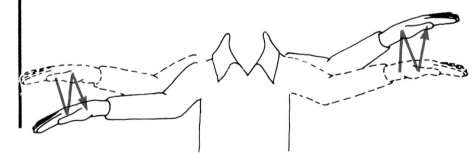

seesaw
B shape both hands left tips left, right tips right. Move up and down alternately.

self
A shape RH knuckles left. Strike against chest.

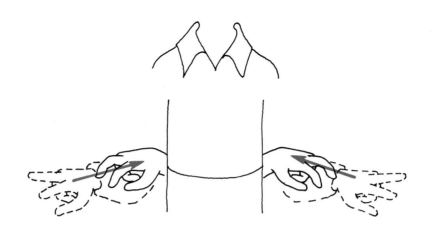

selfish
V shape both hands palms down, tips out. Draw back to waist ending in bent V shapes.

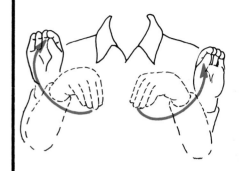

sell
Flat O both hands palms and tips down. Swing up and out.

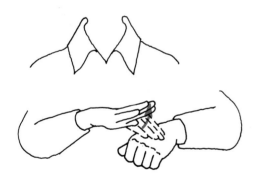

send
A shape LH palm down, knuckles right. Bent B RH palm right, tips down. Place tips on back of left A and swing out once.

September
Open B RH palm in. Place right S against left palm, slide over fingers and down.

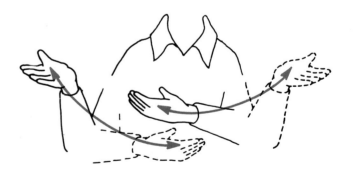

serve
Open B both hands palms up, left tips right, right tips out. Swing to left and back.

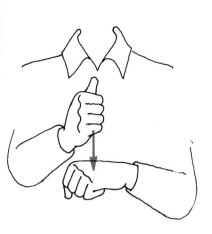

set (verb)
S shape LH knuckles down. A shape RH knuckles left, thumb extended. Place right A on left S.

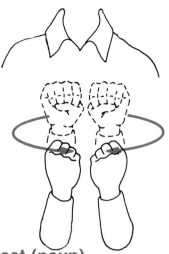

set (noun)
S shape both hands palms down, thumbs touching. Circle out and around ending with little fingers touching.

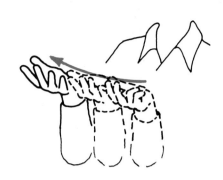

several
"Loose" A shape RH palm up. Pass thumb along the fingers while opening them up.

sew
Niné shape both hands palms facing, tips out. Make motion of stitching with needle and thread.

shade
S shape LH palm out, knuckles up. Open B RH palm in, tips left. Pass right B down in front of left S.

shadow
Open B LH plam out, tips up. W shape RH palm in, tips left. Pass right W down in front of left B.

shake
Five shape both hands palms down, tips out. Shake.

219

shame
Place back of RH on cheek, thumb up. Turn forward opening fingers (i.e. blush spreading).

shampoo
Claw shape both hands. Place tips on head and rub back and forth as if shampooing hair.

shape
A shape both hands. Curve downward outlining shape of body.

share
Open B both hands, left palm right, tips out; right palm in, tips left. Brush little finger side of right B between left thumb and forefinger.

shark
Open B both hands, left palm down, tips out; right palm left, tips up. Place between left middle and fourth fingers and move forward in swimming motion.

sharp
Open B LH palm down, tips out. Five shape RH palm down, tips left. Place right middle finger on back of LH and jerk up and out.

shave
Y shape RH palm left. Draw thumb down right cheek as if shaving.

she
E shape RH knuckles left. Place on right cheek then move out.

220

sheep
Chip left forearm with right V twice.

sheet
S shape both hands knuckles down. Draw up from waist to shoulders as if pulling up sheet.

shelf
Open B both hands held high, palms down, tips out. Hold together then move apart in straight line.

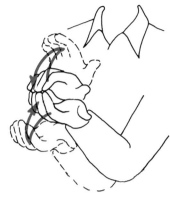

shell
Curved open B shapes both hands, left palm up, right palm down. Place hands together, open up, then close slightly.

she'll
E shape RH knuckles left. Place on right cheek. Move out, form L and twist inward.

she's
E shape RH knuckles left. Place on right cheek. Move out, form S and twist in.

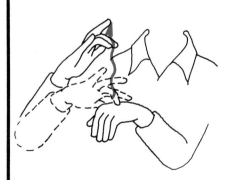

shine
Open B LH palm down, tip out. Five shape RH palm down, tips left. Place right middle finger on back of LH then move up in shimmering motion.

ship
Open B LH palm up, tips out. Place right 3 in left palm and move forward twice.

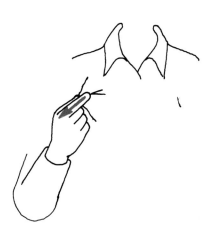

shirt
L shape RH palm in. Grasp clothing with thumb and forefinger and shake slightly.

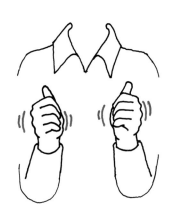

shiver
A shape both hands thumbs up. Hold close to body and "shiver."

shock
Place right index finger on right temple. Then form claw shape both hands, palms down.

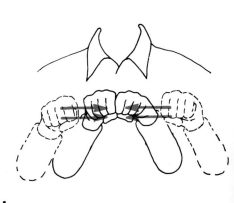

shoe
S shape both hands knuckles down. Strike together several times.

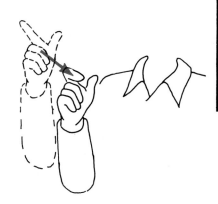

shoot
L shape RH palm left, thumb up. Change to X shape as if pulling trigger.

shop
Open B LH palm up, tips out. Place back of right flat O on left palm and move out twice.

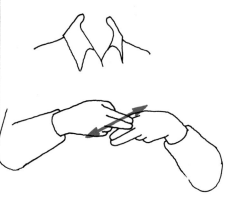

short
H shape both hands left palm right, tips out; right palm in, tips left. Rub right H back and forth on top of left H.

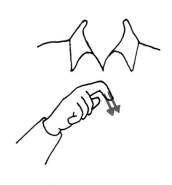

should
X shape RH knuckles down. Move down. Repeat.

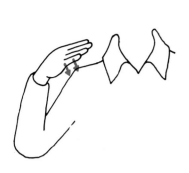

shoulder
Pat shoulder twice with right open B.

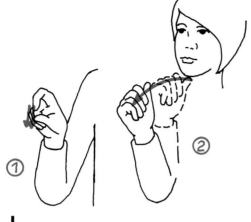

shouldn't
(Exception — made with two signs.) Dip right X down twice then form right A knuckles left, thumb extended. Place thumb under chin and flick out.

shout
Claw shape RH palm and tips in. Hold in front of mouth, then raise up and out.

shovel
Open B both hands left palm up, tips out; right palm up, tips left. Dip back of right B into left palm and turn over toward body.

show
Open B LH palm right, tips up. Place right index tip in middle of left palm and move both hands forward.

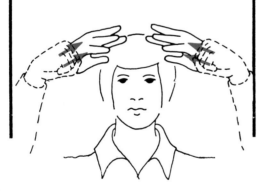

shower
S shape both hands knuckles facing. Hold at sides of head and open into five shapes. Repeat.

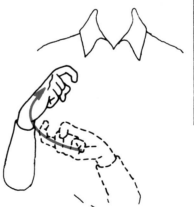

shrimp
X shape RH palm up. Circle up and turn palm down.

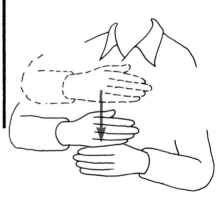

shut
B shape both hands palms in, left tips right; right tips left. Bring little finger side of RH down on index side of LH.

223

shy
Place knuckles of right A on right cheek and twist forward slightly.

sick
Five shape RH palm in. Tap forehead with middle finger.

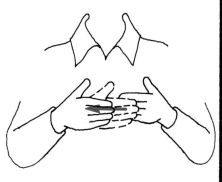

side
Open B both hands palms in, left tips right; right tips left. Place RH on back of LH and slide to right.

sight
S shape both hands knuckles facing. Place right S between the eyes and left S on little finger of right S. Draw apart into five shapes palms out.

sign (noun)
S shape LH. Place right index on base of left thumb then move both hands forward.

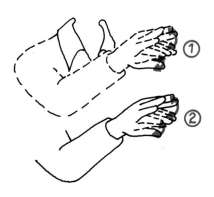

signal
Flat O palm and tips out. Move forward opening into five shape. Lower and repat.

silly
Y shape RH. Shake in front of nose.

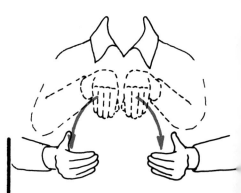

silo
Bent B both hands palms and tips down, index fingers touching. Draw apart and down outlining shape of silo.

silver

Hold right S against right temple then zig-zag out and down.

silverware

Open B LH palm down, tips right. Hold right S against right temple, zig-zag out and down, change into W shape and slide across back of left hand to the right.

sing

Open B LH palm up, tips out. Swing fingers of right open B over left palm in rhythmic motion without touching.

sink

C shape LH palm and tips right, the little finger side down. S shape RH. Place right arm in left C and slowly wiggle down (sink out of sight).

siren

Bent B RH fingers spread. Twist and turn just above head (i.e. blinker).

sister

L shape both hands, thumbs up; left palm right, right palm left. Touch cheek with right thumb then place right L on top of left L.

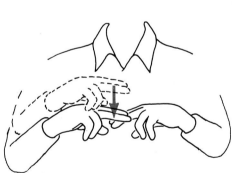

sit

H shape both hands palms down, left tips slanted right; right tips slanted left. Rest right H on left.

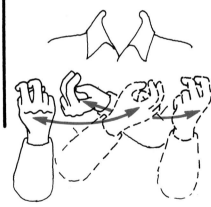

skate

Bent V both hands palms up. Swing back and forth alternately.

skeleton
Bent V shape both hands. Cross wrists on chest and tap shoulders with V's.

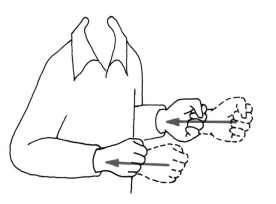

ski
S shape both hands knuckles facing. Mime grasping and using ski poles.

skin
Pull at right cheek with thumb and index of right A.

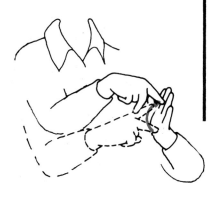

skip
Open B LH palm and tips slanted right. Place middle finger of right K on base of left palm, then twist forward quickly so that index tip rests on fingers.

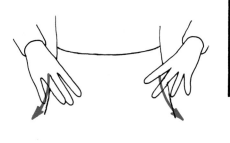

skirt
Five shape both hands, thumbs on waist. Brush down.

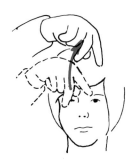

skunk
P shape RH palm down, index tip left. Place thumb on forehead and draw back over crown of head.

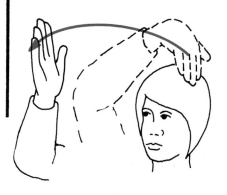

sky
Open B RH palm angled down, tips left. Move up and right pointing to sky.

226

slap
One shape LH. Slap with right open B once.

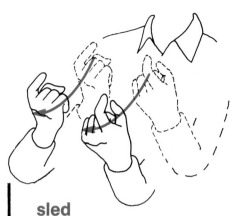

sled
X shape both hands palms up. Move slightly down and out (runners).

sleep
Draw open fingers down over face ending in flat O.

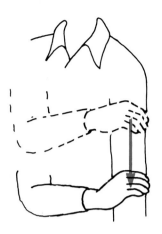

sleeve
Grasp upper left arm with right hand and slide down to left wrist.

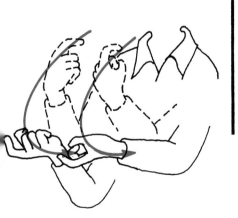

sleigh
X shape both hands palms in, tips up. Arc outward ending with palms up and draw back to body.

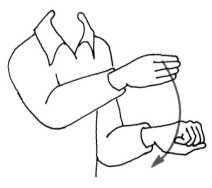

slice
S shape LH palm down. B shape RH palm left, tips out. Move down past left S in "slicing" motion.

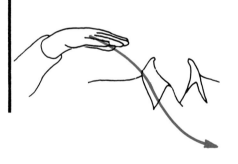

slide
B shape RH palm down held at shoulder. Bring down in sweeping movement (i.e. sliding board).

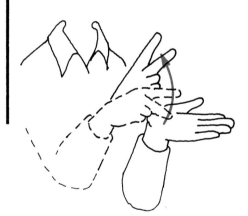

slip
Open B LH palm up, tips out. Place middle finger of right P in left palm, slip forward and up.

227

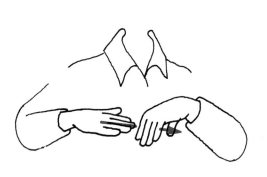

slipper
C shape LH palm down. Open B RH palm down, tips left. Slide under left palm.

slow
Draw palm of RH slowly across back of LH.

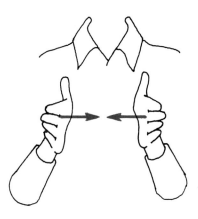

small
Open B both hands palms facing, tips out. Draw close together.

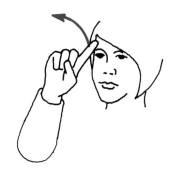

smart
Place right index on right temple then move out quickly.

smell
Open B RH palm up, tips left. Hold under nose and brush upward.

smile
L shape both hands. Place index fingers at sides of mouth and move up to cheeks.

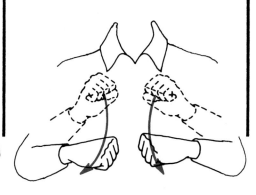

smock
S shape both hands knuckles facing. Hold at shoulders, then swing down and out.

smog
S shape LH. Five shape RH palm in. Brush across fingers of left S.

smoke
Five shape both hands left palm up, tips slanted right; right palm down, tips slanted left. Place right tips in left palm and move up in spiraling motion.

smooth
Flat O both hands palms and tips up. Move forward while changing into A shapes.

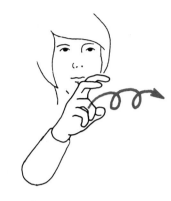

snack
Open B LH palm up, tips out. Place thumb and index tips of right F in left palm, then raise to mouth.

snake
Place back of bent V under chin then circle forward.

snap
Snap right thumb and middle finger.

sneak
Open B LH palm in. Slide right index finger past left little finger then around back of left hand.

sneeze
Hold right index under nose and bob head.

sniff
Place right X against nose and sniff.

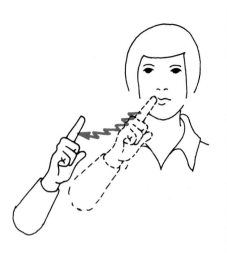

snore
Place right index against mouth, then move out in a zig-zag motion.

snow
Five shape both hands palms down. Wiggle fingers while moving down slowly.

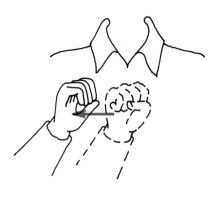

so
Form the letters S and O in quick succession as if one movement.

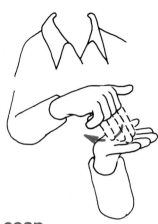

soap
Open B both hands left palm up, tips out, right palm in, tips down. Draw right fingers backwards across left palm ending in A shape.

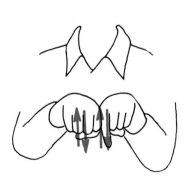

sock
S shape RH palm down. Brush back and forth along side of left index which is held palm down, tip out.

soda
C shape LH palm and tips right, little finger side down. Place RH in left C, tips down, then pull up and out fluttering fingers.

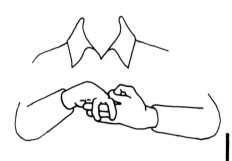

sofa
F shape LH palm right, tips out. Hang right V over left middle finger.

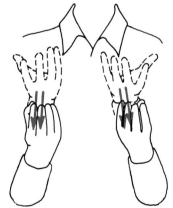

soft
Claw shape both hands palms up. Lower into flat O's palms up. Repeat.

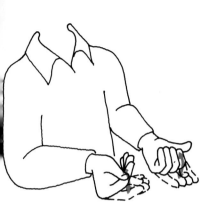

soil
"Loose" flat O both hands palms up. Rub thumbs across fingers beginning with little fingers.

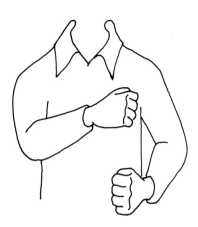

soldier
S shape both hands palms in, left knuckles right, right knuckles left. Place right S on left shoulder and left S just underneath as if holding a gun.

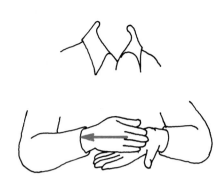

some
Open B LH palm up, tips slanted right. Draw little finger side of right open B across left palm.

somersault
Place tips of right V in left palm, lift up into a bent V, circle around and land tips back in center of left palm.

sometimes
Open B LH palm right, tips out. Strike with right index finger twice.

son
Place thumb side of right flat O on forehead then arc down to crook of left elbow.

song
Open B LH palm up, tips out. Swing right S over left palm back and forth without touching.

soon
Open B LH palm right, tips up. Place side of right S in left palm and make a one-quarter turn forward.

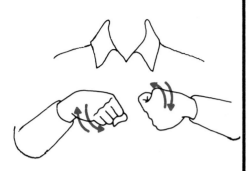

sore
S shape both hands knuckles down. Twist back and forth alternately.

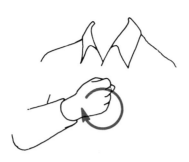

sorry
Circle right S on chest.

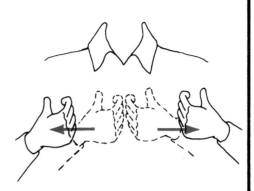

sort
Bent B both hands palms and tips in, fingers back to back. Draw apart.

sound
Hold right S at right ear.

soup
Place back of RH in left palm, then move up to mouth as if eating soup.

sour
Place right index finger on chin, palm left. Twist so that palm faces right.

South
S shape RH. Lower in front of body.

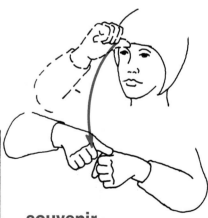

souvenir
S shape LH knuckles right. S shape RH thumb extended. Place thumb on forehead then place on left S.

space
S shape both hands knuckles down, fingers touching. Circle back to body and touch again.

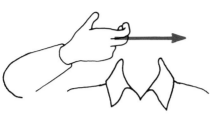

spaceship
H shape RH palm in, tips left, thumb extended. Bend fingers and move swiftly to the left.

spade
Open B both hands left palm up, tips out. Place back of right B in left palm, then lift up and back.

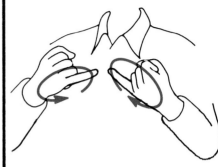

spaghetti
I shape both hands knuckles in, tips facing. Dig in and up.

spank
Strike palm of right open B against palm of left open B.

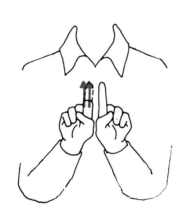

spark
One shape LH, S shape RH. Hold together, then flick right index finger up twice.

sparrow
S shape RH. Change to G shape, then place on chin and snap index and thumb together twice.

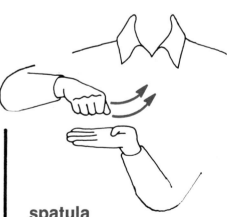

spatula
Open B LH palm up, tips slanted right. A shape RH palm down. Dip over left palm twice.

233

speak
Four shape RH palm left. Move in and out from mouth.

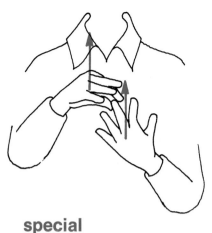

special
Five shape LH palm right. Grasp middle finger with right index finger and thumb and pull up.

speech
S shape RH. Change to bent V, palm in and circle at mouth.

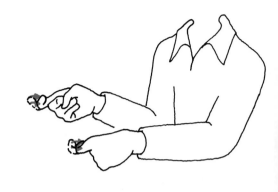

speed
S shape both hands palms facing, little finger sides down, RH a little ahead of LH. Crook index fingers quickly twice.

spell
Five shape RH palm down, tips out. Wiggle fingers while moving hand to right.

spend
Open B LH palm up, tips out. Place back of right flat O in left palm and lift out changing to A shape.

spider
Five shape both hands palms down, tips out. Cross RH over LH, interlock little fingers and wiggle all fingers (i.e. legs of spider.)

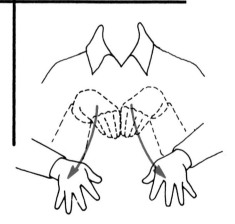

spill
Flat O both hands palms and tips down, index fingers touching. Drop into five shapes.

234

spit
S shape RH knuckles left. Place on mouth then arc out ending in one shape, tip out.

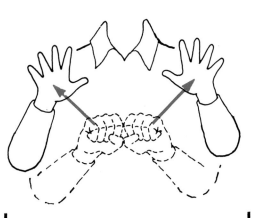

splash
S shape both hands knuckles down, index fingers touching. Open up into five shapes while moving hands apart and up.

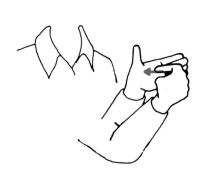

splinter
Open B LH palm right, tips out. Place tips of right index on left palm and push backward.

split
Hold LH up palm in. Now split the middle and fourth fingers apart with little finger side of right open B, palm left, tips out.

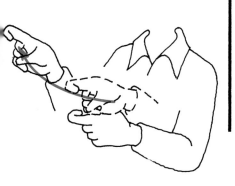

spoil
X shape both hands left palm right, right palm left, knuckles out. Place right X on top of left, then slide forward and off.

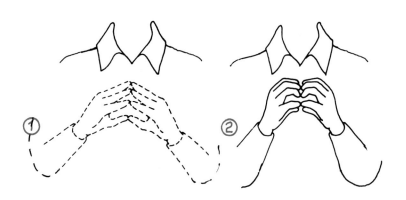

sponge
Place tips of open hands together and close as if squeezing sponge.

spool
S shape LH palm in, knuckles right. Circle right index over left S.

spoon
Open B LH palm up, tips right. Place back of right H on left tips then raise H (thumb up) to mouth as if eating with spoon.

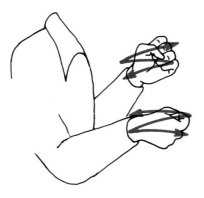

sport
S shape both hands palms facing. Move back and forth alternately.

spot
F shape RH palm down, tips left, index finger curved inside thumb. Place on chest.

sprain
Bent V shape both hands left palm in, right palm down. Twist left V down and right V up.

spray
A shape RH palm left, thumb extended. Move from left to right while pushing thumb down.

spring
Push right flat O up through left C twice opening into five shape.

sprinkle
S shape RH. Open into five shape palm down, tips out. Repeat.

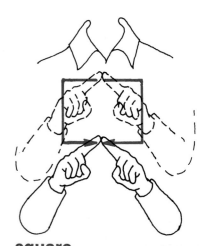

square
One shape both hands palms down, tips out. Hold together, move apart, down and back together outlining shape of square.

squash
C shape both hands palms and tips out, index fingers touching. Swing right C away and up to the right.

squeak
Grasp throat with right C and wiggle slightly.

squirm
B shape LH palm and tips slanted right. Place thumb side of right X in left palm and scratch fingers with tip of right index.

squirrel
Bent V shape both hands palms facing, wrists touching. Tap tips of V's together at mouth.

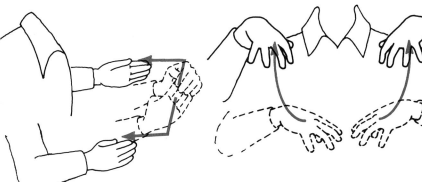

stable
Bent B both hands palms in, tips opposite. Place right B inside left B. Now draw apart, straighten tips and move back toward body.

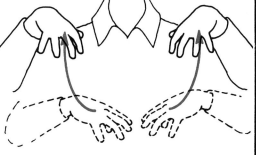

stadium
Five shape both hands palms down, tips facing, fingers slightly curved. Move apart and up in semi-circular motion.

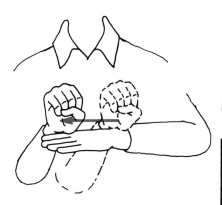

stage
Open B LH palm down, tips right. Slide base of right S forward along side of left B beginning at wrist.

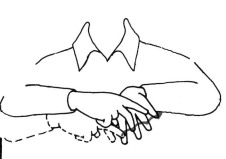

stair
Five shape LH palm down, tips out. "Walk" over back of left fingers with right middle index fingers.

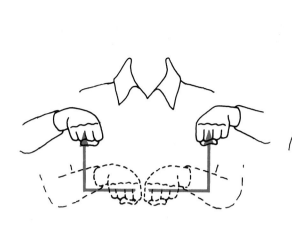

stall
S shape both hands palms down, knuckles out. Place together, then move apart and up outlining shape of stall.

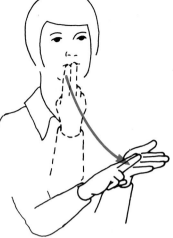

stamp
Open B LH palm up, tips out. Place tips of right H on lips, then move down and place in left palm.

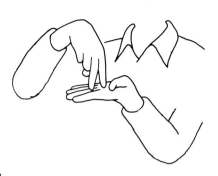

stand
Open B LH palm up, tips right. Stand right V on left palm.

staple
Open B both hands, left palm up, tips out; right palm down, tips left and slightly bent. Strike base of left palm with base of right.

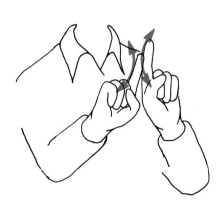

star
One shape both hands palms out. Raise tips up and down alternately.

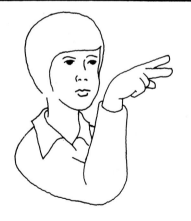

stare
V shape RH palm down, tips out. Hold in front of face.

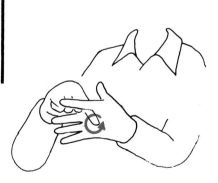

start
Five shape LH palm and tips slanted right. Place right index between left index and middle fingers and make half turn.

startle
S shape both hands. Hold at eyes then open into C shape suddenly.

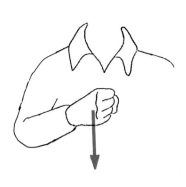

starve
S shape RH palm in. Place on upper chest and slide down slowly.

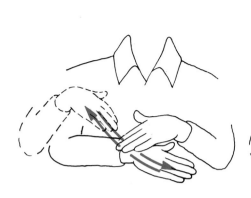

station
Open B both hands palms down, left tips right, right tips out. Slide RH under LH and out again several times.

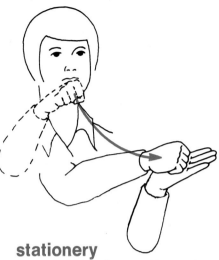

stationery
Open B LH palm up, tips out. Place back of right S on mouth then move down to left palm.

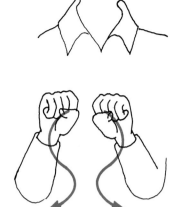

statue
A shape both hands. Move down outlining shape of statue.

stay
Y shape both hands palms down, thumbs touching. Move right Y forward.

steak
S shape LH palm down. Grasp with right thumb and index finger and shake slightly.

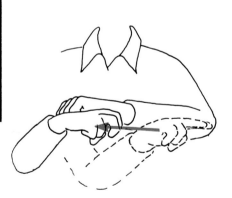

steal
Place right V palm down against left elbow. Snatch toward wrist ending in bent V.

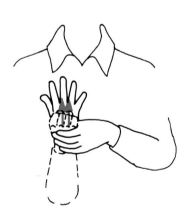

steam
S shape RH palm in. Grasp with LH, then open right S into five shape and move up. Repeat.

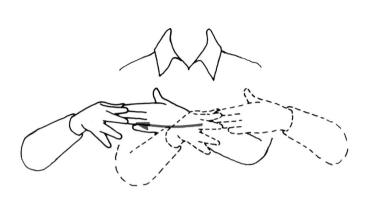

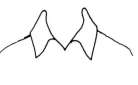

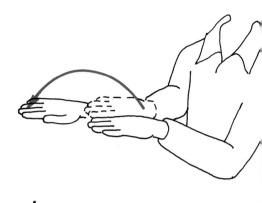

steer
Open B LH palm in, tips right. Grasp tips with thumb and index finger of right F and pull to right.

stem
One shape LH. Place right thumb and index at base of left index and slide up.

step
Open B both hands palms down, tips out. Move right B forward.

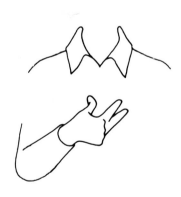

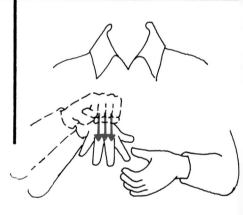

stereo
Five shape both hands left palm left, right palm right. Twist in and place on ears.

stethoscope
Three shape RH palm in, tips left. Place tips on chest and take a deep breath.

stew
C shape LH palm and tips right, little finger side down. Hold right S over left C and open into five shape several times.

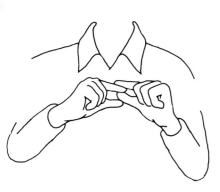

stick
G shape both hands tips facing. Fit together.

still
Y shape RH palm down. Move forward.

sting
S shape LH palm down. Pinch with right index finger and thumb.

stir
C shape LH palm and tips right, little finger side down. Stir right A over left C.

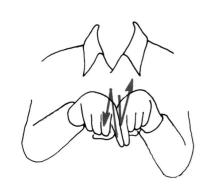

stocking
Place index fingers together palms down. Rub back and forth (i.e. knitting).

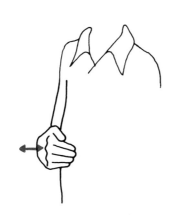

stomach
Pat stomach with palm of right open B.

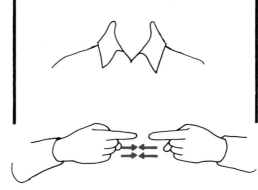

stomachache
One shape both hands palms in, tips facing. Move toward one another in front of stomach.

stone
S shape both hands knuckles down. Tap back of left S with right S twice.

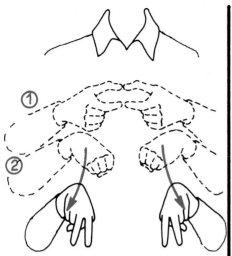

stool
Outline round seat of stool with thumbs and forefingers. Now drop into S shapes, then V shapes pointed down.

stop
Open B LH palm up fingers, slanted right. Chop with little finger side of right open B palm in, tips out.

store
Flat O's both hands tips down. Swing out twice.

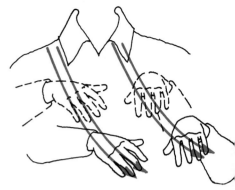

storm
Five shape both hands palms left, tips out. Sweep to the left. Repeat.

story
Beginning with open hands facing one another come down into nine shapes and move apart twice.

stove
S shape RH knuckles left. Place on mouth, then twist out and down.

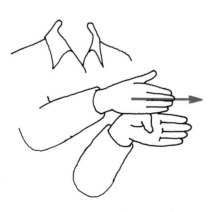

straight
B shape both hands left palm right, right palm left, tips out. Move little finger side of right B straight out across index finger of left B.

strange
C shape RH. Place on right side of face and move across nose to lower left side of face.

242

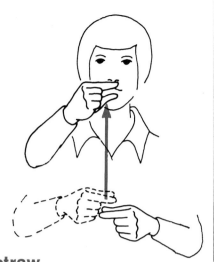

straw
G shape both hands tips facing. Place right G on left G, then raise to mouth.

strawberry
Nine shape RH. Place index and thumb on mouth and flick out.

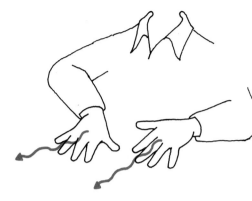

stream
Five shape both hands palms down, tips out. Move forward in rippling motion.

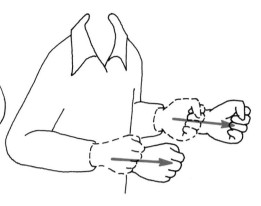

street
S shape both hands knuckles facing. Move forward.

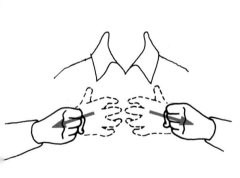

stretch
Claw shape both hands palms in, tips facing. Pull apart into S shapes.

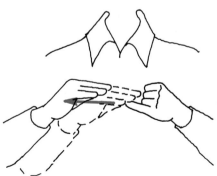

string
I shape LH palm in, tip right. Grasp left little finger with right fingers, then slide fingers off to the right.

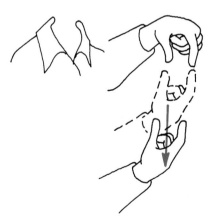

strip
G shape both hands left tips down, right tips up. Place right G under left G, then drop down outlining film strip.

strong
S shape both hands knuckles in. Draw up in front of shoulders holding muscles tight.

 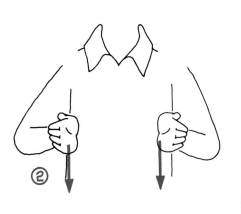

student
Open B LH palm up, tips slanted right. Place right tips in left palm then lift up to forehead closing into flat O. Folow with agent marker.

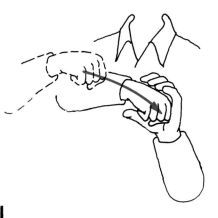

stuff
Stuff right S thumb down into left C.

stupid
V shape RH palm out, tips left. Place on forehead.

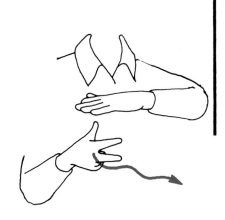

submarine
Open B LH palm down, tips right. Three shape RH palm and tips slanted left. Slide RH forward under left in wavy motion.

subway
Open B LH palm down, tips right. One shape RH palm down, tip out. Slide forward under left B.

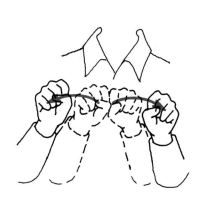

such
S shape both hands knuckles out, index fingers touching. Draw up and apart.

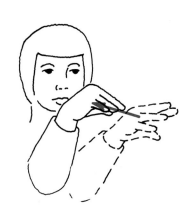

suck
Hold RH palm down, then draw up to mouth ending in flat O.

sugar

H shape RH palm in, tips up. Stroke chin with tips twice.

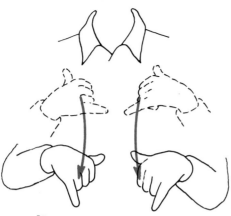

suit

Y shape both hands palms in, thumbs up. Place on chest and slide down to waist.

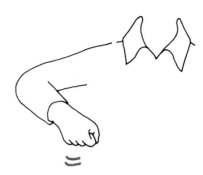

suitcase

Hold right arm down by side with fist clinched as if carrying a heavy suitcase.

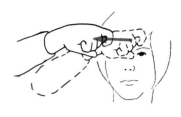

summer

X shape RH palm down, knuckles left. Draw across forehead from left to right.

sun

Place right C against right eye.

sundae

C shape LH palm and tips right, little finger side down. A shape RH palm down, thumb extended. Circle over left C while spiraling upward.

Sunday

Open B both hands palms out. Circle away from each other.

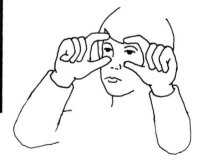

sunglasses

Circle eyes with index fingers and thumbs.

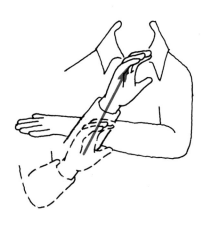

sunrise
Open B LH palm down, tips right. C shape RH palm and tips left. Place right C against outer side of left wrist then move up slowly.

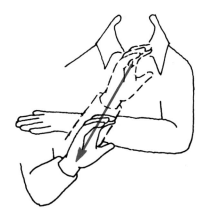

sunset
Open B LH palm down, tips right. C shape RH palm and tips left. Place right C just above outer side of left wrist then lower slowly.

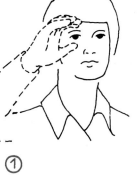

①　②

sunshine
Place right C against right eye. Change into flat O palm down, then open into five shape palm down, tips out.

super
Open B LH palm down, tips right. Make semi-circle with right S over LH.

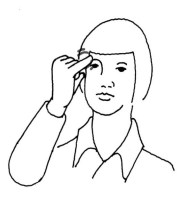

suppose
Tap right temple gently with right little finger.

sure
One shape RH palm left. Place index finger on mouth then arc up and out.

surprise
Place index fingers and thumbs at edges of eyes. Snap open into L shapes.

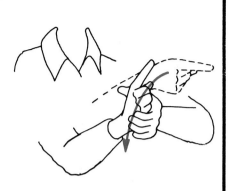

swallow
C shape LH palm and tips right, little finger side down. One shape RH palm left, tip out. Hold over left C then draw back and down into left C.

swan
Open B LH palm down, tips right. Flat O RH palm down, tips slanted down and left. Place right elbow on back of left hand.

swat
Mime using fly swatter.

sweat
Four shape both hands palms down, tips out. Place right four on forehead and left four a little in front. Flutter both hands forward and down.

sweater
Claw shape both hands palms in, tips in. Place on chest and move to waist ending in A shapes.

sweep
Open B both hands left palm up, tips right; right palm and tips slanted left. Sweep little finger side of right B over left palm twice toward body.

sweet
Open B RH palm in, tips up. Place tips on chin and bring down curving fingers.

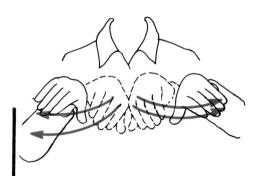

swim
Hands together palms down. Move forward and out (i.e. breast stroke).

247

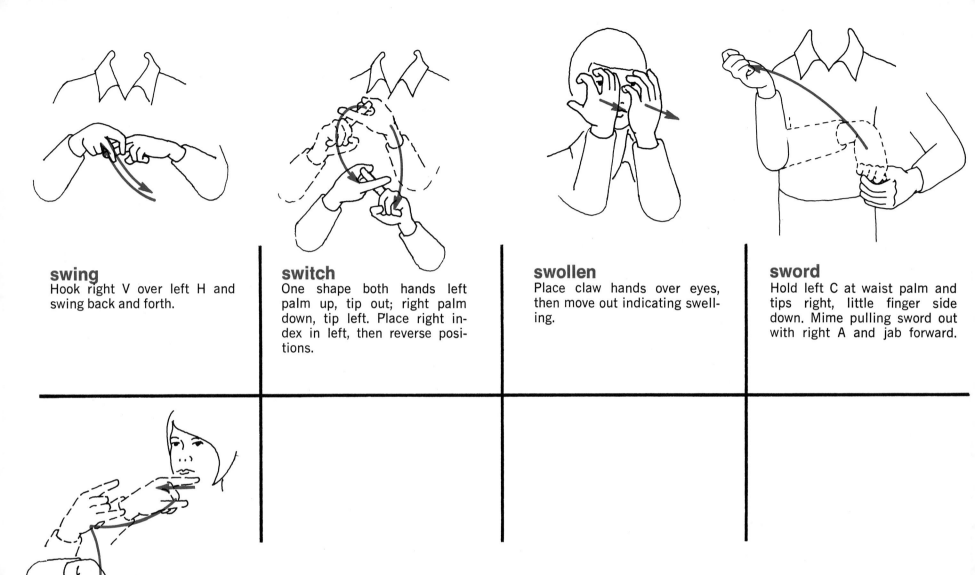

swing
Hook right V over left H and swing back and forth.

switch
One shape both hands left palm up, tip out; right palm down, tip left. Place right index in left, then reverse positions.

swollen
Place claw hands over eyes, then move out indicating swelling.

sword
Hold left C at waist palm and tips right, little finger side down. Mime pulling sword out with right A and jab forward.

syrup
Extend right little and index fingers. Wipe chin with index and flip wrist out.

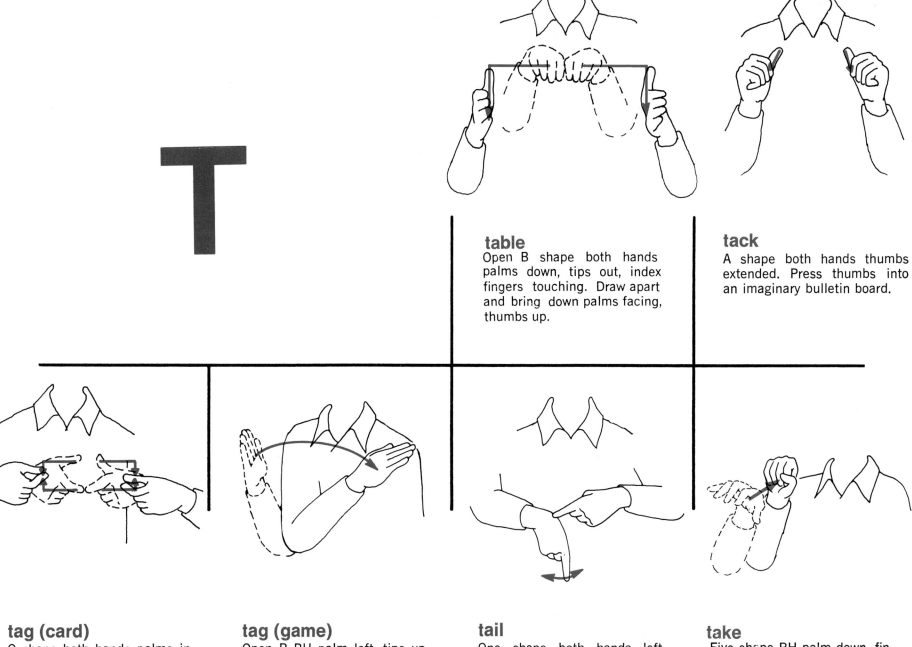

T

table
Open B shape both hands palms down, tips out, index fingers touching. Draw apart and bring down palms facing, thumbs up.

tack
A shape both hands thumbs extended. Press thumbs into an imaginary bulletin board.

tag (card)
G shape both hands palms in. Place tips on upper left chest, then draw apart closing tips.

tag (game)
Open B RH palm left, tips up. "Tag" left shoulder with right hand once.

tail
One shape both hands left palm in, tip right; right palm in, tip down. Place left tip on right wrist then wag right hand from left to right.

take
Five shape RH palm down, fingers slightly curved. Draw up quickly ending in fist.

tale
Nine shape LH palm right, tips out. T shape RH. Arc toward one another and back. Repeat.

talk
Place index tips on mouth alternately, moving back and forth.

tall
Open B LH palm out, tips up. Run right index finger up left palm.

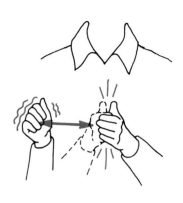

tambourine
Open B LH palm right, tips out. Hit with right A, then shake hand.

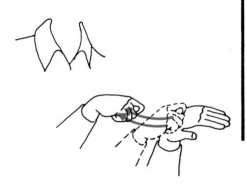

tame
Open B LH palm down, tips out. Rub back of left hand with knuckles of right T twice toward body.

tan
Place index finger of right T on right cheek and slide down.

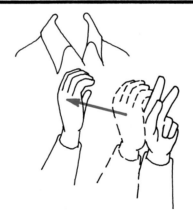

tank
K shape LH palm slanted right. Place little finger side of right C against K, then draw away to the right.

tap
Open B LH palm up, tips out. Tap left palm with tip of right X.

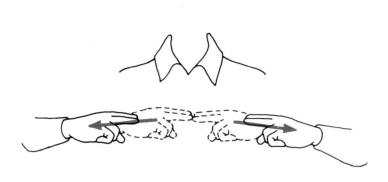

tape
H shape both hands palms down, tips touching. Draw apart in straight line.

tart (adj.)
Twist right T on chin.

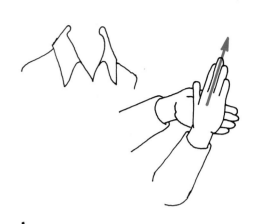

tart (noun)
Open B both hands, left palm right, tips out; right palm left, tips up. Place palms together then slide right B up quickly.

taste
Five shape RH palm in, tips up. Tap middle finger on chin once.

taxicab
X shape LH palm slanted right. Place little finger side of right C on left X then draw back toward body.

tea
Place thumb and index finger of right 9 in left C and stir.

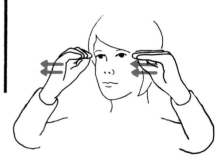

teach
Flat O's both hands. Hold at temples and move out twice.

251

tear
A shape both hands knuckles facing. Bring right A over and halfway around left as if tearing a piece of paper.

tease
X shape both hands left palm right, right palm left, little finger sides down. Slide right X forward on left X twice.

teddy bear
T shape both hands palms in. Cross on chest then rub T's up and down.

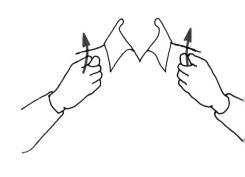

teenager
T shape both hands palms and knuckles in. Place knuckles on shoulders and brush upwards.

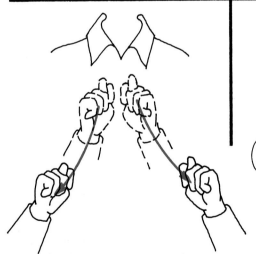

teepee
T shape both hands palms facing, knuckles touching. Draw down and apart outlining shape of teepee.

telephone
Y shape RH. Place thumb on ear and little finger on mouth.

television
Form the letters T and V in quick succession as if in one movement.

tell
One shape RH palm in. Place index tip on chin then move out ending with palm up.

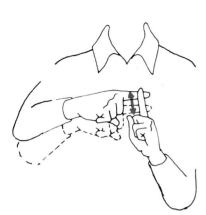

temperature

One shape both hands right palm down, tip left. Rub right index up and down on left.

tempt

Hold left arm up palm in, fingers closed. Now tap elbow with right X.

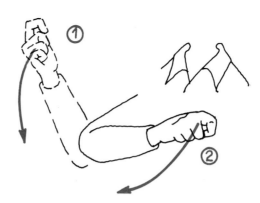

tennis

Mime swinging tennis racket.

tent

V shape both hands palms facing, tips touching. Draw apart ending with palms down.

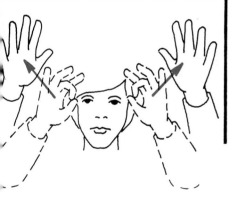

terrible

Eight shape both hands. Place on temples. Snap forward into five shapes, palms out.

thank

Open B RH palm in, tips up. Place tips on chin or lips. Move out as it throwing a kiss.

Thanksgiving

Open B both hands palms in. Place tips on mouth, then arc out and down and up again.

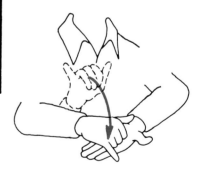

that

Place knuckles of right Y on upturned left palm.

the
T shape RH palm in. Twist out.

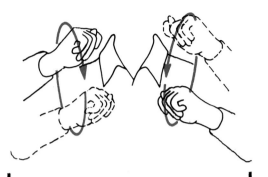

theater
T shape both hands. Move alternately in circular motions toward body.

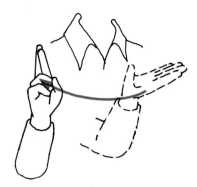

their
Open B RH palm up, tips out. Slide to right and form the letter R.

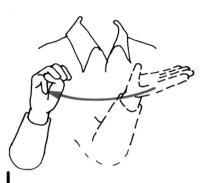

them
Open B RH palm up, tips out. Slide to right and form the letter M.

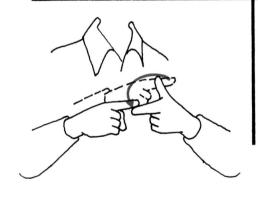

then
L shape LH palm in, thumb up. Place right index behind left thumb and move to left index.

there
Point index finger out.

thermometer
One shape LH. T shape RH knuckles left. Rub right T up and down on left index.

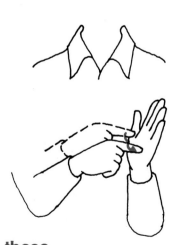

these
Open B LH palm up, tips out. Place right index tip in left palm and jump forward several times.

254

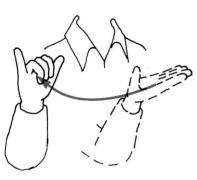

they
Open B RH palm up, tips out. Slide to right and turn over into Y shape.

they'll
Open B RH palm up, tips out. Slide to right, turn over into Y shape, form L and twist in.

they're
Open B RH palm up, tips out. Slide to right, turn over into Y shape, form R and twist in.

thick
Place right thumb and index on chin. Move up a little above mouth, then out.

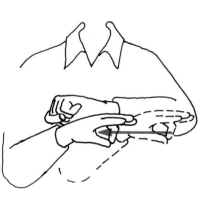

thief
Place right F palm down, tips left, against left elbow then snatch back to wrist.

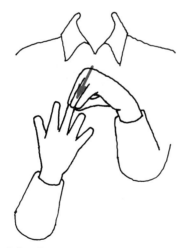

thimble
Mime pushing thimble on middle finger.

thin
Five shape RH palm in, tips left. Draw index finger and thumb down sides of mouth.

thing
Open B RH palm up, tips out. Move slightly out and to the right in small movement.

think

Place tip of index finger on forehead.

thirst

Point right index finger to throat and draw down.

this

Open B LH palm up, tips out. Tap with right index finger.

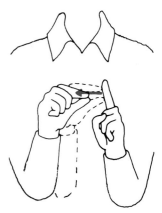

thorn

One shape LH. Place tips of right thumb and index on left index, then pull back to right as if pulling thorn out.

those

Open B LH palm up, tips out. Tap knuckles of right Y on base of left palm, then on fingers.

thread

T shape LH. Place tip of right little finger (other fingers closed) on base of left T, then draw away to right in wavy motion.

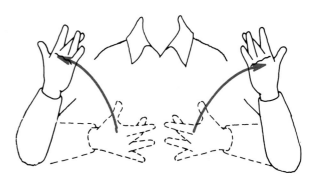

thrill

Five shape both hands palms in, tips facing. Place tips of middle fingers on chest, then brush up and away from each other.

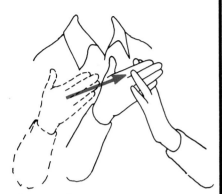

through
Open B both hands left palm right, tips up; right palm in, tips left. Pass right tips through left middle and fourth fingers.

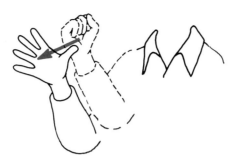

throw
Hold right S over shoulder. Move forward into open handshape (i.e. throwing ball).

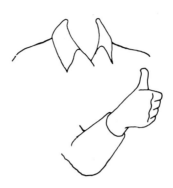

thumb
A shape RH palm left, thumb extended.

thunder
S shape both hands. Draw left S back while moving right S forward. Repeat.

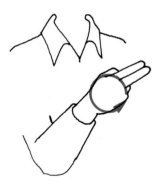

Thursday
Circle right H clockwise.

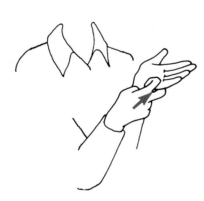

ticket
Open B LH palm up tips out. Bent V RH palm in, knuckles left. Slide onto side of left palm.

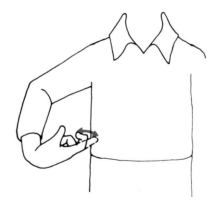

tickle
Make "tickling" motion at right side of waist with right index finger.

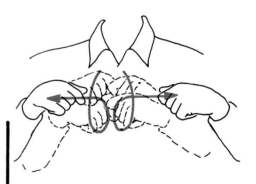

tie
Make motion of tying a knot in a string and pull tight.

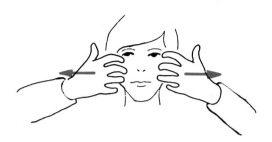

tiger
Claw shape both hands palms in. Place tips on cheeks then move out.

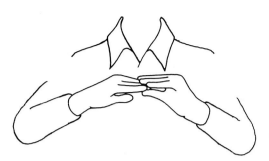

tight
Open B RH palm down, tips left. Grasp with left fingers and hold tightly.

tightrope walker
One shape LH palm right, tip out. "Walk" along left index with right middle and index fingers.

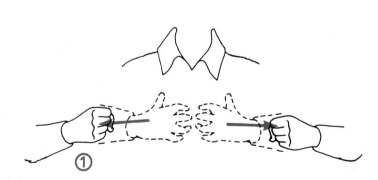

①

tights
Claw shape both hands palms in, tips facing. Draw apart closing into S shapes, then mime pulling on tights.

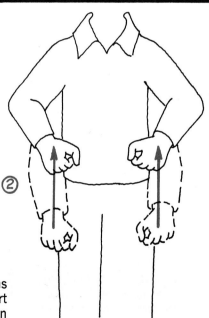

②

time
Tap back of left wrist with right index finger which is slightly bent.

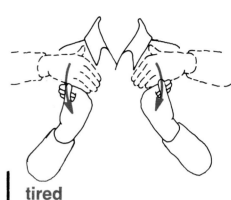

tiny
Claw shape RH palm up. Flick little finger with thumb.

tiptoe
One shape both hands palms in, tips down. Move forward alternately as if tiptoeing.

tire
C shape both hands palms and tips down, index fingers touching. Circle down and turn up ending with little fingers touching.

tired
Bent open B shapes both hands palms in. Place tips just under shoulders and let hands droop slightly.

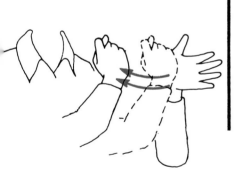
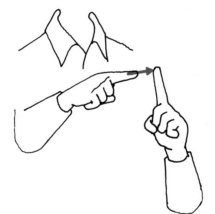

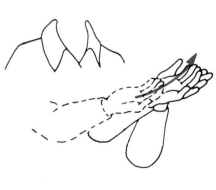

tissue
Open B LH palm up, tips out. T shape RH palm down, knuckles left. Brush base of right T across base of left palm twice.

to
One shape both hands left palm right, right palm down. Direct right index toward left and touch.

toast
Place tips of right V in left palm, circle under and touch back of LH.

toboggan
Open B both hands palms up, tips out. Slide right B forward on left palm.

259

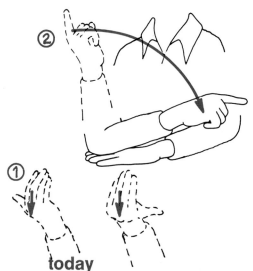

today
Hold cupped hands in front of body with palms up. Then, rest right elbow on back of LH, index finger up, and arc down to inside of left elbow.

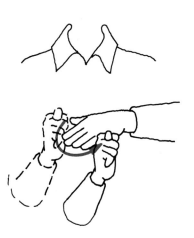

toe
Five shape LH palm and tips slanted right. Place right T on left thumb, then circle around to little finger.

together
T shape both hands, thumbs out. Bring together.

toilet
Shake right T from left to right.

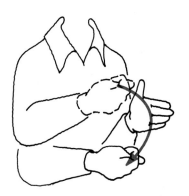

toll
Open B LH palm and tips slanted right. T shape RH. Move across left palm in downward semicircular motion.

tomato
Flat O LH palm and tips down. Place back of right index on lips then brush across side of left flat O.

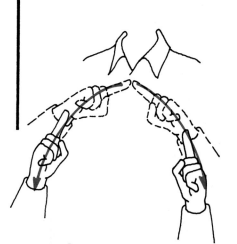

tomb
Place tips of index fingers together palms facing. Draw apart and down outlining shape of tomb.

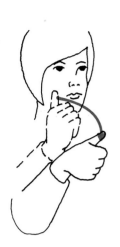

tomorrow
A shape RH. Place thumb side on right cheek and move forward.

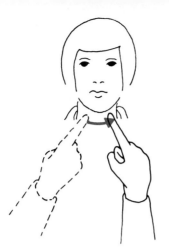

tonsil
Place tip of right index on right side of neck then circle across to left side.

too
One shape LH palm right, tip up. O shape RH tips left. Move toward and touch left index.

tool
T shape RH palm up. Move to right in short jumps.

toot
Hold right S in front of body, then pull down once or twice as if pulling a cord.

tooth
Touch front teeth with index finger of right X.

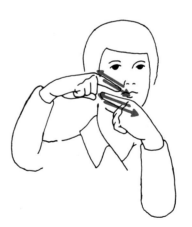

toothache
One shape both hands palms in, tips facing. Move back and forth at lower side of right cheek.

toothbrush
Rub edge of right index finger back and forth over teeth.

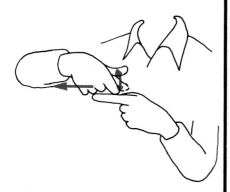

toothpaste
Mime spreading paste on toothbrush.

top
B shape both hands left palm right, tips up; right palm down, tips left. Rest right palm on left tips.

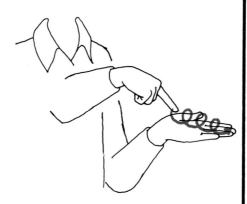

tornado
Open B LH palm up, tips out. Hold tip of right index over base of left palm then move out over fingers in whirling motion.

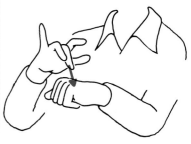

touch
A shape LH palm down. Touch back with tip of right middle finger.

tough
S shape LH palm down. Bent V RH palm in, knuckles left. Slide forward on back of left S.

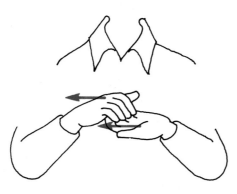

tow
Open B both hands fingers bent at second joint; left palm up, right palm down. Hook right fingers over left and pull to right.

towel
Open B both hands palms facing, tips up. Circle palms on cheeks.

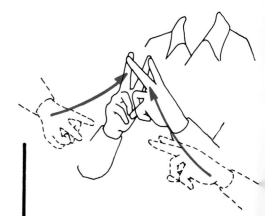

tower
V shape both hands palms down, tips facing. Move up ending with palms facing and tips touching.

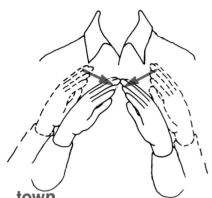

town

Open B both hands palms facing, tips up. Tap tips together (i.e. roofs of many buildings).

toy

T shape both hands knuckles out. Swing back and forth.

trace

Open B LH palm right. Slide right T down left palm as if tracing something.

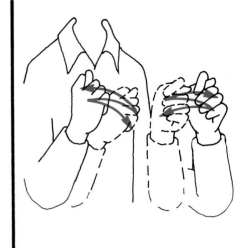

track

T shape both hands palms facing. Twist back and forth alternately.

tractor

S shape both hands. Mime holding large steering wheel and turn in bouncy motions.

trade

Flat O both hands palms in, tips up, left ahead of right. Reverse positions.

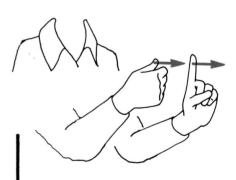

traffic

Five shape both hands. Place hands together and move back and forth alternately in rapid succession.

trail

One shape LH palm right. A shape RH palm left. Place behind left index then move both hands forward.

263

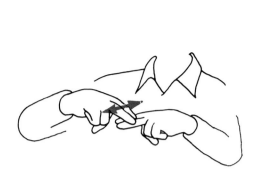

train
H shape both hands palms down, left tips out, right tips left. Rub right H over left.

trap
Place tips of right V on throat.

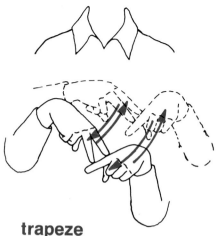

trapeze
One shape LH palm down, tips slanted right. V shape RH palm down, tips left. Place on left index then swing both hands back and forth.

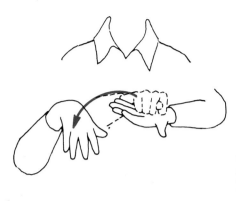

trash
Open B LH palm up, tips right. Place right T in left palm, lift out, then drop into five shape palm in, tips down.

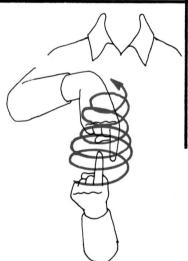

travel
One shape both hands palms in, right tip down. Circle around one another while spiraling upward.

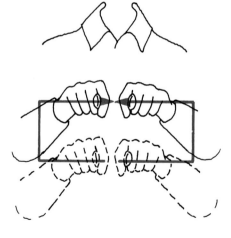

tray
T shape both hands palms down, knuckles out. Draw apart, back to body and then together outlining shape of tray.

treat
T shape both hands. Turn forward and up.

treasure
Open B LH palm up, tips slanted right. Curved open B RH palm in. Scrape back over left palm twice.

264

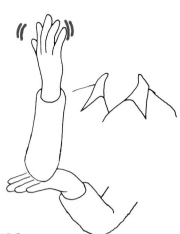

tree
Five shape RH palm left. Place right elbow on back of LH and shake five rapidly.

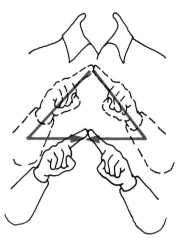

triangle
One shape both hands palms out, tips touching. Outline shape of triangle.

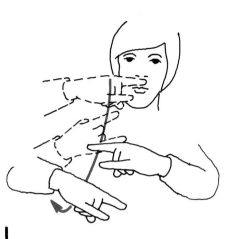

trick
Extend little and index fingers both hands, left palm down, right palm in, tips opposite. Place right index under nose then pass under LH.

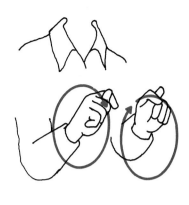

tricycle
T shape both hands knuckles down, LH below RH. Push up and down as if pedaling.

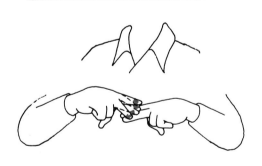

trim
H shape LH palm down, tips right. V shape RH palm down, tips left. Make snipping motion with right V on back of left H.

trip
Bent V RH. Bob up and down while moving around.

truck
T shape LH palm right. Place little finger of right C on left index and draw away.

true
Place right index on mouth then move straight out. Repeat.

trunk
Open B LH palm down, tips out. Bent B RH palm down, knuckles left. Place tips on back of left B, then lift fingers up.

try
T shape both hands. Hold in front of chest then twist out forcibly.

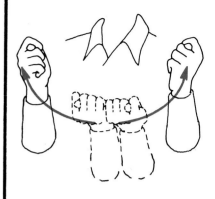

tub
T shape both hands palms up, little fingers touching. Move apart and up outlining shape of tub.

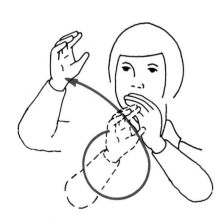

tuba
C shape both hands left palm right, right palm left, left C held at mouth. Place right C against left, then circle out, under and up again, outining shape of tuba.

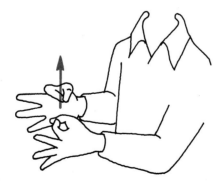

tube
F shape both hands palms facing, tips out. Place right F on left, then move up.

Tuesday
Move right T in small circle.

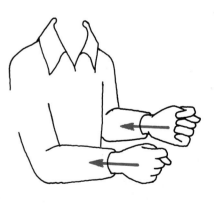

tug
T shape both hands palms facing. Pull back to body.

266

tulip
Place right T at right side of nose then move to left side.

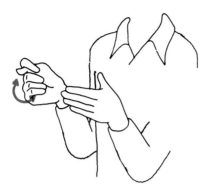

tuna
Open B LH palm in, tips right. T shape RH palm left, knuckles out. Place left tips on right wrist, then move both hands forward, fluttering right T.

tunnel
Hold LH palm down fingers slightly curved. Pass right T under and out.

turkey
Place back of right Q on tip of nose then shake down in front of chest.

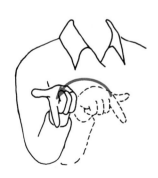

turn
L shape RH palm down. Turn so that palm faces up.

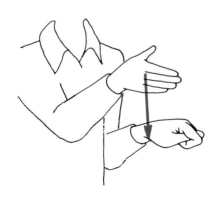

turnip
T shape LH knuckles down. Open B RH palm left, tips out. Slice down beside left T.

turtle
Place right A under curved LH. Extend thumb and wiggle.

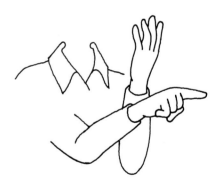

twig
Four shape LH palm in. One shape RH palm in, tip left. Place against left wrist.

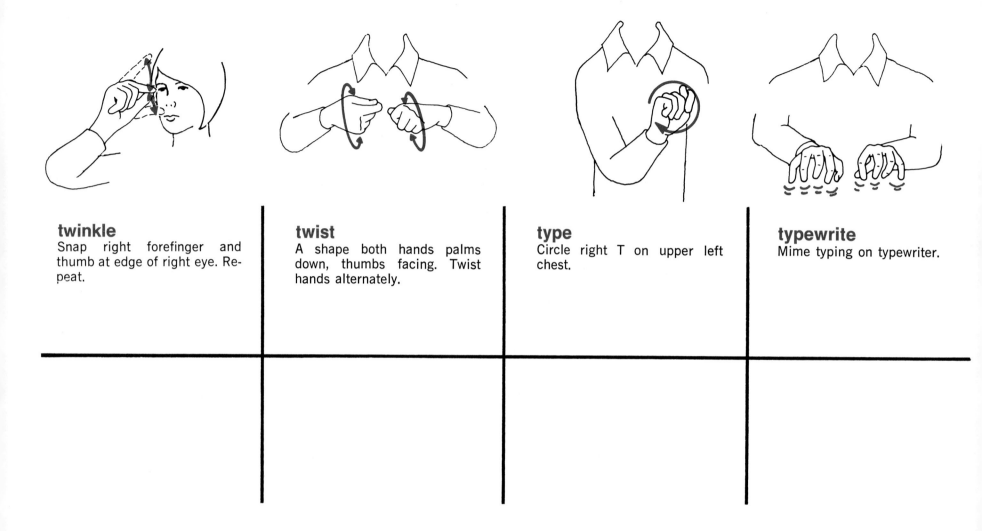

twinkle
Snap right forefinger and thumb at edge of right eye. Repeat.

twist
A shape both hands palms down, thumbs facing. Twist hands alternately.

type
Circle right T on upper left chest.

typewrite
Mime typing on typewriter.

U

ugly
X shape RH palm down. Draw across nose from left to right.

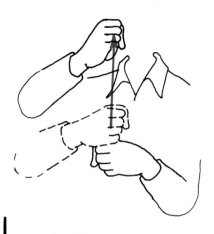

umbrella
Rest right S on left S and move up as if opening umbrella.

uncle
Shake right U at right temple in small counter-clockwise circles.

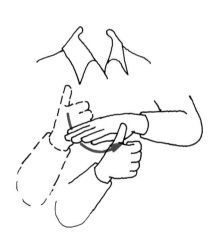

under
Open B LH palm down, tips right. Pass right A thumb up under left palm.

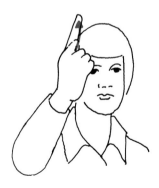

understand
S shape RH palm in. Place on forehead, then snap index finger up.

underwear
C shape LH palm in, tips on chest. Open B RH palm in, tips down. Slide into left C.

269

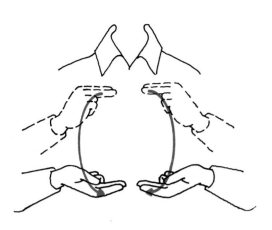

uniform
H shape both hands palms down, tips facing. Hold in front of chest, then arc out and turn over.

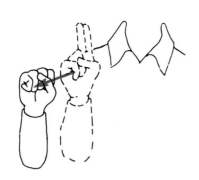

United States
Form the letters U and S in quick succession as if in one movement.

unlock
F shape both hands palms facing, right thumb and forefinger enclosed by left. Snap open and apart.

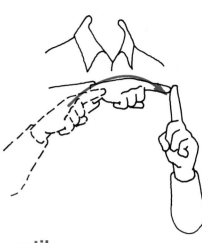

until
One shape both hands palms facing. Arc right index over to left.

up
Point index finger up.

upstairs
One shape RH. Move up in two short movements.

us
U shape RH palm in. Place tips on right side of chest then arc over to left side.

use
U shape RH. Move in circular motion counter-clockwise.

V

vacation
Five shape both hands palms facing, tips out. Tap armpits with thumbs.

vaccination
Scratch left upper arm with right thumb and forefinger.

vacuum
Open B LH palm down, tips out. Place base of right V on back of left B then slide forward.

valentine
One shape both hands palms in, tips slanted down and touching. Outline valentine on chest.

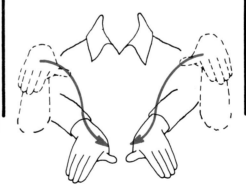

valley
Open B both hands palms down, tips out. Swoop down and level off outlining shape of valley.

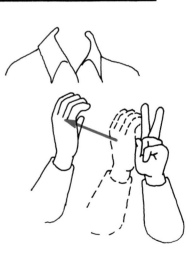

van
V shape LH, C shape RH palm left. Place right C against left V, then pull back to the right.

271

vane
V shape RH palm in, tips left. Place back of wrist on left one shape and wave back and forth two times.

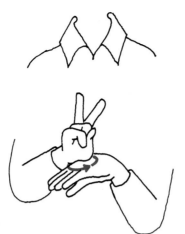

vanilla
Open B LH palm down, tips out. Circle right V on back of left B counterclockwise.

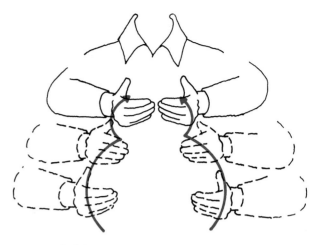

vase
Curved open B shape both hands palms and tips facing. Move up outlining shape of vase.

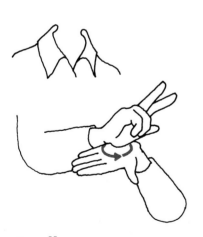

vaseline
Open B LH palm up, tips out. Circle right V in left palm clockwise.

veal
V shape LH. Grasp side with right thumb and forefinger and shake.

vegetable
V shape RH palm left. Touch right side of chin with index finger then middle of chin with middle finger.

very
V shape both hands palms facing. Place tips together and draw apart.

272

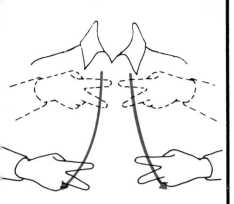

vest
V shape both hands palms in, tips facing. Place on chest, then move down and apart.

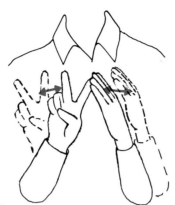

village
Open B LH, palm right, tips up. V shape RH, palm left. Tap hands together twice.

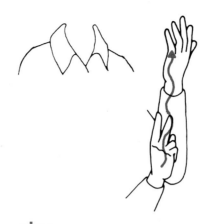

vine
Open B LH palm in. Run right V up left arm from elbow to fingers in wavy motion.

vinegar
V shape RH palm left. Tap chin with index finger.

violet
Place index finger of right V on right side of nose, then the middle finger on left side of nose.

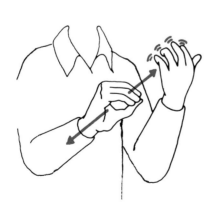

violin
Mime holding and playing a violin.

visit
V shape both hands palms in, tips up. Rotate away from body alternately.

vitamin
Shake right V from left to right.

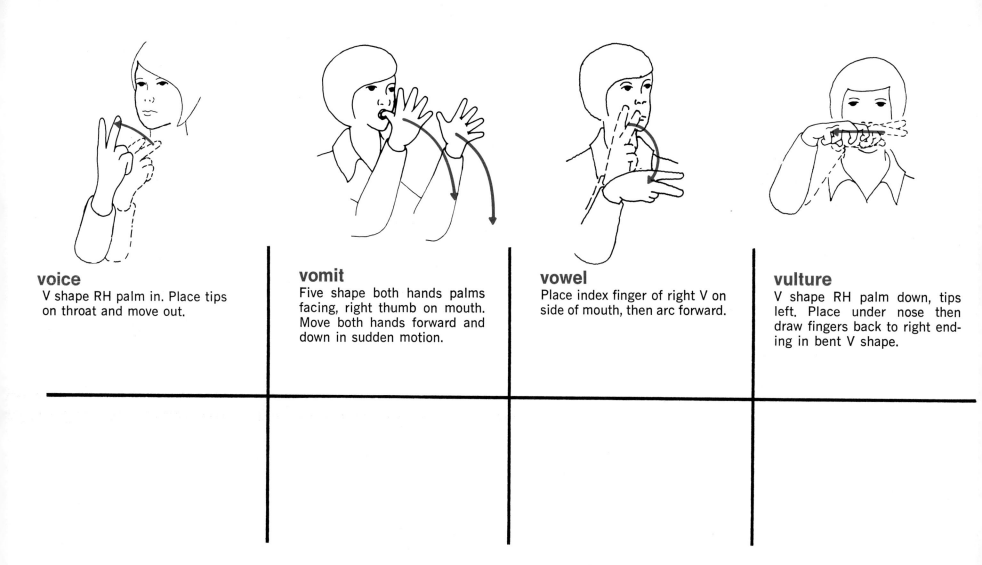

voice

V shape RH palm in. Place tips on throat and move out.

vomit

Five shape both hands palms facing, right thumb on mouth. Move both hands forward and down in sudden motion.

vowel

Place index finger of right V on side of mouth, then arc forward.

vulture

V shape RH palm down, tips left. Place under nose then draw fingers back to right ending in bent V shape.

W

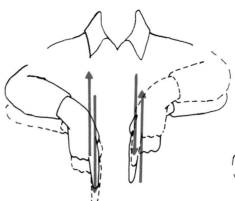

wade
One shape both hands palms in, tips down. Move up and down alternately.

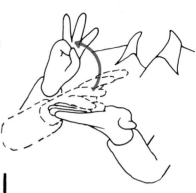

waffle
Open B LH palm up, tips out. Place right W, palm down, in left palm then lift back up.

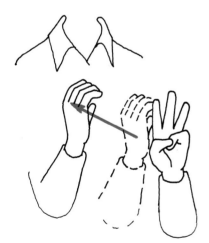

wagon
W shape LH palm right. C shape RH palm left. Place little finger side of right C on left W and draw back.

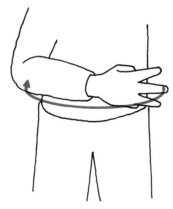

waist
W shape RH palm in, tips left. Draw fingers across waist from left to right.

wait
Hold open hands palms up in front of body, left a little ahead of right. Wiggle fingers slightly.

waiter
Snap right flat O on forehead, then change to open B palm up, tips slanted back as if balancing tray.

waitress
Brush thumb of right A down right cheek, then change to open B shape palm up, tips slanted back as if balancing tray.

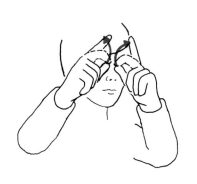

wake
Hold index fingers and thumbs over eyes. Snap open into L shapes.

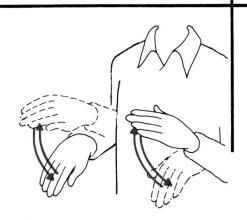

walk
Open B both hands palms down, tips out. Flap forward several times alternately.

walkie-talkie
C shape RH palm and tips in. Place on mouth, then move to right ear as if holding ear piece.

wall
B shape both hands left palm right, right palm left. Place right little finger on left index and draw apart.

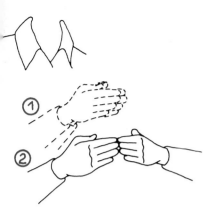

wallet
Open B both hands palms together, tips out. Open so that palms face in and tips touch.

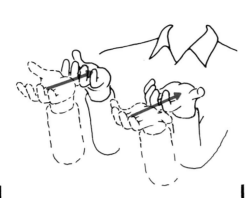

want
Five shape both hands palms up, fingers slightly curved. Draw back to body.

warm
Place tips of right claw at mouth then open up fingers into five shape.

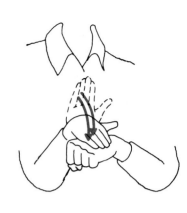

warn
S shape LH palm down, knuckles out. Tap twice with tips of right open B.

was
Place index finger of right W on lips and move back to right cheek.

wash
Rub right S in circular motion on upturned left palm.

wasn't
Place index finger of right W on lips and move back to right cheek. Then form N shape and twist in.

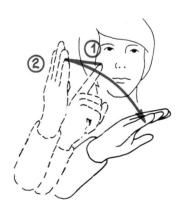

wasp
Place right index on right cheek. Move away into B shape palm slightly left, tips up, then brush right cheek lightly.

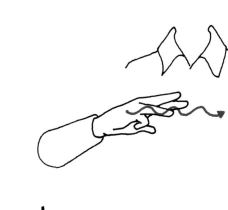

waste
Open B LH palm up, tips slanted right. Flat O RH palm and tips up. Place in left palm, then slide out into five shape palm up, tips out.

watch
Place back of right V just under right eye. Move out over left hand which is held palm down.

water
Tap lips twice with index finger of right W.

wave
W shape RH palm down, tips left. Move in wavy motion to the left.

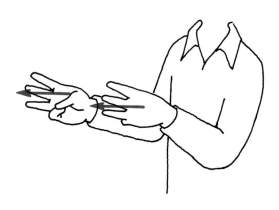

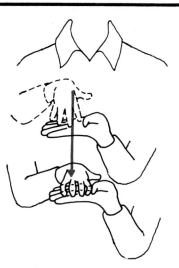

way
W shape both hands palms facing, tips out. Move forward.

we
Touch right index finger to right side of chest and arc to left.

weak
Open B LH palm up, tips right. Place tips of right fingers in left palm and bend suddenly.

278

wear
A shape LH knuckles down. Circle right W over back of left A.

weather
W shape both hands left palm up, tips out; right palm down, tips left. Place right wrist on left then reverse.

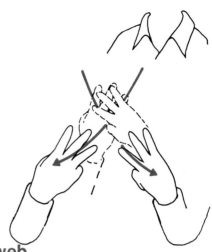

web
W shape both hands palms in, tips slanted up. Place right W on back of left and draw down and apart.

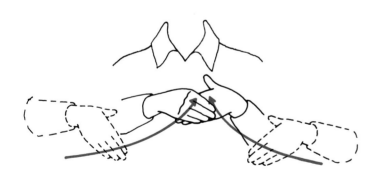

wed
Open B both hands palms slanted in, tips slanted down. Arc toward one another ending with right hand on back of left.

Wednesday
Move right W, in small circle counter-clockwise.

weed
Place index finger of right W on right side of nose, then move to left side.

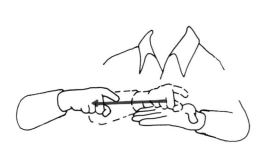

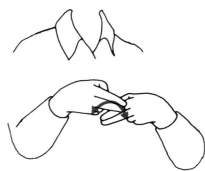

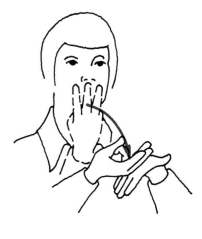

week
Open B LH palm up, tips slanted right. One shape RH knuckles down, tip out. Pass across left palm from base to tips.

weigh
H shape both hands palms slanted in, left tips slanted right, right tips slanted left. Place right H on left and see-saw back and forth as if balancing.

welcome
W shape RH palm in. Place tips on mouth, then move out.

well (adv.)
Open B LH palm and tips slanted up. W shape RH palm in. Place tips on mouth, then move out and down to left palm.

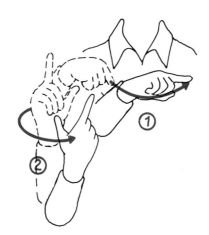

well (noun)
W shape both hands palms facing, tips slanted up. Point tips out and drop hands down.

we'll
Place right index finger on right side of chest and arc to left side. Form L and twist in.

were
Place right R on lips and move back to right cheek.

we're
Touch right index finger to right side of chest and arc to left. Then form R and twist in.

weren't
Place right R on lips and move back to cheek. Then form N and twist in.

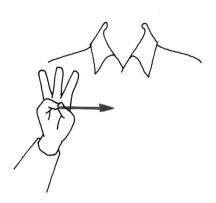

west
W shape RH. Move to left.

wet
Five shape both hands palms in, fingers slightly curved. Place right index tip on mouth then drop both hands into flat O shapes.

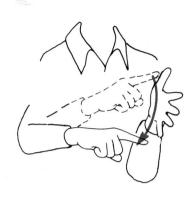

what
Five shape LH palm up, fingers slanted right. Draw right index tip across left fingers.

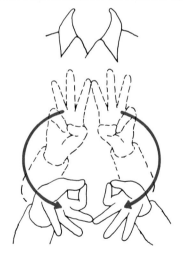

wheel
W shape both hands index tips touching. Circle out and over ending with palms up.

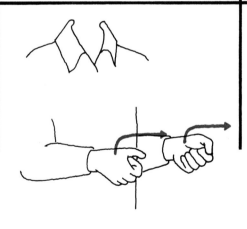

wheelbarrow
S shape both hands knuckles facing. Hold some distance apart and push forward as if pushing a wheelbarrow.

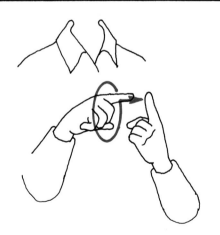

when
Hold left index finger up palm in. Circle with right index finger and then touch tips.

where
One shape RH hand. Wave from left to right.

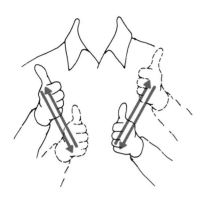

which
A shape both hands palms facing, thumbs up. Move up and down alternately.

whip
C shape LH palm down. Make whipping motion at side of left C with right A.

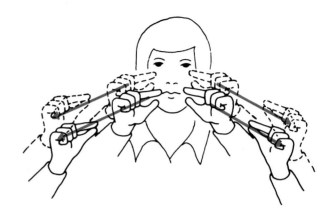

whisker
G shape both hands palms and tips facing. Place on cheeks, then draw away. Repeat.

whisper
B shape RH palm left. Place on left side of nose.

whistle
Place tips of right bent V on lips and mime whistling.

white
Five shape RH palm in, tips left. Place tips on chest and bring out into flat O shape.

who
Circle right index finger around mouth clockwise.

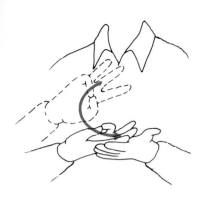

whole

Open B LH palm up, tips out. Hold right W up, turn and rest in left palm.

whom

Circle right index finger around mouth and form right M.

whose

Circle right index finger around mouth and form right S.

why

Open B RH palm in, tips up. Place tips on forehead and move out into Y shape.

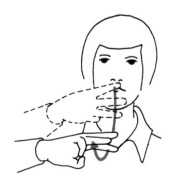

wicked

W shape RH palm in, tips left. Place on mouth then twist out and down.

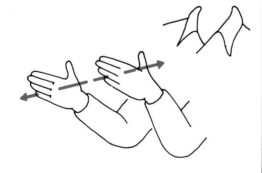

wide

Open B shape both hands palms facing, tips out. Move apart.

wife

Curved open B both hands, left palm up, tips slanted right; right palm down, thumb touching right cheek. Move down and clasp left hand.

wig

One shape LH palm in. Claw shape RH palm down. Hold over left index, then lower slightly.

283

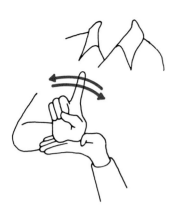

wiggle
Open B LH palm up, tips slanted right. One shape RH. Place base of right one in left palm and shake back and forth.

wild
Place tips of right W on right temple then loop forward and up.

will
Place palm of right open B on right cheek and move out.

win
S shape LH knuckles right. Make sweeping pass with right C over left S closing into S shape.

wind (verb)
Mime winding a wrist watch.

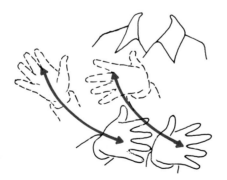

wind
Five shape both hands palms facing, tips out. Swing back and forth.

window
Open B both hands palms in, tips opposite. Place right little finger on left index. Move up then down.

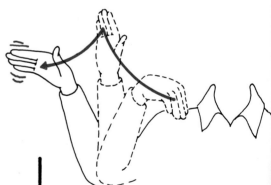

wing
Bent B shape RH palm down, tips on right shoulder. Swing out and up straightening fingers, slightly.

wink
Snap right thumb and forefinger in front of right eye. Open slightly and snap again.

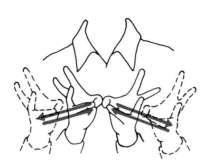

winter
W shape both hands palms facing, tips up. Tap little fingers and thumbs together several times.

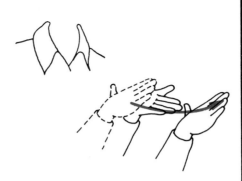

wipe
Open B LH palm and tips slanted out. Slide right palm over left in "wiping" motion.

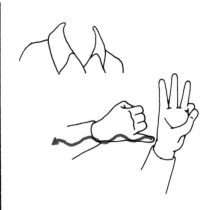

wire
W shape LH. I shape RH palm in, tip left. Place tip of right little finger on inside of left wrist, then draw back to the right in wavy line.

wise
Move right X up and down on forehead several times.

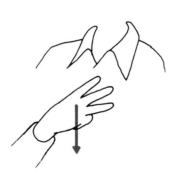

wish
W shape RH palm in. Place on chest and move down slightly.

wishbone
One shape both hands palms facing. Place tips together.

witch
X shape both hands, left palm up; right palm down. Place back of right X on nose, move out and down and tap left X, twice.

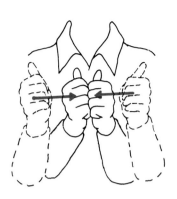

with

A shape both hands knuckles facing, thumbs up. Bring together.

without

A shape both hands knuckles facing, thumbs up. Draw apart, spread hands, palms up.

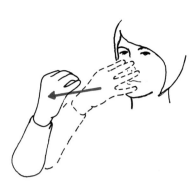

wolf

Five shape RH palm in, tips up. Place tips on nose and draw away into flat O shape.

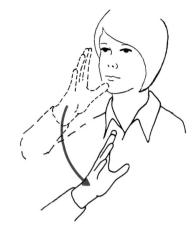

woman

Open B RH palm left. Brush thumb against chin and bring down to chest.

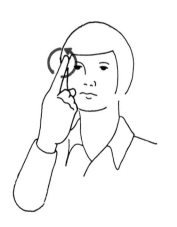

wonder

Circle right index tip on right side of forehead.

wonderful

Five shape both hands palms out, tips up. Move up and out away from center.

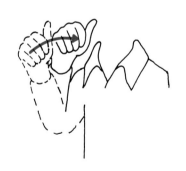

won't

A shape RH knuckles left. Jerk back over right shoulder.

woods

Rest right elbow on back of LH which is held before you, tips right. Form right W and flutter fingers from left to right.

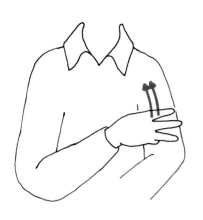

wool
W shape RH palm in, tips left. Brush left upper arm. Repeat.

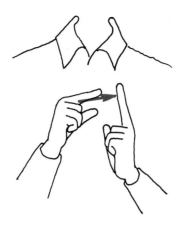

word
One shape LH. G shape RH palm down, tips left. Place tips of right G against left index finger.

work
S shape both hands palms down. Hit back of left S with right S.

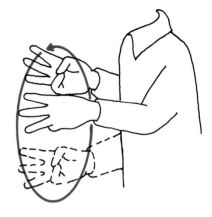

world
W shape both hands tips slanted out, left palm right, right palm left. Cross right wrist over left. Now, circle right W forward and under left W returning to original position.

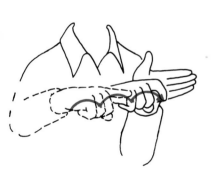

worm
Open B LH palm right, tips out. Place side of right index against left palm and move forward in crawling motion.

worry
W shape both hands palms slanted out. Circle toward one another in front of face.

would
Place palm of right open B on right cheek then move out. Repeat.

wouldn't
A shape RH knuckles left. Jerk back over right shoulder then form irregular marker.

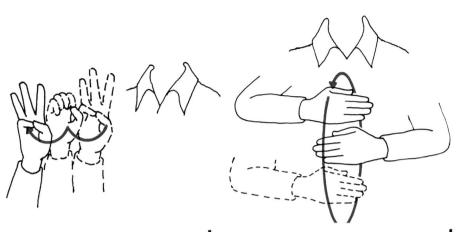

wow

Form the letters W-O-W in rapid succession.

wrap

Open B both hands palms in, left tips right, right tips left. Circle left hand with right.

wreath

C shape both hands palms out, tips up, thumbs touching. Circle down so that little fingers touch.

wreck

One shape LH. W shape RH palm in, tips left. Strike left index with back of right W.

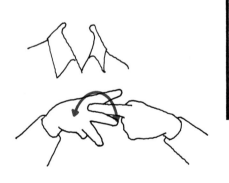

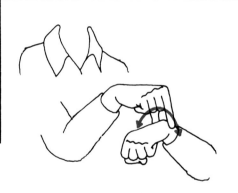

wrench

One shape LH palm in, tip slanted right. W shape RH. Place left index between index and middle fingers of right W, then twist right W up and down.

wrinkle

Open B LH palm right. Slide tips of right four down left palm in wavy motion.

wrist

S shape LH palm down. Place right thumb and forefinger around left wrist and twist from left to right.

write

Mime "writing" in upturned left palm with thumb and forefinger of RH (other fingers closed).

288

wrong
Strike chin with knuckles of right Y.

X

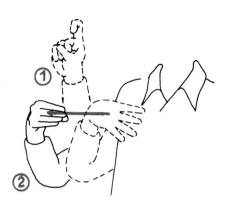

x-ray

X shape RH. Change to five shape palm in, tips left and place on chest. Now, move out into flat O shape.

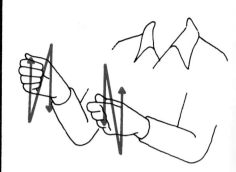

xylophone

A shape both hands palms facing. Mime playing a xylophone.

Y

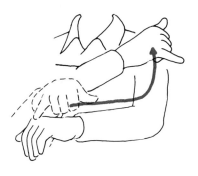

yard
Place knuckles of right Y on back of left wrist. Move up to shoulder.

① ②

yawn
Hold right S at mouth then open up into bent three shape.

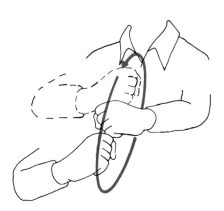

year
S shape both hands, left knuckles right, right knuckles left. Place right S on top of left. Circle forward and under ending in original position.

yell
Claw shape RH palm in, tips left. Place over mouth, then move up and out quickly. Repeat.

yellow
Y shape RH. Shake in and out.

yes
S shape RH. Shake up and down.

291

yesterday
Place thumb of right A on right cheek. Move back in semi-circle toward ear. Y shape is sometimes used.

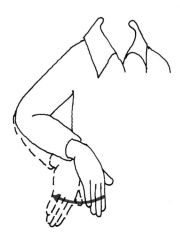

yet
Hold right open B down by side and flick back once.

you
Point index finger at person being addressed.

young
Bent B shape both hands thumbs up. Place tips of fingers on shoulders and move up.

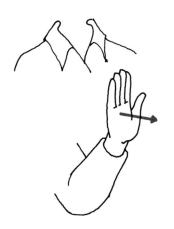

your
Face palm directly at person being addressed.

you're
Point index finger at person being addressed then form R and twist in.

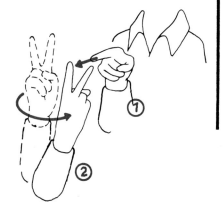

you've
Point index finger at person being addressed then form V and twist in.

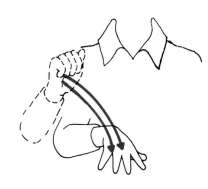

yo-yo
A shape RH. Drop down into five shape palm and tips slanted down. Repeat.

Z

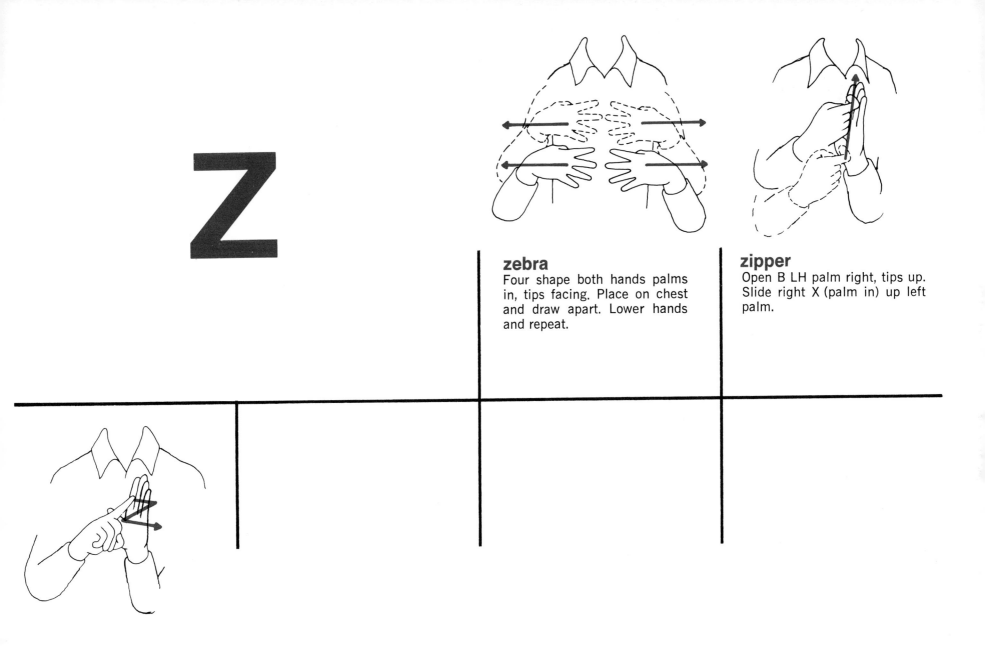

zebra
Four shape both hands palms in, tips facing. Place on chest and draw apart. Lower hands and repeat.

zipper
Open B LH palm right, tips up. Slide right X (palm in) up left palm.

zoo
Open B LH palm right, tips up. Trace Z on left palm with right index finger.

APPENDIX

The Origins and Nature of Signed English

The basic idea of representing English manually is not original with *Signed English*. Over the years, many people have made important contributions in this area. We have tried to use these contributions wherever they would help us meet our goal: an easily learned gesture system for use by and with preschool and elementary level deaf children. So that you can better appreciate the origins of our work, we will describe briefly and simply the history of the manual representation of English. More technical discussions can be found in such journals as *Sign Language Studies* and the *American Annals of the Deaf*.

As far as we know, Richard Paget was the first to develop such a system. He worked in England in the nineteen thirties and forties. He called his system the *Systematic Sign Language* and published an account in 1951. Paget first proposed that a sign represent an English word, that signs be ordered in the same way that English words are ordered, and that a special children's vocabulary be included. He also briefly considered using Ogden's *Basic English* vocabulary as a basic part of his system, but decided against it. Many of his signs were synthetic, however. By that we mean that the signs were specially devised by him on a logical basis for international use. For the most part, he did not include the natural signs used by the English deaf. For a variety of reasons, the *Systematic Sign Language* has not been used very much in England or elsewhere. Recently, however, it has received renewed attention. The system has been renamed the *Paget-Gorman Sign System* after *Pierre Gorman,* an Australian who has continued to work on the system.

About a decade after the formal publication of a description of the *Systematic Sign Language,* David Anthony began work with the deaf retarded in Michigan with a similar set of ideas and goals. He chose, however, to use the gestures of the American Sign Language as well as the American Manual Alphabet as his basic building tools. Anthony and his associates devised a system called *Seeing Essential English* (SEE) which seeks to represent the sound, spelling and meaning of parts of English words: more specifically, word roots, prefixes and suffixes. *Seeing Essential English* is a very comprehensive and ambitious system. It seeks to mirror English as fully as possible. It consists of more than a hundred prefixes and suffixes and has a sign vocabulary of several thousand words. Anthony and his associates are regularly engaged in developing more SEE vocabulary. Anthony clearly pioneered in this field in the U.S.A. and deserves credit for keeping the very idea of a manual representation of English alive when few regarded it as a method with much promise for educating deaf children. We admire the ingenuity and thoroughness which is characteristic of the *Seeing Essential English* system, and have borrowed many of their signs. We do not believe, however, that *Seeing Essential English* or any of the somewhat similar systems that are mentioned below, quite meet the needs of a preschool child and his parents as we see those needs, i.e., a tool which is powerful enough for the language of the young child and at the same time simple enough to be learned quickly by hearing parents. We also feel that gesture or sign system should represent meaning or concepts only. The English alphabet is surely well represented by the manual alphabet and other techniques seem better suited to represent sound. By attempting to represent sound and spelling as well as meaning, *Seeing Essential English* necessarily has had to create a large number of synthetic signs which differ from those in the American Sign Language.

Some of Anthony's former associates have formulated systems of their own. They have, however, retained the basic sound, spelling, and meaning framework of the *Seeing Essential English* system. Dennis Wampler and others have developed a system called *Linguistics of Visual English* (LVE) in which the basic gesture now represents either free or bound morphemes. Signs have been developed for a relatively small number of morphemes at this writing. Gerilee Gustason and her associates have recently prepared a book named *Signing Exact English* which is a smaller and simpler illustrated alternative to *Seeing Essential English*. A great many signs are common to all systems. Where appropriate we have borrowed signs from these systems as well. Our reservations about these systems are essentially the same as stated above for SEE.

The rationale for *Signed English,* on the other hand, is really very simple. Gestures or signs are used to represent the meaning of words in a set of 2500 English words used most frequently by and with pre-school children. Gestures do not represent sounds, syllables, or phonemes, nor do they represent English spelling.

English, of course, consists of more than a set of words. Words are ordered and marked in certain regular ways to show tense, case, comparison, etc. The order of sign words in *Signed English* follows exactly the order of English words and we have devised a set of 14 "markers" which parallel or represent certain structural features of English.

Of course, 2500 words are not all the words in the English language and 14 markers do not reflect all the structural features of English. (You will remember that we even suggested only seven markers for those parents who find it difficult to learn a new language system.) Observation of children's language behavior suggests, however, that this system is large and flexible enough to meet most of the needs of preschool and elementary grade children. And we know that learning an artificial system is a very difficult task even for the most devoted parents. Consequently, we have purposely devised a limited system which can be supplemented with the use of a very simple existing technique: the manual alphabet. It can be used to spell any words that cannot be handled by the *Signed English* system.

It may be of interest to you to know how we developed and/or selected the signs for *Signed English*. First, we began with the cardinal rule in this work, i.e., one sign (gesture) is designated to represent one English word. Second, where possible a sign from the American Sign Language is used for this purpose. Please note again that a sign represents the meaning and not the sound or spelling of a word. Consequently, sign words do not necessarily have the same constituent parts as do English words. For example, the sign words that represent the English words "today" and "yesterday" do NOT have a common gesture element that represents "day". Some sign words do have elements in common, but this reflects either a convenience or is the result of the usual growth of a natural language, i.e., the American Sign Language. Remember common gesture elements from sign word to sign word are a convenience and not a rule in *Signed English*. (See Endpaper VI.) We choose the natural sign from ASL for a simple reason. We want to make it easier for the child to communicate with users of the American Sign Language. This is an important property of *Signed English* because most deaf adults use some variant of the American Sign Language when they communicate with each other. This may be an uncomfortable truth for some readers, but it seems best to state it clearly and explicitly.

Since the American Sign Language is not English, there is not a perfect relationship between the word in the spoken language and the gesture in the signed language. Moreover, there are some concepts present in one language which are not directly present in the other. The articles "the", "an", and "a" are examples of words that do not exist in the American Sign Language. We have either invented signs for such words or used those invented by other system makers. Additionally, there are a great many cases where one American sign is now used for more than one English word, e.g., "glad" and "happy". We arbitrarily decided that the American sign would represent only one of these words, "happy" and invented a sign, a variant of the original sign, to represent the second word "glad". This, of course, applies to other like cases.

We have followed standard English dictionary practice in treating words as separate entries. With rare exceptions, one sign word represents one separate dictionary entry. For example, we have assigned two signs for each of such English words as "mean" and "rock".

When only one of two similar dictionary entries is used frequently by preschool children, we offer only one sign word. The infrequently used word is spelled as are other infrequently used words in *Signed English*. For example, we have a sign word for the animal "bear", but no sign for the second dictionary entry for this word form.

Probably the greatest departure from American Sign Language usage consists of using signs in English word order and in using sign markers to represent or parallel English structural meanings. This is not to suggest that American sign order is totally different from English order or that the American Sign Language does not have structural markers. There are some similarities in order and structure. The comparative marker, as one example, is taken directly from the American Sign Language and retains the same meaning.

All of the exceptions to the rules described in this Appendix are given in the introduction: About *Signed English*.

A few final words about the American Sign Language: it is a living natural language. It changes over time and it changes in ways that are not necessarily logical or convenient from our point of view. Some of the signs that are included in this system may eventually find their way into the American Sign Language. This should not surprise you. Nor should it surprise you to learn that the meaning of some signs vary from one region of the country to another. Even more than that, you should anticipate that a skilled signer will sign somewhat differently in different social situations. In short, expect the same kind of variation you would meet with different speakers of English.

REFERENCES

Anthony, D. A., *Signing Essential English,* Eastern Michigan University, Ypsilanti, Michigan, 1966. Unpublished Master's Thesis.

Anthony, D. A., and Associates (editors) *Seeing Essential English.* Educational Services Division, Anaheim Union High School District, P.O. Box 3520, Anaheim, California 92803, 1971, Volumes 1 and 2.

Beier, Ernst G., Starkweather, John A., and Miller, Don E. Analysis of word frequencies in spoken language of children. *Language and Speech,* Vol. 10, 1967, pp. 217-227.

Bornstein, H., *Reading the Manual Alphabet.* Washington, D.C. 1965, Gallaudet College Press.

Bornstein, H., and Kannapell, B. M., *New Signs for Instructional Purposes.* Office of Education Report 6-1924, Washington, D.C. 1969.

Bornstein, H., A description of some current sign systems designed to represent English. *The American Annals of the Deaf,* June 1973, Vol. 118, No. 3.

Bornstein, H. and Hamilton, Lillian B., Recent national dictionaries of signs, *Sign Language Studies,* 1, pp. 42-63, The Hague, Mouton Press, 1973.

Bornstein, H., Signed English: A manual approach to English language development. *Journal of Speech and Hearing Disorders,* xxxix, 3, 1974, pp. 330-343.

Bornstein, H., Sign language in the education of the deaf. In I. M. Schlesinger and L. Namir (Eds.) *Current Trends in the Study of Sign Languages of the Deaf.* The Hague, Mouton Press (in press).

Fant, L. J., Jr., Ameslan: *An Introduction to the American Sign Language.* National Association of the Deaf, Silver Spring, Md. 1972.

Gentile, A., and DiFrancesca, S. *Academic Achievement Test Performance of Hearing Impaired Students in the United States: Spring 1969, (Series D, No. 1)* Washington, D.C. Gallaudet College, Office of Demographic Studies, 1969.

Gorman, P., and Paget, G., *A Systematic Sign Language.* Royal National Institute for the Deaf, London, 1964 (mimeographed).

Gustason, G., Pfetzing, D., and Sawoldow, E., *Signing Exact English.* Modern Signs Press, 3131 Walker Lee Drive, Rossmoor, California 94720, 1972.

Hoemann, H.W., (editor) *Improved Techniques of Manual Communication: For Use With Severely Handicapped Deaf Clients.* Bowling Green State University, Bowling Green, Ohio, 1970.

Howes, Davis H., A word count of spoken English. *Journal of Verbal Learning and Verbal Behavior,* Vol. 5, 1966, pp. 572-606.

Kannapell, B. M., Hamilton, L. B., and Bornstein H. *Signs for Instructional Purposes.* Gallaudet College Press, Washington, D.C. 1969.

Madsen, W., *Conversational Sign Language: An Intermediate Manual,* Gallaudet College Press, Washington, D.C. 1972.

Murphy, Helen A., *The Spontaneous Speaking Vocabulary of Children in Primary Grades.* Boston Univ. Journal of Education, Boston, Mass. No. 140, Dec. 1957, pp. 105.

O'Rourke, T. J., (editor) *Psycholinguistics and Total Communication: The State of the Art.* American Annals of the Deaf, Washington, D.C., Oct. 1972, pp. 134.

Paget, R., *The New Sign Language.* The Wellcome Foundation, London, 1951.

Stokoe, W. C., Jr., Casterline, D. C., and Croneberg, C. G., *A Dictionary of American Sign Language on Linguistic Principles.* Gallaudet College Press, Washington, D.C. 1965.

Wampler, D. W., *Linguistics of Visual English.* Linguistics of Visual English, 2322 Maher Drive, No. 35, Santa Rosa, California 95405 Booklets): *Morpheme List One, An Introduction to the Spatial Symbol System, Questions and Answers.*

Wepman, Joseph M., and Hass, W., *A Spoken Word Count* (children—ages 5, 6, and 7). Language Research Associates, Chicago, Ill., 1969, pp. 94.

INDEX*

*sign changed from previous edition

298

* sign changed from previous edition

* sign changed from previous edition

* sign changed from previous edition

* sign changed from previous edition

* sign changed from previous edition

* sign changed from previous edition

* sign changed from previous edition

* sign changed from previous edition

A MODEL FOR THE VISUAL REPRESENTATION OF SPEECH

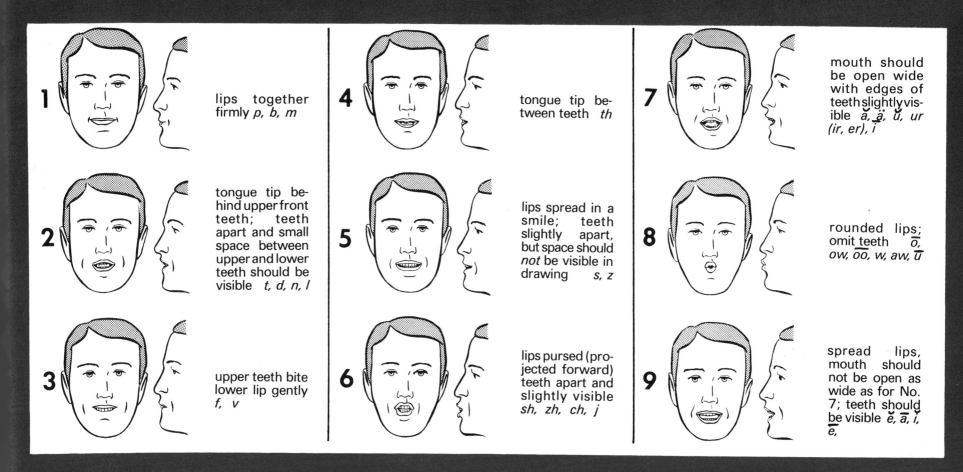

1 — lips together firmly *p, b, m*

2 — tongue tip behind upper front teeth; teeth apart and small space between upper and lower teeth should be visible *t, d, n, l*

3 — upper teeth bite lower lip gently *f, v*

4 — tongue tip between teeth *th*

5 — lips spread in a smile; teeth slightly apart, but space should *not* be visible in drawing *s, z*

6 — lips pursed (projected forward) teeth apart and slightly visible *sh, zh, ch, j*

7 — mouth should be open wide with edges of teeth slightly visible *ă, ä, ŭ, ur (ir, er), ī*

8 — rounded lips; omit teeth *ō, ow, ōō, w, aw, ū*

9 — spread lips, mouth should not be open as wide as for No. 7; teeth should be visible *ĕ, ā, ĭ, ē,*

Signed English is intended to be an aid to language development and a supplement to speech. We want, therefore, to present to the child consistent and accurate relationships between printed word, signed word, and appearance of the lips while that word is spoken. To do this we have shown the most distinctive shape of the first visible lip movement for most words in this book.

Because some different sounds appear the same on the lips, we decided that nine different lip shapes could be used to represent reasonably the speech sounds. These nine shapes are shown above. By consulting the model you can tell which sound has been drawn for any word in the text. There are certain exceptions, however. When an emotion such as surprise or excitement is involved, the drawing usually represents the emotion rather than the sound.

CONTRACTIONS

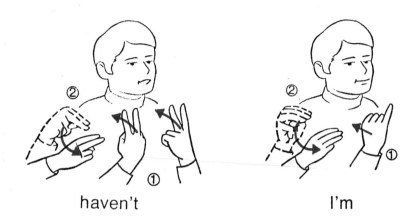

haven't   I'm

A simple and widely used technique is followed in forming most contractions. As shown above, you first execute the sign word, then add, with a twisted motion, the appropriate manual letter. The table below gives all of the contraction parallels.

English spelling	'd	'll	'm	'nt	're	've	's
Manual letter	d	l	m	n	r	v	s

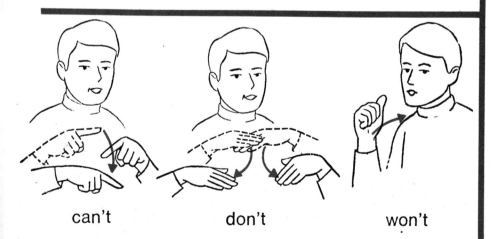

can't   don't   won't

There are three well-established exceptions taken from the American Sign language: *can't*, *don't*, and *won't*. These signs are also involved in the sign contractions on the right.

do   does   did

don't   doesn't   didn't

If the technique described at the upper left were followed, *doesn't* would be represented by do + third person singular + 'nt and *didn't* by do + irregular past + 'nt. This violates our one sign plus one marker rule (and incidentally, demonstrates how clumsy unlimited combinations of sign markers can be). Therefore, *doesn't* and *didn't* are formed by marking *don't* with the appropriate markers. Similarly, *wouldn't* and *couldn't* are the marked sign words, *won't* and *can't*. We have not been able to devise an acceptable composite sign to represent *shouldn't* so we simply use *should* + *not*.

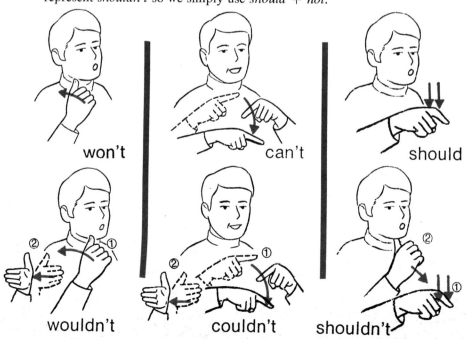

won't   can't   should

wouldn't   couldn't   shouldn't

v